Dr. Syama Prasad Mookerjee

The Great Educationist

Dr. Syama Prasad Mookerjee

The Great Educationist

Dr. Nand Kishore Garg

Namarta Sharma

Published by
PRABHAT PRAKASHAN PVT. LTD.
4/19 Asaf Ali Road,
New Delhi-110 002 (INDIA)
e-mail: prabhatbooks@gmail.com

ISBN 978-93-90101-82-5
Dr. Syama Prasad Mookerjee
THE GREAT EDUCATIONIST
by Dr. Nand Kishore Garg • Namarta Sharma

Edition
2025

Price
₹ 600.00 (Rupees Six Hundred only)

Printed at
Shree Sai Printers, Sahibabad

त्वदीयं वस्तु गोविन्दं तुभ्यमेव समर्पये।
तेन त्वदंघ्रिकमले रतिं मे यच्छ शाश्वतिम्॥

Twadiyam vastu govindam tubhyamev samarpaye
ten twadanghrikamale ratin me yachchh shashwatim.

(Meaning: O God 'Govind', everything that I have is given to me by You and I submit everything to You. Please give me only one thing that I get affection in Your lotus like feet timelessly.)

The Devoutness of Dr. Mookerjee

I thank God for whatever He has given me, and I pray to Him to provide me with the strength and devotion to dedicate myself to Him. I have now come to realise that one's ailments and sorrows vanish if one just concentrates on Him. I feel a sense of serenity that I could never have imagined I was capable of attaining. But I am still unable to invoke Him in right earnest. I suppose that profound ability too lies in His hands. Previously, I had never felt the urge to invoke Him thus. It is His grace that has taught me to feel this way. So, I am confident that He, in His infinite mercy, will show me the right way to do it. I do not aspire for wealth, fame or glory. I will get only what I deserve and what I have laboured for, and I only seek the right to offer myself to Him. I do not wish to make any irrational demands on those whom I love dearly and whom I crave to have around me. I wish them happiness and peace. Living in this world is like living in a world of make-believe. It contains both truth and falsehood if one achieves truth, which I have had the good fortune to attain, why should he wish to forsake it? I want to cling to it with all my might.

—Dr. Syama Prasad Mookerjee

Leaves from a Diary, 27 January 1946, p. 166

Dr. Mookerjee in the eyes of his Contemporaries

"Like Shiva who drank the poison after churning the sea, somebody must be there to drink the poison of Indian politics. It can be you (Dr. Mookerjee)."

—Mahatma Gandhi

~•~

"I know you have a very strong mind...I pray that you receive that message of renunciation, which serves as the bridge between this world and the next."

—Gurudev Rabindranath Tagore

~•~

"His (Dr. Mookerjee's) religion was not of narrow kind. He was catholic in his sympathies, and broad-minded in his outlook...That man (Dr. Mookerjee) has a spiritual dimension...It is Indian and not merely Hindu."

—Dr. Sarvapalli Radhakrishnan

~•~

"I have whole-hearted respect for you, and I also have a sincere affection for you...I believe that one day, we shall make India fully independent. On that glorious day, Bengalis will remember foremost you and Subhas Bose—you will be the Country's true Leaders."

—Kazi Nazrul Islam,

National Poet of Bangladesh

~•~

"You seem to have emerged as a real bap ka beta in the university! No one is prepared to work so hard and so selflessly as you are now doing."

—Acharya Prafulla Chandra Ray,

An Eminent Scientist

~•~

"Like your father, you (Dr. Mookerjee) are the personification of generosity. You always help the destitute just like your father. You want to throw the communalism outside the nation."

—Maulavi Kazi Abdul Qadas,

Vice President, Islamia College Union

~•~

"He has the making of a public man. He has tact, common sense, organising capacity, readiness in the debate and a robust sense of humour."

—Praphulla C. Ghosh,

Teacher of Dr. Mookerjee in Presidency College

प्रधान मंत्री

Prime Minister

MESSAGE

I am happy to learn that the Maharaja Agrasen University, Himachal Pradesh is publishing a book on the life and works of Dr. Syama Prasad Mookerjee.

Dr. Syama Prasad Mookerjee was a statesman, profound thinker and great leader who devoted his life to the development of India. I am sure, this book will go a long way in generating renewed interest in his thoughts and vision, especially among the youth.

On this occasion, I extend my best wishes for the success of the book.

(Narendra Modi)

New Delhi
18 May, 2016

Asutosh Mookerjee Memorial Institute

77, Asutosh Mookerjee Road, Kolkata – 700025.
E-mail : ammibb@bsnl.in Ph. : (033) 24766668

20.06.2016

A research project has been taken up by Maharaja Agrasen Institute of Technology on the life and times of Dr. Syama Prasad Mookerjee to be published in two volumes, first volume being 'Dr. Syama Prasad Mookerjee: the Educationist'. The research project has been undertaken by Dr. Nand Kishore Garg, Chancellor, Maharaja Agrasen University (H.P.) and Sm. Namrata Singh Sharma, Assistant Professor , Department of Humanities, Maharaja Agrasen Institute of Technology, which is a highly commendable effort. The topic they have selected is extremely important in the present day situation. They have selected one of the most important aspects of Dr. Mookerjee's life. I am sure their joint effort will be highly recommended by the Academia.

Reena Bhaduri

Reena Bhaduri
Secretary
Asutosh Mookerjee Memorial Institute

Secretary
Asutosh Mookerjee
Memorial Institute
Calcutta-25

Brief Profile of Dr. Syama Prasad Mookerjee

Educationist, Parliamentarian, Administrator and Leader of the Hindu Mahasabha and Jan Sangh was born at Calcutta on 6 July 1901 and educated at Calcutta and London; elected to Senate and Syndicate of the Calcutta University, 1924; Vice Chancellor, Calcutta University, 1934-38.

Member: Bengal Legislative Council 1929-1937, 1937-1942 and 1946, Finance Minister, Bengal Government, 1941-42, Resigned in 1942; Joined the All-India Hindu Mahasabha, 1939, its working President, 1940-44, 1944-46; Constituent Assembly 1946 and Lok Sabha, 1952-53.

Elected to the House of People from Calcutta (South-East) continuously; Minister of Industry and Supply, Govt. of India, 1947-50; resigned from Cabinet in Protest against Nehru-Liaquat Pact, 1950; formed the Bharatiya Jan Sangh, 1951 and became its President; President 'The Royal Asiatic Society' 1943-46; President Mahabodhi Society, 1942-53, Founded 'The Nationalist', an English daily and Bangla daily 'Hindustan'.

Books Published: 'Leaves from a Diary', 'Integrated Kashmir', 'A Phase of the Indian Struggle', 'Awake Hindustan', 'Educational Speeches', 'A Volume of Convocation and Other Speeches'.

Placed under house arrest in a guest house in Kashmir, 1953 and died in detention on 23rd June 1953.

Acknowledgement

From the stage of conception to its culmination, with all the attributes required to transform this writing into a proper book, we have been blessed with insights and guidance of those who are arguably the best people to have studied or known the life of Dr. Mookerjee. The first name which occurs in our mind is that of Dr. Reena Bhaduri, niece of Dr. Syama Prasad Mookerjee and the Secretary, Asutosh Mookerjee Memorial Institute, Calcutta.

Another beacon to have lighted the portals the book has travelled during its making is the Hon'ble Governor of Meghalaya, Sh. Tathagata Roy who encouraged us whenever we groped in the dark for facts and information about Dr. Mookerjee. We are grateful to Sh. Gyanendra Shrivastava, Retd. IAS and Chief Executive, MATES, for his unremitting support.

We are also indebted to our Guru Sh. B.L. Mahajan for his continuous blessings and active support.

Another set of names which provided us with invaluable support consists of Smt. Usha Garg, Trustee, MATES, and Sh. R.P. Singh, Advocate, Lucknow High Court.

We are also grateful to Sh. Vikas Garg, Sh. Vivek Garg and Sh. Sanjay Singh for their moral support.

We also express our gratitude to the following institutions which equipped us with all the relevant material for the book:

Asutosh Mookerjee Memorial Institute, Calcutta.
Asutosh Museum, Calcutta University, Calcutta.
Dr. Mookerjee Smruti Nyas, New Delhi.
Dr. Syama Prasad Mookerjee Research Foundation, New Delhi.
Indira Gandhi National Centre for Arts.
Nehru Memorial Museum and Library, New Delhi.
Satya Pal Gupta Memorial Library, MAIT, Delhi
Swami Vivekanand Chair, Maharaja Agrasen University, Himachal Pradesh.

Dr. Syama Prasad Mookerjee: The Great Educationist

A Brief Synopsis

Whatever has been written about Dr. Syama Prasad Mookerjee so far doesn't do justice to his grand and multi-faceted personality. This leading sentiment is behind the motivation of writing the present book. A lot has been written on Dr. Mookerjee's political endeavours. However, his persona is immeasurably significant beyond his political life. The simplest explanation of his life proclaims him master of social, educational and economic thought.

Through this book, we have tried to know how Dr. Mookerjee became a powerful personality, an educationist, a thinker, and an administrator. We see a happy blending of tolerance, humanity, and tradition, together with the scientific outlook and a broad understanding of all that is best in the life and ideals of the West in his personality. He moulded his character and future by inheriting a rich tradition of erudite scholarship, fervent nationalism, and fearlessness from his father, Sir Asutosh Mookerjee, who was the Vice Chancellor of Calcutta University and justice of Calcutta High Court. Dr. Mookerjee's latent qualities and brilliance could be shone forth with the help of hard training he received at his home and school, coupled with the filial care of his father. The death of his father caused him to bring him into the educational field, even while he was still a student.

By becoming the youngest Vice Chancellor of Calcutta University in 1934, Syama Prasad took advantage of the opportunity to put his aims and ideas regarding the education of his people in practise. It was under his tenure that Gurudev Rabindranath delivered his convocation address in Bengali, which was not less than a revolution in British India.

Dr. Mookerjee's fame as a devoted educationist, intellectual and orator had by this time began to spread beyond the boundaries of Bengal. He was elected a member of the court and council of the Indian Institute of Science, Bangalore, in 1935 and also became a member and then Chairman of the Inter-University Board in the creation of which he had played a leading role. He was also nominated by the Government of India to the Committee of Intellectual Co-operation of the League of Nations as India's representative in 1938. In 1943, he was elected President of the Royal Asiatic Society of Bengal.

The following quotes from Dr. Mookerjee's speeches better explain his outlook towards education:

"The university must be a national organisation, looking at educational problems not from the narrow outlook of any particular community, but solely from the standpoint of national advancement and must cater to the needs of all communities and sects..." (Bengal Legislative Council Proceedings, vol; 43, No.5, 19.03.34, P.404)

What is education worth if our youth, in general, are physically weak or unfit, unable to stand the stress and strain of modern life? What is education worth if we cannot turn them into men physically strong and well-equipped sane and robust?"—(Calcutta University, Convocation address, 1935)

"It is incorrect to look upon educational institutions as factories to produce potential clerks and leadership to our staff. We have to turn out students who are capable of providing leadership to our self-governing institutions, such as municipal corporations, provincial and central legislatures and also of directing the affairs in various fields of life, such as financial, commercial and also of directing the affairs

in various fields of life, such as financial, commercial and industrial zones. India today badly needs people who are imbued with the spirit of service and also innovative, courageous and liberal in outlook...It is also for you not only to inculcate in the minds of youth the passion for knowledge and truth and spirit of reverence, but also to foster in them the love of their motherland—that real patriotism—which implies one to sacrifice everything for the good of one's country". (All-India Education Conference at Nagpur in 1935)

Dr. Mookerjee always saw the role of education as of utmost importance in the process of national regeneration. Throughout his life, he spoke in favour of education, teachers and students. Dr. Mookerjee was an educationist in his true spirits. How did he emerge in a great thinker of education, which new experiments he brought out into the world of education and which educational and cultural organisations saw him as their life force? Study of these topics is the focal point of the present book.

Contents

1
Introduction

To say that the past has always been perfectly portrayed in the annals is indeed very tough, nay impossible. The reasons may vary from the remoteness of that past in question to willfully written account with lopsided views on events described; from intent to hide a few facts to undermining heroes by not according them a place they deserve in historical accounts.

Not in so distant a past lived Dr. Syama Prasad Mookerjee, a resplendent educationist, and policy-maker who was subjected to this historical injustice and apathy by being denied a place he deserved in the pantheon of patriots who shaped the course of our Motherland during the freedom struggle and after Independence. It is not that his persona did not attract people to write on his works and times, but it is felt that whatever has been written about him and his deeds is not at all sufficient. If we analyse the matter written about him, then we will find that many important facets of his personality have either been unnoticed or deliberately left for some or the other reason. An iota of analysis of Dr. Mookerjee's life and his works is sufficient to place him as an ace amongst luminaries India has witnessed in the last Century.

Why India became so radiant in producing a plethora of valiant heroes during an age of its freedom struggle covering roughly a century or a little more? Perhaps the most straightforward answer to the question lies in the unusual times when the country in distress calls for her youth to come out and save her from any disgrace. India too called her youth to wage war against colonial oppression she has been crumbling under. The simplest of youth emerged as heroes during that great struggle for Independence waged against the mighty imperialist power Great Britain. Methods varied from non-violence to violent means to throw the imperialist yoke.

Dr. Mookerjee, too, had his share of heroism, although unnoticed to a great extent, in lending a hand to carve out a future for his Motherland by contributing in the field of education as he felt pen to wield enormous power to wage a war against injustice and atrocities. Born during times, which we can comfortably call, first significant momentum towards Swaraj, Dr. Mookerjee was destined to imbibe the patriotic ethos in the air all over the country. Therefore, to understand his formative days, we will discuss in some detail the prevailing conditions around the time of his birth and succeeding early years of his childhood.

19th Century and the first half of the 20th Century were under simmering against the oppression of every conceivable sort, economic, political, social and cultural. The intensity of British domination was such that the people of India were living in utterly miserable and oppressive conditions, and yet they believed for many decades that the British Raj was benevolent for them. 'White Man's burden' and other such tricks created a complete hegemony over the native people. During the British Raj, the two constants were working day and night against the subjugated masses, namely Despair and Death. The British policies vis-à-vis India were a typical manifestation of a parasitical relation between colonies feeding its master empire. The implementation of the policies took recourse to all draconian measures to extract and maximise unlawful gains for the Empire. Noticeably, the Indian rulers who were not under direct British subjugation too were mere instruments in the hands of the British representatives often placed in the courts of former. The power and value of such rulers were mostly decorative. In the areas within the purview of the British Raj, higher echelon of administration was invariably manned by the British. The lower stratum was meant for the local people, however, with excessive discrimination is not only wages, but in general treatment they were meted out.

The repressive regime of the British, however, led a section of Indian people to have access to what Europe was witnessing during the 19th and 20th centuries. A part of the Indian middle class gradually acquired education on western lines and understood socio-political changes happening in Europe of their times. The resurgence of nationalist movements across the European continent in the wake of Napoleonic victories and unification of Germany and Italy, etc., were a few remarkable events which had an imprint on the literate Indian minds. Such sections were the first to break the hegemonic barriers of 'White Man's Burden' and the real nature of seemingly benevolent policies of the white administration. The native population also started understanding how their religious and cultural practises were being attacked. The biggest flashpoint was provided by Enfield cartridges which were believed to be made of pork and cow meat. The result was known to all of us as India's the first war of Independence. However, there were several other instances of armed rebellions, even in the 18th Century itself. First such to blow the war trumpet against the rule was Sannyasi Revolt in the East India Company controlled Bengal. Although many a time, these revolts were aimed at local power magnets, the real reason for such uprising was the repressive policies of the new rule which was least bothered about the weal of its subjects. The apparent instruments of authoritarianism were Zamindars, money-lenders and other middlemen who made every pretext to earn revenue applying worst of measures to realise revenue from the poor peasants, artisans even when crop or business did not yield even for their subsistence. The most significant aspect of these revolts was their broad swath and multiple sections of people. This fact in itself is an index of how the sentiments were simmering against the foreign yoke. The self-glorified rule of the British was gradually coming under intense scrutiny, and the veil of their benevolent government was getting torn.

Having seen the failure of armed resistance during the great revolt of 1857, which had seen both overt and covert support by people, it was realised that the method to challenge foreign rule needs a change. Moreover, after this failed armed battle, there was no political leadership or the will from the erstwhile rulers and other power centres to carry forward the struggle against the British. Apart from the above, the East India Company too ceased to the ruler of India, though deriving legality and power from the Empire. After the revolt of 1857, India was placed under the direct rule of the British Crown. This new political arrangement for the country was put in place to instil faith in the minds of the subjects about the impartiality of the rule of the Crown. However, the new educated middle class was gradually becoming more and more aware of the inherent flaws of the colonial state.

Now, the lead was taken by the newly emerging class of educated Indians, and they gradually laid the first bricks of the foundation of the Indian struggle for Independence. The threads of the struggle were to be woven around the tenets of Nationalism. Nationalism, as against the widespread belief that it was an import of the West in our country was always a deep-rooted political and more so a cultural phenomenon of our land inhabited by people representing many cultures and diverse ethnicities within the all-encompassing Indian ethos. Nationalism was entrenched even at the times of the Vedas which have multiple references to the word 'Rashtra' referring to specific territoriality in the term.

India was the first country where any term referring to a nation was used. In Atharva Veda, earth is treated as the mother "माता भूमिः पुत्रो अहं पृथिव्या".

As is well known, the territory is a key element of a nation, even in its most modern connotations. Then, there was a unique oneness of the Indian religious belief system, with all its differences yet encompassing the entire life of the polity, formed another great element of the country's national ethos. Moreover, the building of a nation in the strictly political sense began when the small tribal and other such polities started taking the shape of a nation at least in its rudimentary appearance around 5th and 6th century BC. Moreover, by the 3rd century BC, India was to witness a far-flung empire. This was the famous Mauryan Empire which gave us the first emperor of the country in Ashoka the great who

set the tone, at least in India, to what political scientists call benevolent kingship. Noticeably, the Empire was founded by Chandragupta Maurya, who was mentored in statecraft by Kautilya, one of the most prominent political thinkers the world has ever produced. Even when India was in a state of political disarray, her religious unity provided a much-needed base for being afloat by and large as one polity. In this regard, the great philosopher Adi Guru Shankaracharya was foremost by providing the cultural and religious glue to the county. He founded *Char-dham* pilgrimages which even today serve the same purpose. Adi Guru's efforts significantly undermined the fissiparous tendencies like different languages and geographical divisions. Perhaps his was an effort to establish unity in diversity.

The political chaos during the medieval period was more than alluring for the Muslim adventurers of central Asia who initially resorted to plunder the wealth and capture the humans for slavery. However, a few of them also began to harbour the thought of territorial aggrandisement and expansion of their faith, Islam. In the series of such invasions from central Asia came Zahir ud-Din Muhammad Babur. Babur founded Mughal dynasty which during the reign of Akbar grew as one of the mightiest empires of the contemporary world. This geopolitical stability during Mughal rule too is an index of India being a nation much before the British set their foot on the Indian soil. Even after Aurangzeb, when Mughal dynasty began losing power, their predecessors wielded once, the writ of their rule and their affirmations were needed by provincial powers to legitimise their political authority over their respective areas of influence. Moreover, as we have said earlier, the culture and the religion have always been such that these provided the pearls of diversity, a string of unity, strong enough even in times of political duress to hold the nation as one. Perhaps this was the strength behind India's first struggle for Independence in 1857 as it did witness cultural and religious undercurrents aimed at solidifying the efforts of the natives trying to come out of the colonial yoke. Noticeably, these cultural and socio-religious undercurrents were providing the people of India the foundation and faith in their ability to rise in rebellions which occurred before 1857. One of the most prominent of such rebellions was the one known to us as Sannyasin Rebellion. This armed upheaval happened in Bengal in the first half of the 1770s. This uprising was fated to acquire mythical proportions when the famous Bengali author Bankim Chandra Chatterjee penned a novel based on the Sannyasin Revolt. The novel was 'Anand Math,' and its song 'Vande Mataram' was destined to become the war cry for the rebellious masses, a symbol of the country's pride and eventually its national song.

Interestingly, imperialistic political thinkers and writers tried to impress a point that India was not at all a nation until the advent of the West in the Indian subcontinent, of course, as a power enforcing on the Indian people as masters of their fate. What is more surprising is the fact that many people believed in the western political outlook about Indian Nationalism, such was the hegemony exercised by the colonial power over the colonised. Such hegemonic influences often called colonial hangover continue even today and as a result of this disturbing trend, Indian Nationalism with its well-established antiquity has not been portrayed in a historically correct perspective.

It is pertinent to note the fact that many rebellions were being waged against the enemy in zamindars and other local power magnets responsible for their miseries as people initially failed to see the colonial power, the real enemy. However, this foresight was not going to be an everlasting deprivation as there emerged a class not only educated, but thoroughly inbred in the western ethos but still Indian at heart. This class was to lead what was dubbed as the Bengal Renaissance. In the first few decades of the 19th Century, many educated people of India believed that the country was in shambles because of many archaic socio-cultural practises which over a while not only lost meaning, but also turned into evil practises. Child marriage, sati and the overall treatment meted out to the widows were prominent among them. Then there were also questions on the relevance of the Indian education system and what was being taught to the students. The flag bearer of Bengal Renaissance was Raja Ram Mohan Roy. Henri Louise Vivian Derozio (1809-31) and his father, Francis Derozio, Debendranath Tagore, Ishwar Chand Vidhyasagar, Micheal Madhusudan Dutt and Bankimchandra Chatterjee, etc., were certain other leading faces of the Bengal Renaissance. This class of educated people was proud to be an Indian, a fact that Henri Derozio's lament can testify that for the lost pride of his Motherland and his prayer that the toil of Indians like him begets a boon of the betterment of the country.

My country! In thy days of glory past
A beauteous halo circled round thy brow
and worshipped as a deity thou wast—
Where is thy glory, where the reverence now?
Thy eagle pinion is chained down at last,
And grovelling in the lowly dust art thou,
Thy minstrel hath no wreath to weave for thee
Save the sad story of thy misery!
Well—let me dive into the depths of time
And bring from out the ages, that have rolled
A few small fragments of these wrecks sublime
Which human eye may never more behold
And let the guerdon of my labour be,
My fallen country! One kind wish for thee!

They ardently felt that western education could be of immense advantage for the Indians to come out of the deep slumber and forge ahead in all walks of life. They also had belief in the benevolent nature of the British rule. The first half of the 19th Century witnessed an intellectually intense period, and a host of initiatives were taken up by these leaders to address the socio-cultural and educational ailments of the Indian society.

However, their understanding could not penetrate beyond the mask of British benevolence which was out to cater to her greed even by virtually sucking the blood of the colonised Indian subjects. The first-ever realisations about the real intentions of the British rule came to the fore not out of sudden divine realisation. It was to come from people who toiled hard to understand this evil facet of colonial rule through proper research and observations. Now the time was ripe for the new crop of Indian leaders who were all set to take the struggle against the imperial power to an entirely new level. Bengal of the second half of the 19th Century was now consecrated with patriotism, and it was ready to lead the country in her struggle against the British Raj. This particular period gave several new leaders in luminaries from Bengal alone like Rabindranath Tagore, Swami Ramakrishna Paramhansa, Swami Vivekanand, Dr. Mahendra Lal Sarkar, Rajendra Lal, W.C. Banerjee, Anand Mohan Bose and Surendranath Banerjee.

This was also the time when Indian Nationalism was for the first time being firmly entrenched across the whole nation. The new class of Indian freedom fighters got a new understanding of the real face of the British economic policies, which eventually help them wage the long war against colonial oppression. For the first time in 1867, Dada Bhai Naoroji and R.C. Dutt, in their respective books, namely 'The Poverty and British Rule in India' and 'The Economic History of India', laid exploitation by the British threadbare. This exposition of the economic exploitation by the colonial power was pitted and used against the tyranny of the Englishmen. Both Naoroji and R.C. Dutt proved that the miseries of Indian people were not because of any divine curse, but were the result of the Imperial policies thoroughly orchestrated and intended to exploit the subjugated masses of the colony. Interestingly, with such elucidations of economic nature of the British rule, there began a long series of efforts aimed at exposing the truth behind the so-called compassion of the 'White Man's Burden' especially its real economic countenance. The leaders representing almost every part of the country mounted severe attacks on the Raj based on such economic critiques. Among those who took the lead were prominent figures like Gopal Krishna Gokhale, G.B. Joshi, Surendranath Banerjee, Mahadev Govind Ranade, D.I. Wacha, Bal Gangadhar Tilak, and G. Subramaniyam Aiyyar, etc. Even more interesting was the fact that now not only Indian economic analysts, but literati also included a few offshore names too. Bharatendu Harishchandra, the father of modern Hindi literature, satirised in 1880:

अंग्रेज राज सुख साज सबे सब भारी।
पै धन विदेश चलि जात इहै अति खारी।।

(The pleasure of English rule overpowers all, but the painful and sorrowful thing is that our wealth drains to the foreign land.)

Similar were the echoes from nowhere else, but Britain itself when the famous English poet Thomas Campbell composed...

"Rich in the gems of India's gaudy zone
And plunder piled from kingdoms not their own."

The Bengal Plunder, as Adams describes it in 'The Law of Civilisation and Decay', arrived in London soon after the Battle of Plassey and offered a foundation on which the industrial regeneration of England was based.

This was also the time when winds of Nationalism and unification of Italy and Germany were blowing across the oceans. The winds of change also reached the Indian shores. The monumental efforts of Bismarck for German unification and of Cavour, Garibaldi, and Mazzini for Italian unification were mesmerising enough to catch the attention of the Indian freedom fighters. With their excellent understanding of western knowledge and wisdom, the Indian leaders were smart in taking the lessons of Nationalism from Europe and the eventual application of the same to make the Indian freedom struggle more potent. India's struggle for Independence, which till then was fragmented and to a great extent localised, started becoming pan-Indian. The leaders gradually started looking beyond their provinces by not only taking up issues which had an impact on people of other states and also began travelling to other parts of the country to provide the people much-needed stimuli to rise against the oppressive regime.

India's first war of Independence, 1857 was remarkable not only because of its scale, strategising and courage to fight against an enemy which over a period of time assumed monstrous proportion, but also for the fact that communal cordiality was to the forefront as Hindu and Muslim communities fought hand in hand against the enemy whom they believed was the reason behind their economic, social, cultural and religious impoverishment. This communal camaraderie during 1857 made the British not only fearful for their future as masters of this resource yielding colony, but also devise a strategy, notoriously known as 'Divide and Rule', to make their fortunes in India everlasting. The most revealing statement on the 'Divide and Rule' game of the British came in 1881 from Sir John Strachey, who said, "The existence side by the side of the hostile creeds is one of the strongest points in our political position in India.[1]" The most prominent example of the implantation of the policy came as a shock to the people of Bengal, as they were at the vanguard of the Nationalist Movement, which was growing leaps and bounds. In 1905, with Lord Curzon at the helm of affairs in India, Bengal was partitioned, apparently for administrative comforts as the state was too large for the British to run it efficiently.

Lord Durham said, "It seems to have been the considered policy of the British Government to govern its colonies by means of division and to break them down as much as possible into petty isolated communities incapable of combination and possessing no sufficient strength for individual resistance to the Empire."

However, in the womb of the partition of Bengal was Swadeshi Movement which was to transform the cinders of India's struggle for Independence in conflagration inciting the imagination of almost every Indian for a life free from subjugation. Writing on the Bengal Partition in his book 'Hind Swaraj', Mahatma Gandhi says, "True renaissance came after the partition of Bengal. We are

indebted to Lord Curzon for that." Bengal was to receive another dent by the British when in 1911, Calcutta (Kolkata) was stripped of its status as the capital of India under the English rule. This was, of course, another attempt to weaken the resistance they were facing from the people of Bengal who by now began to use revolutionary methods preached by new leaders like Aurobindo Ghosh.

Nevertheless, the roots of resistance gained unfathomable depth, and the all-encompassing nature of the struggle had in it the cementing force of literature, art, education, in fact, culture in its entirety. The impact of such an all-inclusive struggle meant that more and more people could understand the real face of the rule. The reflections of the same can be gauged from the fact that this was the time when Bengal becomes the soil giving birth to the most fervent minds of the time. Rabindra Nath Tagore's 'Gitanjali' winning him the Nobel Prize for literature in 1913 was perhaps a crowning glory.

Shri Aurobindo, in his famous book 'The Ideal of Human Unity' says, "Bengal has given the gift of greatest and creative talent to the English language. Bengal gave birth to the first modern Indian poet who became world-famous." The artists like Gaganendranath and Abanindranath rose to fame during this time. Nandlal Bose was yet another son of the soil who was busy contributing with his paintbrush, beautiful hues to the cultural contour of Bengal. This was also the time when Vivekanand and Shri Aurobindo were trying to teach the masses about India's spiritual heritage and its ability to answer the vexed questions of life.

Noticeably, the initiatives were not confined to literature, fine arts, etc., but there was a conscious effort made by the contemporary intelligentsia to promote and imbibe the new trends of science as well. The leaders believed that the scientific temper of the people too needed an overhaul to make them befitting to the times the world succeeded after Industrial Revolution. This was also felt that growth of science and technology was synonymous to success. Toeing to this line, the nationalist leaders, supported by donations from like-minded rich people, began to open institutions for research and development. The first name that comes to our mind is that of the prominent scientist Prafulla Chandra Ray who lived and immensely contributed to the growth of sciences during the heyday of the Indian freedom struggle. His efforts yielded a new branch of Chemistry. Jagdish Chandra Bose was yet another luminary in the sphere of sciences whose contribution gave the Indian people a self-belief in their capabilities to forge ahead in all walks of life. The nationalist leaders had firm faith that through the expansion of education among the masses, the movement will gain immense strength. Therefore, they preached an all-encompassing education.

The leaders of the Indian struggle for Independence knew that the education proposed by the British proved the most potent tool for them to expand the colonial hegemony. They also understood the fact that the intellectual and educational liberty precedes all kinds of liberty, including economic and political liberty. The freedom fighters also had the insight to see the truth behind the process of indoctrination of the people of India in the principles of the sham benevolence of White man's burden'. The British always tried to hold the strings of higher education in their hands. How the British wanted to control education can be summed up in the words of none other than Sir Charles Wood. He was against imparting higher education to all Indians. He only wanted to educate the rich people of India. He was against giving facilities to the future critics, challengers and complainants. Wood's Dispatch (1864) was no less significant that Lord Macaulay's 'Minutes' on Indian education (1835).

Sir Charles Wood's opinion is a clear index of how Britain perceived the spread of education among the masses and how a literate mass could acquire potency to rise against the Empire. The Dispatch, in reality, promoted Western literature and knowledge, and government offices showed preferences for persons educated in English. The education planning and management schemes remained only in black and white. It neglected general education. Only the privileged class could receive education. Indigenous schools remained neglected. Priority was given to people educated on English pattern about government posts. The Dispatch did not aim at education for leadership, education for the industrial regeneration of India, education for the defence of the Motherland, in short, education required by the people of a self-governing nation. Departments of Education were opened in the five provinces, but they could not promote the real interest of education. The system of grants-in-aid did not operate in the proper sense, i.e., there was always the paucity of funds, the irregularity of their release and biased attitude towards the privately managed schools. The idea of providing vocational education as advocated by the Dispatch was, in reality, absent. People were facing the problem of unemployment. The Wood's Dispatch could not remove the imbalance in the Indian education system. The rich people sent their children to English-medium schools, and the government gradually stopped financial aid to the indigenous schools, and so the existence of these schools became jeopardised. It failed to develop character initiative and leadership among students. The Dispatch succeeded in only producing a class of clerks and accountants.

Therefore, it was not surprising that the leaders, including the pioneer of 'Bengal Renaissance', not only aspired for a broader base of education, but prophesied how vital it could be for emancipation. Writing to Mr. Wynn, one of his English friends, Raja Ram Mohan Roy said, "Supposing that some 100 years hence the Native character becomes elevated from constant intercourse with Europeans and acquirements of general and political knowledge as well as of modern arts and sciences, is it possible that they will not have the spirit as well as the inclination to resist effectually unjust and oppressive measures serving to degrade them in the scale of society." The prediction began to gain stable soil underneath in the first half of the 20th Century as a large number of educated Indians took the torch of learning and education to the fellow countrymen and taught them to march together for freedom. Leaders like Raja Ram Mohan Roy thought that western education, art and culture could be beneficial for the upliftment of the Indian society. They also believed that such contact with Europe will also make Indian people prudent enough to understand the oppressive nature of the colonial regime, but will also help them come up with the knowledge to wage a struggle against it. This presage was not far from turning into a truth.

The Indian intelligentsia was also aware of the fact that a large country like India slipped into slavery because of internal strife and other such frailties of the Indian society. That's why they resorted to putting first their own house in order before taking the bull of Imperialism by its horns. They not only criticised the shortcomings of their social system, but also put new ideas, like humanism, equality for all, reason and scientific temper, etc., on the anvil. However, it was carefully taken enterprise which witnessed a delicate balance between tradition and modernity. Therefore, the leader-scholars like Tilak and several others also brought to the fore the time-tested virtues of Indian culture. Now there was a conscious effort on their part to promote the Indian languages and vernaculars along with modern education to give these ideas a much-needed reach to the ordinary people.

It is pertinent to note here that the first half of the 19th Century was witnessing an unprecedented spree of social, religious, cultural and political movements led by people who wanted to acclimatise the best practises and policies of the West. However, amidst all such causes and effects developed a class of western educated people who were rooted in the clutches of the preaching of people like Macaulay and eventually lost the sense of Nationalism and, as a result, foresight and will to fight the enemy present in the guise of the benefactor. There was also an assemblage of people who blindly opposed the benefits of western education as they wanted to cling to their past thoughtlessly and opposed even the most positive changes aimed at the betterment of the country. Fortunately enough, such classes of people were fast losing ground vis-à-vis the far-sighted nationalists.

Amongst such nationalist Sir Asutosh Mookerjee was foremost. Sir Asutosh Mookerjee, the first Indian to become Vice Chancellor of Calcutta University, had a firm belief what Indian philosophy advocates as a tool for mankind's emancipation, *'Sa Vidya ya vimuktaye* (सा विद्या या विमुक्तये)*'*. Sir Asutosh knew that equipping Indian educational institute with a reasonable approach towards modern pedagogy was the need of the hour. It was also needed that the learned men need to be made part of academic facilities. As a result of his endeavour, eminent scholars like Sir C. V. Raman, Dr. Rajendra Prasad, and Dr. Sarvepalli Radhakrishnan found an academic platform which catapulted the ethos of learning in India to newer heights. Above all, he was, both by his sheer presence in a household and his deliberate efforts, shaping a leader and an educationist par excellence in Syama Prasad Mookerjee, his son. It was no surprise that his son Syama was destined to become the foremost flag-bearer of the Indian education.

Endnotes

1. Sir John Strachey, India. London: 1888. p. 225.

□

2

Ancestry and Heritage

"The last eight years, in truth, have been years of unremitting struggle; difficulties and obstacles kept springing up like the heads of Hydra, each head armed with sharp and often venomous fangs. A late lamented member of the Syndicate once very aptly alluded to the toil of the Syndicate and the Vice Chancellor as truly Herculean. Of myself, I may say with good conscience that if often I have not spared others, I have never spared myself. For years now, every hour, every minute I could spare from other unavoidable duties—foremost among them the duties of my judicial office—has been devoted by me to university work. Plans and schemes to heighten the efficiency of the university have been the subject of my daydreams into which even a busy man lapses from time to time; they have haunted me in the hours of nightly rest. To university concerns I have sacrificed all chances of study and research, possibly, to some extent, the interests of my family and friends, and certainly, I regret to say, a good part of my health and vitality. Do not imagine, however, that I repine at the sacrifices made. I have had my reward in many ways. I need not remind you that great comfort springs from the consciousness of rectitude of purpose, from the conviction, that the cause to which one devotes all his strength and for which one renounces the ordinary delight of life, is a high and sacred one. But, also, I have enjoyed many bright moments of a more definite character."

—Sir Asutosh Mookerjee

(from convocation address of Calcutta University; 28 March 1914)

On an intellectual level, roots of the Mookerjee family lie in Bengal's 'New Renaissance'. This is like a big tree the roots of which are deep spread on earth. A human being's achievement can touch the sky; however, his relation remains forever with the mother earth.

There were many established erudite scholars of Sanskrit and Bangla literature in the ancestors of Syama Prasad. His ancestor Ram Mookerjee was the brother of Narsingh Ojha, great grandfather of Krittibas Ojha, the celebrated translator of the epic Ramayana into Bengali. Due to an unendurable political situation, Narsingh Ojha left his father's house in Sonar village of East Bengal and came to the village of Phulia near Shantipur in Navadwip district of West Bengal. Vishwanath, the great grandfather of Syama Prasad, was brought up in his maternal uncle's home in Jirat, Hugli district (West Bengal). He settled himself permanently in Jirat, and it became the realm of his genealogy.

Ramchandra Tarkalankar, the brother of Syama Prasad's great grandfather, was a renowned professor of Sanskrit in Calcutta. Navgopal, son of Ramchandra, was also a teacher in a Sanskrit college. Vishwanath, Syama Prasad's great grandfather, is also credited with writing one of the earliest travelogues in Bengali, describing his travel by boat from Kalna to Rangpur. This book is an example of a simple prose style, whereas Bangla prose was still in the developing stage. Durgaprasad, Vishwanath's brother, memorised so many old creations of Bangla. Hariprasad, another brother of Vishwanath, too wrote prose and poetry in Bangla. His book 'Vichitra Bangchitra' was published in 1887.

Vishwanath and his wife went for their final journey in early stage leaving behind their four sons, Durga Prasad, Hari Prasad, Ganga Prasad and Radhika Prasad when they were seventeen, fifteen, thirteen and ten years old, respectively. All the boys were very bright and pursued their study with great vigour in spite of odds and hurdles in their lives. Durga Prasad, the elder of brothers, moved to a place called Andul in Howrah district to work as a school teacher and brought his brothers along too. He was a parent to his brothers at this stage. He moved to other places like Tamlak, and also tried to train himself in more lucrative and chose to study civil engineering, and eventually rose to be the district engineer in Ghazipur in the United Provinces (now Uttar Pradesh). He finally moved to Calcutta. Here he got his brothers admitted to schools to complete their education.

Ganga Prasad got admitted to the Hare school, the best school in the city. Ganga Prasad took the entrance exam conducted by Calcutta University in the year 1857, the year Calcutta University was founded. He not only cleared the exam, but also won a scholarship. He got admitted to Presidency College. He qualified Bachelor's degree in Arts in 1861. After that, he decided to study medicine and enrolled himself at the newly established medical college in Kolkata and cleared medicine degree with credit in 1866. For some time, he studied Law also. In medical college, he proved himself a meritorious student and won a medal for that.

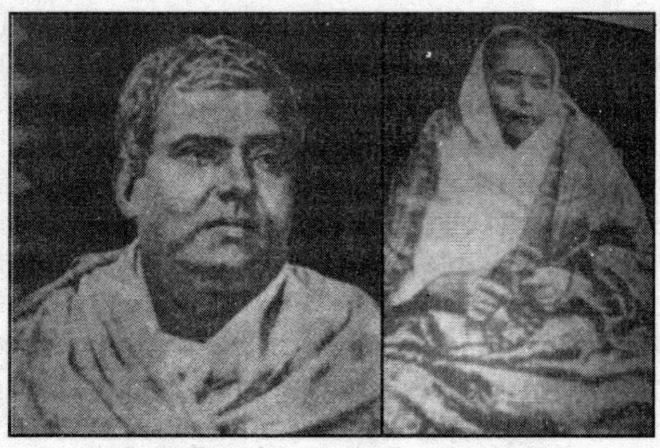

Ganga Prasad *Jagattarini*

He got married to Jagattariani, and their first son Asutosh was born on 29 June 1864 at rented premises at Malanga Lane, Bow Bazar, Kolkata. That age was of Bengali new Renaissance, and it was not a surprise that the son of Ganga Prasad would be one of the great sons of Bengal and a notable personality (Syama Prasad, great-grandson of Ganga Prasad) would be born in the year to come about whom this book has been penned down. Asutosh received full guidance and proper direction from his father, Dr. Ganga Prasad. Asutosh proved to be a talented student in his school.

Madhusudan Das was his home tutor, who, in later years, emerged as a popular leader.

For primary education, Asutosh got admission in South Suburban School. He became a member of the London Mathematical Society while still he was in school. His original contribution in the mathematical research field was named after him as 'Mookerjee theorem'. He was the first of his kind who got two post-graduate degrees in Physics & Mathematics. Apart from that, he became proficient in Physical Science, Law and Sanskrit language. His contemporaries started calling him an incarnation of goddess Saraswati. He received the title of Shastra-vachaspati. He had the quality of a good administrator as well as a good statesman; he accepted to be an educationist. The then Viceroy, Lord Curzon had been immensely impressed by his work as a member of Indian universities' commission that he decided to appoint him Vice Chancellor of the premier University of Calcutta as well as chief justice of the Calcutta high court.

Syama Prasad inherited self-esteem, robust uncompromising nationalism and his fearlessness from his father and great grandfather Ganga Prasad who refused to join Government service. It would be interesting to recount here an incident in the early life of Ganga Prasad which shows from where Asutosh had imbibed his strong spirit of self-respect. Once Ganga Prasad was asked to join the viceroy's establishment as a doctor. However, the military Secertary to the viceroy asked him to come in proper western dress code. He was asked to wear a pair of trousers in place of wearing dhoti. Ganga Prasad told his Principal that although he had been very kindly received by the Military Secretary, the latter did not want a good doctor, he only wanted a pair of trousers. He had, therefore, decided not to accept the appointment. Though he was under great financial stress, he would, he said, rather start an independent practise in his profession. Bhawanipur was then the residence of many eminent Bengalese of the time. Ganga Prasad decided to set up practise there. He soon acquired a large practice. He emerged as a good and renowned private physician. Sir Asutosh, father of Syama Prasad, too lived a life of utmost simplicity. He always dressed in the most ordinary *dhoti* and a short coat. In the High Court itself, he used to change his trousers after finishing his days' work. It was a remarkable sight to see him walking vigorously down the staircase reserved for his majesty judges, dressed in *dhoti* with the chadar carelessly thrown on one of his broad shoulders. He had agony over ruining of the Indian textile industry. Bharatendu Harishchandra (1850-1885), the father of modern Hindi literature, represented the agonies of Indian people and their exploitation by the British.

कल के कलबल छल सों इते के लोग।
नित-नित धन सों घटत हैं बाढ़त हैं दुःख सोग।।
मारकीन मलमल बिना चलत नहीं कछु काम।
परदेशी जुलहान कै मानहु भये गुलाम।।

(Spinning machines, crafty and foxy people
deceasing our poor weavers
decreasing wealth, increasing sorrow
people here, becoming slaves of foreign loomers.)

True Nationalists wanted to stay away from foreign clothes.

Rabindranath's poetry shows his anguish over the declining of the Indian textile industry. He described the pathetic condition of the time in his poetry. "My beloved nation, they (Britishers) live here indifferently, disdaining you, moreover, we just to get a promotion, have become their sycophants, and we wear their foreign clothes (shame!)"

Syama Prasad always wore swadeshi like his father and grandfather barring some occasions like when he was studying in Lincon's Inn in England.

Syama Prasad's grandfather flourished, and soon he purchased land in Bhawanipur and built his home in 1872. Ganga Prasad established his reputation as a writer also. He wrote books on Biology. He had a great love for his mother-tongue and completed a Bengali edition of the Ramayana. He was one of the earliest in Bengal to write books in vernacular dealing with the theory and practise of medicine and the health and proper development of the future mothers like *'Matrashiksha'*. He had a great love for literature. Asutosh's passion for books was steadily encouraged by his watchful father. Ganga Prasad's love for books transmitted in his son Asutosh who used to get up from bed very early and go for a walk together. Ganga Prasad used to tell his son the stories of great men. Asutosh was gifted with a prodigious memory. Even before he had reached his age fifteen, Asutosh memorised Defoe's 'Robinson Crusoe', Swift's 'Gulliver's Travels', Campbell's 'Pleasure of Hope', the first chapter of Pope's translation of the 'Iliad' and the first canto of Milton's 'Paradise Lost'.

Dr. Syama Prasad built a library in his house. He spent a good portion of his earning on the books. This characteristic was transmitted in his son Asutosh and grandson Syama Prasad. The exchange of letters between Ganga Prasad and Asutosh has been kept safely at microfilms division of Nehru Memorial Museum and Library, Teen Murti Bhavan, New Delhi. There have been kept so many bills of stationers which testify that he used to purchase books for Asutosh and least bothered about how expensive the book might be. The bill of 424 rupees 4 aana and seven pie, of 21 December, 1880 has the names of the following books: Trigonometry, Optics,

Modern Geometry, Conics, Linguistic, English Literature of Bernard Shaw, Literature of Chaucer, Anglo Saxon Dictionary (2. vols.) of Joseph Bosworth, Full Positive Philosophy, etc.

Bow Bazar

He used to purchase from Sumbhoo Chunder, a bookseller stationer, shop no. 58, Wellington Street, Bow Bazar, Calcutta.

Letter of 26 October 1882, written by Ganga Prasad, when he was in Gazipur to his sons Asutosh and Hemanto testify his opinion for literature. He wrote, "I spent the greater part of my time here in translating Roberts. This day I read the greater portion of Lethbridge's book on higher education. His advocacy of this cause and his defence of the educated natives entitle him to gratitude and respect of all." Asutosh replied on 28 October, "I have also read Lethbridge, and he stands single against the best so-called politician who is against state education... I want Demorgen's Double Algebra. I have just finished Markby's Jurisprudence for the last there weeks. It is not a book of a high order; besides the fundamental doctrine seems to be erroneous because inconsistent with modern ideas and of individuality and liberty.

I am reading Shakespeare's Sonnets which will be done by tomorrow. Hemanto, Fani, Girdhar and Harilal went for Wilson's circus in the night. If one is to keep up nights at all, it's far better to read than to see a ball or circus, of course, the case with Shakespeare's play is far different."

The exchange of letters explains that our hero's mental capabilities' foundation had been laid on. In the Mookerjee family, father-son relation was not about the fulfilling of the son's needs, but father had taken the responsibility of satiating the knowledge thirst of the son; in this manner, father was fully involved in growing up of his son.

Asutosh got admission in Presidency college for higher education where his classmate was Narendranath Dutt (Swami Vivekanand). The third roll of Asutosh papers, kept in Nehru Memorial Museum and Library, has his essays and lectures kept intact, among those are—Napoleon, Newton, William Scott, Emerson and classical education.

Asutosh was married as was the custom then while he was still a student (in his early 20s) to Jogmaya, the daughter of a simple and learned brahmin Ram Narayan Bhattacharya of Krishnanagar. To Asutosh's gladness, he didn't take a paisa in dowry.

A rare occasion when Asutosh took part in a political demonstration was in May 1883 when he was still a student of the Presidency College. The occasion was afforded by the well-known contempt of court case against Surendranath Banerjee, the famous nationalist leader. In his English daily, 'The Bengalee', Surendranath had made strong critical remarks against Mr. Justice Norris of the Calcutta High Court for having caused the household deity of a Hindu family to be produced in the court and, thereby, having hurt the religious feelings of the Hindus. He was charged with contempt of court and tried before a full bench of the High Court on 5 May 1883 and sentenced to imprisonment. In the words of Surendranath:

"The student community had mustered in strong force, and among them, I noticed some who rose to high distinction as servants of the crown. In the demonstration that followed the passing of the sentence, they took a leading part in a fashion, common among young men all over the world, smashing windows and pelting the police with stones. One of these rowdy youths was Asutosh Mookerjee." The religious, as well as the nationalist sentiments of young Asutosh, had been deeply touched.

Asutosh received Premchand Roychand studentship as early as in 1883. He topped the list in the B.A. examination of 1884. He was the first student to receive post-graduate degree in two subjects Physics and Mathematics. It is worthy to note that Asutosh was appointed examiner at the M.A. exam in Mathematics the year after he took his master's degree. He was the first Indian examiner. Asutosh took up the study of Law in 1885. He passed the B.L. examination in 1888. As a student of the Law Department of the City College, Calcutta, he was the pupil of Satyendra Prasanna Sinha, the eminent lawyer who later in life took a seat in the British House of Lords as Baron Sinha of Raipur.

The keen interest taken by Asutosh in legal studies while he was a student is shown by the fact that he attended the Tagore Law Lectures for three successive years and won the gold medal awarded for proficiency in the subject of the lectures. In 1893, he did his PhD under the guidance of Lord Sinha (then Mr. Sinha). In 1898, he delivered his famous Tagore lectures on the Law of Perpetuities, which was highly appreciated.

His book 'Geometry of Conics' was first published in 1893 by Macmillan & Company. The royalty papers of this book are kept in NMML (third roll of Asutosh papers-R-10976). This book is considered as a standard book for undergraduate classes; it has been incorporated in the syllabi of Cambridge University. It is worthy to note that Macmillan & Company also published Syama Prasad's book 'A Volume of Convocations & Other Speeches' in 1938.

For several years, Asutosh devotedly kept himself busy in studying, under the guidance of learned scholars. His eminent success was due to his forceful character and vast in-depth study. He grew up to be a multifaceted genius –Judge and Jurist, Mathematician, Scholar, Linguist, Educationist. For a short period of time, he engaged himself in teaching at Indian Agriculture Research Council. Dr. R.P. Paranjpye, a prominent mathematician of the time, remarked: "If he had made up his mind to devote himself entirely to the study of Mathematics, he was sure to have secured a place in the front rank of world mathematicians." An example of his dedication towards the learning is that he had mastered French and German to study certain treatise in original. He was a polyglot. He had the knowledge of some eighteen or nineteen languages.

Sir Asutosh referred to this aspect of his career while he was addressing the Senate in 1920. "Nothing is dearer to me; nothing has been dearer to me than my university. I began life as a research student in mathematics when the research was practically unknown in this country, and the ambition of my life was to be a research professor at my University. Mr. Justice Gooroodass Banerjee, who was then Vice Chancellor of this university, made a desperate attempt to create a chair for me, but such were the times that he failed to collect even a sum which would yield a modest income of ₹4,000 a year which was all that he and I thought would be sufficient to maintain me as a research professor. The result was that I drifted into Law, but I made a determination at the time that, Heaven willing, I would devote myself to the service of the university, so that in the next generation, any aspiring scholar in my position might not drift into Law, but have full opportunities to serve the cause of letters and Sciences."

In 1913, Asutosh set the seal of academic recognition of the Vernacular of the province by conferring the degree of Doctor of Literature on Rabindranath Tagore, "a loyal and life-long devotee of the most progressive of the Indian vernaculars". In April 1921, the Syndicate of the Calcutta University accepted with thanks a gift from Sir Asutosh to institute a gold medal to be bestowed once in every two years upon the individual deemed by the Syndicate to be most eminent for original contribution to Letters or Science written in the Bengali language. The medal was to be called the 'Jagattarini Medal' after the name of his mother. The first recipient of the medal was Dr. Rabindranath Tagore.

Sir Asutosh had another ability to spot and nurture the different talents. In 1921, Brajendranath Seal was appointed Vice Chancellor of the Mysore University, and Asutosh secured the services of Sarvepalli Radhakrishnan as George V Professor of Philosophy in his place. The great eminence to which Prof. Radhakrishnan rose later on in life showed how keen was Asutosh's faculty of discerning merit.

It was Sir Asutosh who discovered Sir C.V. Raman, India's and Asia's first Nobel laureate in Physics. At that time Raman was engaged in Finance dept. of Indian Govt. Mohammed Shahidullah, a Bengali Muslim youth and a graduate in Sanskrit honours, was practising as an advocate at the sub-divisional court at Basirhat. He was very talented but had been refused admission to the post-graduate clan in Sanskrit on the ground of his religion. Sir Asutosh arranged for him to study Sanskrit in France and, eventually, he turned out to be one of the most brilliant and outstanding scholars of the subcontinent.

Justice Sir Asutosh asked the junior-most lawyer in an important case to open the case, which would normally have been done by the senior lawyers. Sir Asutosh must have seen some spark in this young man, the boy was shy, but once he opened the case, his talent shone forth, and his shyness left him. Later, he called him to his Chamber and offered him a lectureship at the University Law college which he thankfully accepted. The young man was none other than the first President of the Republic of India—Dr. Rajendra Prasad. Sir Asutosh was one of those personalities who discovered the talent of Srinivas Ramanujan.

Likewise, he had also brought in people like Ganesh Prasad (a great mathematician); Brajendra Nath Seal (Classmate of Swami Vivekanand and founder member of Ramkrishan Mission); Dr. Bhandarkar (Prof. of History and Sanskrit); H.S. Suhrawardhi (Chief Minister of Bengal (1946-47) and the fifth Prime Minister of Pakistan (1956-57)); Khudabux (Founder of Khudabux Oriental Library); K.S.

Jaiswal (renowned historian); C.E. Cullis (a great mathematician); Abnindra Nath Tagore (great painter of Bengal school of art); G. Thibaut (astronomer); Yamakani (A sanskrit Scholar); R. Kiyura (Scholar of Hinyan and Mahayan Budhisam); Manoharlal (Historian); W.H. Young (Mathematician); Kazim Shirazi (Litterateur); I.J.S. Taraporevala (Linguist); A.R. Forsyth (Prof. Geometry); etc. Just to name a few.

During his Barrister days, he trained so many junior advocates, Sir Asutosh's clerk was an intelligent, humble student who was like him in Mathematics and Law. He belonged to a Muslim farmer family. He was Abdul Qasim Fazlul Haq who became the chief minister of Bengal in days to come. He was called 'Sher-e-Bengal' in Bangladesh. He had an intimate relationship with Syama Prasad. We will discuss him in later pages of the book.

Sir Asutosh prepared a clan of educated Indians who were ready to follow the footprints of him; besides he started instilling his own qualities in his second son Syama Prasad.

Sir Asutosh had an enviable string of academic degrees and honours bestowed on him. These were written with his name as CIE, CSI, MA, PRS, DSC, DL, FRAS, FRSE, *Saraswati, Shastravachaspati, Sambuddhagam, Bharatmartand,* Dr. in Law, etc.

Institutions were honoured by offering their membership to him. He was a member of the Royal Asiatic Society; a fellow of the Royal Society, Edinburgh; a member of the Syndicate of the Calcutta University in 1889; a judge of the High Court at Calcutta in 1904; and the Vice Chancellor of the University in 1906, and continued in that post till 1914. Again, he adorned that post from 1921-1923. In 1914, he established Calcutta University College of Science. He played a great role in establishing Bengal Technical Institute at Jadavpur (Now Jadavpur University). He opened Calcutta Mathematical Society in 1908. Nobel Laureate Rabindra Nath Tagore said about him, "In the field of Education, Asutosh fought the obstacles with bravery in making our country independent." One of the speeches titled 'The Future of Indian Literature' has a preface by Rabindranath Tagore, which is:

"I have clearly felt the greatness of Asutosh as revealed in his essay 'The Future of Indian Literature' where he has outlined his noblest ideals and aspirations with the whole of India as its background. He boldly employed his creative faculties at the University against all heavy odds. Here he was engaged in the task of liberating the mind of the whole of India and laying the foundation of the treasure house of knowledge. With his extraordinary achievement and breadth of vision, he aimed at providing for the future a stable and permanent haven for the entire country and attempted to set up a lasting memorial on the extended basis of that institution. I have realised the essential nature of his sublime ideal, and I pay homage to the great intellect that has departed forever." (Translation of Jatiya Sahitya by Bharatiya Vidya Bhavan)

In the speech "The Future of Indian Literature", Sir Asutosh had voiced his vision of assimilation of literary ideas among different regions of India, which will ultimately pave the way towards national unity. He called upon his countrymen in the following words:

"Today we have to leave aside the map of Bengal and look at the map of India. Standing on the banks of the Ganges, we have to take an imaginative plunge into the Narmada, Sindhu and Kavery; in the green lap of Bengal, we have to see visions of Rajputana—Stretch your arms and embrace the whole of India and bring it close to your heart. We must be prepared to accept what is good in others. If we have something good to offer, we should be willing to offer it gracefully to others. Without such an exchange, our literature cannot thrive, nor can it attain fullness. We have to find a common means that would help unite in a single thread Bengal, Bihar, Orissa, Madras, Gujarat, Rajputana, Gandhar and Punjab, and they can meet together in the same realm of literature." (Translation of Jatiya Sahitya by Bharatiya Vidya Bhavan)

Sir Asutosh was a great Nationalist. He was proud of being himself an Indian. He realised that the development of National language as distinct from English was essential to create appreciation and love in the new generation for their national life and culture so that the flag of cultural unity be raised up.

In 1906, he introduced 'Bengali language', as a separate subject in University. He started a post-graduate degree in regional languages. Towards the end of his Vice Chancellorship on 8.4.1922, Sir Asutosh said, "I will do everything in my power to train students in Bengal and send them forth in Bengal, and make the people of Bengal realise that they are Bengalis and not Englishmen." On another instance, he said, "We shall learn English quite as well as an Englishman or even better. But that will not prevent us from learning our mother-tongue."

Sir Asutosh was a man of modern thought. Facing a tremendous resistance in getting his widow daughter remarried by the orthodox Hindus, Sir Asutosh remained firm and braved all the resistance.

The staunch Nationalism in Sir Asutosh and spread of good human values in his house had a deep influence on Syama Prasad. His fearlessness and ardent love of freedom impressed Syama Prasad most. The guiding Principal of Sir Asutosh's life was "Freedom first, freedom second, freedom always." Sir Asutosh was perhaps the most fearless of the public figures of India of his time. His fearlessness was seen in provincial and imperial councils where he roared like a lion in putting forth his views untrammelled by any considerations of fear or favour. We will have to quote a classic example of his fearlessness. He was invited by Lord Curzon to go to London as a representative of Calcutta to attend the Coronation of Edward VII. This was undoubtedly a great honour. Asutosh told him that he could not go as his mother would not allow him. Lord Curzon is reported to have asked him to tell his mother that he will have to go under orders of the representative of sovereign India. To this, Asutosh said that his mother would reply that nobody except herself had the right to issue orders to her son. He was noted for his remarkable independence and enjoyed the full confidence of the public.

Syama Prasad inherited the fearlessness from his father. Sir Asutosh gave a tremendous contribution in nurturing and fostering the ideology of Dr. Syama Prasad. For this, the society will always be indebted to him. The natural blending of Indian spiritual and moral values, patience with philosophical and scientific ideology gave birth to a great educationist, a great statesman and a great personality Dr. Syama Prasad Mookerjee.

□

3
Early Life

"Faith in the worth of the smallest fact and the laws that govern the star-beams,
Faith in the beauty of truth and the truth of perfect beauty.
Faith in the God who creates the souls of men, by knowledge and love and worship."
(From a poem referred by Sir Asutosh Mookerjee in his Convocation address, Calcutta University, 18 May 1922.)

What distinctive feature separates a genius from a common man? The genius quickly finds out the answer to the problem which a common man is unable to understand. A genius is generally a man with one supreme gift, a gift which overshadows all other gifts. His abilities lie in more directions than one, all equally developed and all equally noteworthy. What is there in such genius talents which take them beyond the limits of Geography and Time? Why do these personalities' experiences, inspirations and teachings become all-time useful? What ability and thought power do they have that they become successful in realising the highest goals. Why these people become cynosure to all? Lives of great men leave footprints on the sands of time. They inspire others to make their lives sublime too. Such men have the exceptional ability and cognition to realise the highest goals. Such people create their environment, which leads to their splendid success in life. We will try to find the answers to the above significant questions by analysing some unique aspects of the life of Dr. Syama Prasad Mookerjee.

Howrah Bridge-1901

Kolkata (Calcutta) being a significant port city gradually became a truly cosmopolitan city comprising traders, travellers, etc., representing geographies from across the globe. The very fact became raison d' être behind Kolkata's munificent and all-embracing character. The backbone of Indian faith and agriculture, the Ganges completes her journey from the Himalayas and meet the Bay of Bengal in Kolkata on the one hand, while, on the other hand, thalassic spirits brought to the city not only trade and commerce, but also myriad cultures to the city. All the above factors contributed to the city's distinctive character building. Political and Economic factors also contributed to giving Kolkata a unique character. Apart from other factors, this port city also contributed eventually in the personality development of Dr. Syama Prasad Mookerjee.

Childhood

Syama Prasad Mookerjee, second son of Sir Asutosh Mookerjee and Jogmaya Devi, was born in Kolkata at 77, Russa

Road, Bhawanipur (now Asutosh Mookerjee Road) on 6 July 1901. Beni, the nickname of Syama Prasad, grew up to be a stout child. As he was darker in complexion than his brothers, the other children of the family used to tease him by calling him 'Bhutu'. His elder brother Ramaprasad and his cousin Bankda used to call him by this name only even in later years of his life. One person who used to love Syama Prasad dearly was his grandmother's brother Aadhar Chandra Chatterjee. He was very great at storytelling and listening to stories was the passion of little Syama Prasad. Sir Asutosh believed that telling stories to children was like providing them with food for the development of their mind. Whenever he had the opportunity to spend time with children, he used to tell them stories of great men. Syama Prasad also loved to visit his *mamar bari* (mother's parents' house) which was in Krishnanagar. One of the primary reasons for having the pleasure in visiting *mamar bari was* the availability of special sweets (*Sarbhaja* and *Sarpuria*) at Krishnanagar as Syama Prasad was very fond of eating sweets.

Syama Prasad's Father Sir Asutosh Mookerjee and Mother Jogmaya Debi

Syama Prasad's mother and grandmother were strict vegetarians—no onions even. No outside eatables were allowed in Mookerjee house. Food in the Mookerjee household was rice as a staple with much milk. Sir Asutosh was fond of milk and Bengali sweets made out of milk. Sir Asutosh's wife and mother were very orthodox about food and would eat only what they had cooked and drink water only from river Ganges. They specifically took care of hygiene and purity in food. Sir Asutosh stayed clear of tea or food served at the establishment of a foreigner, including the Government House.

Sir Asutosh was a religious Hindu Brahmin, though unorthodox in his way, but he did not try to inculcate his specific kind of religiosity in his children and would rather liked that they grew up according to the beliefs that they developed along the way. He was a great disciplinarian—a disciplined administrator and a disciplined father. His children developed around his set of laws at home. Children of the Mookerjee family were not allowed to roam around the streets. Sir Asutosh had the habit of going for the morning walk daily, the habit he inherited from his father. Syama Prasad adopted this very routine.

Syama Prasad with his father Sir Asutosh Mookerjee

The Ancestral House of Syama Prasad

Russa Road

The Layout and Ambiance of Ancestral Home

The broad but moderately built three-storeyed house, better known as 77, Russa Road, Bhawanipur, can be called aesthetically beautiful. It had been a meeting place of great intellectuals for over half a century. This house still stands. The house had a very long frontage and an enormous gate in front. Inside, on the left, was the main entrance, a staircase to go up to the first floor where offices were built. The ground floor, after the staircase, had mainly areas for storage, dining area, worship rooms, kitchens, and bathrooms. There were two courtyards. Another staircase went up near the dining area to the first floor where there were bedrooms, a long verandah and the only staircase to go to the second floor. Everywhere and every place, of course, had books. This was one of the largest, if not the most extensive, private libraries. The second floor had the main and enormous library and had bedrooms and washrooms.

77, Russa Road

Syama Prasad's grandfather, Dr. Gangaprasad built the left side of the main building and the right side (the New House–*natunbari*) was built by his father Sir Asutosh. They were interconnected and part of each other. In the new house, on the ground floor, but detached were two shops on rent, one was clothing shop and the other a medicine store which was run by Dr. Hem Sen who lived at the back of the house. Besides the main building, there was a sizeable compound where there were quarters for the servants, gatekeepers, drivers, coachmen, etc., besides cowshed, stable and garage. There were two motor cars, one Studebaker and the other a Daimler and a horse cart. There were few cows to give fresh milk to the family. This area was under the control of the main gatekeeper Karan—a huge man who looked like a sumo wrestler. In fact, in early days, he was a wrestler. He used to give physical training to the children of the family.

There were so many cats all over the house; no one was

their patron. Though they were fed but not pampered. Whenever the cat population reached a new high, some of them were put in gunny bags, taken by car and released in a distant part of the town. However, after a lapse of a few days, many cats would return home—covering a distance of five to ten miles! Sir Asutosh would express his appreciation about the intelligence and sense of direction of the homecoming cats! Whatever the case, they were never harmed. The Mookerjee family had sentiments of kindness towards animals.[1]

The above description clears that Mookerjee family was an enriched family economically and intellectually. The atmosphere at home was pious and pure (*Sattvik*). The books got a special and important place at their home. It was evident that children got acquainted with great books in their childhood. Books were available for the sharp and intelligent mind and healthy body there was healthy and pure food plus training of wrestling.

The Mookerjee family, the devotee of God, was a unique amalgamation of human values and professional ethics. The feeling of 'universal welfare' was always the priority of the Mookerjee family. Their inspiration for blissful life lied in the following sloka of Rigveda:

सर्वे भवन्तु सुखिनः
सर्वे सन्तु निरामयाः ।
सर्वे भद्राणि पश्यन्तु
मा कश्चिद्दुःखभाग्भवेत् ।

(May all become happy, May all be free from illness.
May all see what is auspicious, May no one suffer in any way.)

Endnotes

1. Banerjee Purnendu. Sir Asutosh: Our Grandfather. Bhartiya Vidya Bhawan; 1992, p. 9-11.

□

4

From Student to Scholar

"To my mind, the University is a great storehouse of learning, a great bureau of standards, a great workshop of knowledge, a great laboratory for the training as well of men of thought as of men of action. The University is thus the instrument of the State for the conservation of knowledge, for the discovery of knowledge, for the distribution of knowledge, for the applications of knowledge, and, above all, for the creation of knowledge-makers."

—Sir Asutosh Mookerjee

(Excerpt from the convocation address of Calcutta University, 18 March 1922)

The first indication that Syama Prasad was a child prodigy, so far as his extraordinary inclination and love for education are concerned, came from the fact that he was given admission directly in class 2 in the Bhawanipur Mitra Institution when he was 5. This was not such a common practise then, but his learning

habits were such that Sir Asutosh Mookerjee was convinced that his ward would be able to handle this little transition often a big asking from a kid of 5. His father Sir Asutosh inspired his friend Sir Bisheswar Mitra to set up his Mitra

Mitra Institution, Bhawanipur

Institution at Bhawanipur, where Sir Asutosh's sons got their early education. He could easily afford to send him to any of the public schools run by Englishmen in Calcutta or elsewhere. However, his nationalism, grounded as it was on Indian culture and ideas, would not allow him to send his son to public school. He was well aware of the fact that they could de-nationalise even the best and most promising of Indian boys.

Syama Prasad, as it was expected, did exceptionally well in school. The only change from his home and the first formal institution was that in the list of mentors apart from his father were added a few more names. Harshnath Banerjee was credited to have a very positive and lasting impact on his young pupil. He taught him between 1907 and 1910. In his memoir, Banerjee remembered Syama Prasad as a student who was bright and full of potential. According to Banerjee, Syama Prasad never tried to show attitude just as his father was such a big personality. He never used to fight with his classmates. Banerjee used to tell him stories of great men like George Washington and Napoleon Bonaparte. It was a rare interest in the small-aged kid. He would read and adapt more and mix with boys above his age. Satish Chandra Basu, Principal of School, used to teach him English. His other teachers were, Bishweshwar Mitra,

Syama Prasad (right sitting), Ramaprasad (left sitting), Bamaprasad (left standing), Umaprasad (middle standing), Jagattarini Debi (centre sitting), Amala (right standing) – year 1908

Dulal Chandra Sarkar, Pandit Hemchandra Bidyaratan, Nagendra Nath Mitra, Mukund Pada Roy, Kumud Chandra Roychowdhury, Asutosh Ghosh (a freedom fighter), Samarjeet Datta, Pandit Panchanan Bhattacharya. Jatindra Nath Mitra, the Mathematics teacher, used to tell his students to chant *Hari-Naam.* According to a retired teacher of the school, Sri Harshnath Bandyopadhyay, "Syama Prasad had various positive qualities as a student. He never fought with his fellow friends in school. He was quite attentive to his lessons and respected his teachers. He was a diligent student as well."[1]

His teachers' prophecy was to be proved right in a future not so far. By his 20s, when most of the young men and women remain indecisive about their future, Syama Prasad began to tread on the path to the pantheon of leaders who shone brightly over the horizon of the Motherland.

As a child, Syama Prasad was not interested in sports or any activity of that kind. Instead, he was very much interested in reading and was a voracious reader. Though Syama Prasad was just one year elder to Uma Prasad, he was three classes ahead. However, during that time, nobody was allowed to sit for the Matriculation examination before 16 years of age, so he went to his ancestral home[2] in Madhupur for a few months. The peaceful

Sir Asutosh (centre front row), on the ground sitting Syamarasad (4th from right), Ramaprasad (5th from right), Umaprasad (6th from right), Bamaprasad (standing behind Umaprasad) at Calcutta University – year 1908

atmosphere of Madhupur helped Syama Prasad in attaining the truth in his later years.[3]

At Madhupur in 1923: Standing – Syama Prasad.
Sitting left to right : Tara Debi, Kamala Debi (eldest sister), Sudha Debi

Syama Prasad, when he passed Matriculation Examination – 1917

Admission in the Presidency College

Shortly after, he sat for his matriculation examination, which he passed with a first division and a scholarship. He got himself admitted to Presidency College, the most prestigious one in those days. Hereafter, he passed his Intermediate class in Arts in 1919 and acquired the first position in I.A. As the education level was increasing so was developing his mental faculty. Syama Prasad was also learning impeccably from his surroundings as the different academicians and philosophers used to visit Sir Asutosh and discuss the topics of utmost importance. Syama Prasad always listened to them with great interest. Sir Asutosh assigned him the job of his secretary. The learned father used to give dictations to his sophophile and receptive son. This was the training part given to a son by a learned father. Syama Prasad started taking dictations of long letters from his father which were often also typed by Syama Prasad. He also started keeping a record of his father's mail. Even at times, due to the tight schedule of Sir Asutosh, he used to answer letters on his behalf. People had also started correspondence with Syama Prasad to convey their messages to Sir Asutosh. On 26 December 1915, someone from Chandra Nagar, Bengal wrote a similar letter to Syama Prasad, which has been placed in the category of 'unknown papers' of II-IV installations of Mookerjee's private papers in the Nehru Memorial Museum and Library. He was only 14 years old in 1915 when he did not even pass the matriculation examination. This means that Sir Asutosh had started the training of Syama Prasad from the school days. In the category of these 'undeciphered letters', a noteworthy letter (letter no. 17) of Rama Prasad is kept. He wrote this letter to Syama Prasad on 7 June 1920. This letter is an example of a good understanding and humour between the two brothers. In this letter, Rama Prasad has inspired Syama Prasad to become courageous. The elder brother was also contributing in improving Syama Prasad.

The events of this time stirred the mind of young Syama Prasad. However, Syama Prasad was not getting emotional on this State; instead, he was thinking about practical solutions to problems. By this time, his ideas had got a clear direction. In 1919, Bankim Chandra Roy, son of Syama Prasad's *Bua* (paternal aunt), who was used to address as 'Bankda' by Syama Prasad, had gone for research work in Chemistry at Leeds University. Syama Prasad had a long correspondence with Bankda. The study of his letters shows that the events of the period shook the conscience of Syama Prasad. Young Syama Prasad wanted to free the Mother India from the shackles of slavery and eradicate the poverty and sufferings of the Indians. He asked Bankda that he should soon return to India after getting higher education and work for the benefit of the countrymen. In the same letter, Syama Prasad wrote that life should not be meant for pleasure; this life is meant for serving others. Syama Prasad discussed Mahatma Gandhi and the non-cooperation movement with Bankda. About Gandhi, he wrote, "He is a mad man indeed, but he is one of those mad men who come only once in an age." He was interested in boycotting foreign goods, but he criticised the boycott of education. He further wrote that there is only one path to progress, which comes out only through education. If students leave their studies, how will they help in the development work of the country?

"We do not have to build an illiterate society, but we have to grow on with the fearlessness and self-confidence on the path of progress and always remember, Swaraj is our birthright."

The above thoughts of Syama Prasad seem to be the thoughts of a very settled person. The impression of Bal Gangadhar Tilak, the founder of the Swadeshi movement, was evident on the young Syama Prasad. He had openly condemned Jallianwala Bagh in another letter, on which Bankda had mentioned global tragedies in one of his letters. He told Syama Prasad that many Jallianwala Bagh tragedies had happened in Ireland. Syama Prasad condemned Nazism in

Syama Prasad at the age of 18

response. Syama Prasad and Bankda also criticised the British Prime Minister Lloyd George, whose failed policies were exploiting the working class of Britain and almost all the industry was suffering. Syama Prasad had discussed issues like anti-national policies, unemployment and high prices, etc.

He did his B.A. class with honours in English, where he secured the first position in 1921. Besides this, he topped both in the I.A. and B.A. in Bengali as well. For the above feat, he was awarded the Bankim Chandra gold and silver medals. He used to spend his free time in the library where he got a chance to read a lot of Bengali literature and other literature from abroad. Whereas he learned to evaluate emotions in human characters from Shakespeare, Wordsworth's theory of pantheism reminds him of the Vedanta philosophy of India. He found that literature, whether from any country or written in any language, discovered the truth at the root of it all, which was discovered by the sages of India. India's prince Siddhartha abandoned all the glory in search of truth. He went out in the forest, discovered the truth and became Gautama Buddha. The whole literature is based on the concept of Satyam Shivam Sundaram.

Syama Prasad at the age of 19

The brilliant student Syama Prasad was appointed as the General Secretary of the Presidency College magazine. This was a matter of great pride for a student. Syama Prasad also took charge of editing the magazine. He wrote letters to eminent writers for writing articles for the magazine. In this series, he wrote the first letter to Professor Percival on 2 September 1920. After that, the affectionate relationship between Professor and Syama Prasad was established. On 20 November 1920, he wrote to Professor Percival, "Give me your blessings that I may live a pious, virtuous and manly life." Syama Prasad was always pure—the purity of the character, the purity of heart, the mind, the deeds and the purity of the word. His fearlessness, extreme renunciation and struggle for justice-related matters are all manifestations of his manliness.

Vice Chancellor of the University of Leeds and Chairman of the Sadler Commission, M.E. Sadler had an affectionate attitude towards Syama Prasad. In one of his letters, he told Syama Prasad that he was undoubtedly impressed with Indian philosophy. He sent Syama Prasad a copy of Students' Year Book of the Oxford University. When Syama Prasad inquired about Bachelor of Civil Law in Oxford and higher studies in the West, Sadler suggested, "I think it better that Indian students should come to the West when they are mature. It is difficult in any case to achieve a synthesis between the ideals of India and the West. However, it is not impossible, and those who succeed in finding the true synthesis are benefactors, both to India and the West." The exchange of ideas with Sadler was helpful in polishing Syama Prasad's personality. This communication was enriching mental faculty of Syama Prasad. Syama Prasad's rendition of mutual relations with Sadler is a book called 'The Poetic Procession' presented to Syama Prasad by Sadler in 1921.[4]

Syama Prasad with some of his Colleagues

It is essential to mention here that his father, Sir Asutosh, had introduced M.A. classes in Bengali defying many an opposition from various quarters. He was determined to give his mother-tongue a rightful status in the University. Apart from this, to set an example, Asutosh encouraged his son, Syama Prasad to join the M.A. classes in Bengali. He knew very well that this would act as an incentive to fellow students to join this course in Bengali which was till then not very popular. Syama Prasad joined the law classes at the University. Here also he stood first both in Master of Arts in 1923 and Bachelor of Law the next year. It is delightful to mention that in his Bengali classes, he chose to write a thesis on the social plays of Girish Chandra Ghosh, a famous Bengali actor and playwright of the 19th century and also a follower of Sri Ramakrishna Paramhansa.

Coming back to his pursuance of higher studies, Syama Prasad expressed his wish to go to England to become a barrister after passing the B.L. examination in 1924. To this, Asutosh was very much against. During the 1920s particularly, the Mookerjee family lost quite a few of their family members. Kamala, Syama Prasad's eldest sister died in 1923, after which Asutosh was so aggrieved that he stopped celebrating Durga Puja at his household. Sir Asutosh himself left this world in 1924 at the age of 60. However, much before this time, Syama Prasad had already started grooming himself in the affairs of the University under the guidance of his father. He was already a fellow of the University Senate in the faculty of Arts. At this very time, Syama Prasad Mookerjee was about to go to Simla for a conference and Asutosh to Patna. Both of them left for the station together and later departed for their destination. Unfortunately, that was the last time Syama Prasad spoke to his father. Syama Prasad received a telegraph while in Simla, saying that his father was very ill. However, when he reached Patna, Asutosh had already passed away. Syama Prasad left for England in 1925 to study law after his father's demise. He stayed at 112, Gower Street in London and joined the Lincoln's Inn. There his roommate was Surendra Nath Sen (historian) and Jatindra Mohan Majumdar (a friend). It should be mentioned here that though Syama Prasad went to England to study law, his primary motive was to acquire first-hand knowledge of the British and French Universities. He, therefore, sat for his preliminary bar examination in haste, as a result for which he did not fare very well.

At last, in 1927, he became a barrister-at-law and came back to his country. During the time he was in England, a conference was held in 1926 between the English Universities and Syama Prasad. The then professor of the University of Calcutta and later the president of India, Dr. Sarvepalli Radhakrishnan, visited England as a representative from India.

Another stalwart and the great scientist, Sir Prafulla Chandra Roy also had many educational discussions with Syama Prasad. In addition to all these, Syama Prasad went all the way to Paris to gain knowledge of the French Universities, with the help of the British ambassador Lord Krew, who was a great friend of Sir Asutosh. Syama Prasad's stay in England proved to be quite positive about several significant friendships with outstanding personalities. One of them was Sarvepalli Radhakrishnan. Syama Prasad already knew him, back in Calcutta though. Sir Asutosh had already seated him on the George V Chair Professorship of Mental and Moral Sciences of Calcutta University. While in England, this friendship grew more profound in the years to come.

The Marriage of the Elder Brother

Rama Prasad (Judge, Calcutta High Court and member, Senate, Calcutta University), elder brother of Syama Prasad got married to Tara Devi in 1920. Purnendu Banerjee, the nephew of Syama Prasad, made a fascinating reference of this marriage in his book. Ramaprasad's classmates Subhash Chandra Bose, Dilip Kumar Roy and Kshitij Chandra Chatterjee were having a bet, who could have eaten more? Syama Prasad was offering them different food items with great enthusiasm. All of them were making great fun. Sir Asutosh was delighted to see this. He said he would have to give prizes along with a digestive Churna (Lavan Bhaskar) to all three of them.

Tara Devi was a duty-oriented woman. In the later life of Syama Prasad, she played a vital role in his life. She was very trust-worthy of him in all his family and public affairs. Tara Devi used to call Syama Prasad *Mejo thakurpo* (second son of her father-in-law), while he used to call her *Boudi* (Bhabhi).

Friendship with Subhash Chandra Bose

It is interesting to note that Subhash Chandra Bose was a good friend of both Rama Prasad and Syama Prasad. However, once in 1916, he was punished in the Presidency college by Sir Asutosh as he was involved in a protest against an English teacher, Mr. Oaten. The house of Subhash Chandra, 38/2 Elgin Road, was near to Mookerjee's house. His father Janki Nath Bose was a renowned advocate. Both Syama Prasad and Subhash Chandra wanted to get India free from the British Raj. Both of them did not believe in extreme non-violence as they opined that the internal policy of non-violence could ruin any society. At one place, Syama Prasad said, "Ahimsa doubtless implies abstention from selfish and aggressive violence. However, does it signify inertia and pacifism under all circumstances? Did not Sree Ramachandra, so kind to righteous men and women, including even Nishadas and Savaras, wage war to punish the arrogant evil-doer who insulted womanhood and violated the sanctity of the peaceful hermitage? Let us not forget that valour was greatly esteemed by the sages and free rulers of India in olden times. When valour languished, the entire polity weakened. When the sword and the book of knowledge kept together, justice, equity and liberty ruled the affairs of the State." Though the working style of Syama Prasad was different from that of Subhash Chandra, they were friends for a long time. When Subhash Chandra was captive in Darjeeling Jail in 1936, Syama Prasad took permission from jailor to meet him. Syama Prasad got only one-hour permission to meet him on 11 June 1936, but in the presence of police officer P.S. Kursiong. Subhash Chandra asked Syama Prasad to arrange some books for him. Subhash Chandra wrote on 17 June 1936 to Syama Prasad and requested to send him more books along with Dr. Dinesh

Sen's 'Brihat Bang'. He sent a catalogue of books attached with his letter to Syama Prasad. (See Appendix)

Though Syama Prasad had differences with him on political issues, they had no reservations from each other. Syama Prasad pressurised the administration to free Subhash Chandra and his brother Sharat Chandra from jail. Both brothers were not keeping good health when they were in jail.

Paying tribute to Subhash Chandra, Syama Prasad wrote on 21 October 1944 in his diary:

"We, especially I, had no grudge against Subhash. Indeed I had for him admiration and affection and genuinely believed that there was no other person who could be near him in the political field of India... In any case, his name is today associated with unique romantic adventure—a man, a patriot who so hated foreign rule and so eager to see his country free, that he risked all, and ultimately identified himself with the enemy, Whether his methods will lead to any success or not, it is extremely doubtful.

Today it must be admitted that taking him as he is, he is one of the foremost Indians of his time who regarded no means or method as bad if he felt he could thereby attain the power to wrest the freedom of his country... A national hero in exile to serve his country's cause—that is how he appeals to many of his countrymen who may not agree with him always."

The Literary Impact on Syama Prasad

Almost invariably, we find across all ages and geographies that the making of great men has a common strand of being the receptacle of the wisdom of stored in the form of writings of the scholars of yore. The bookshelves of libraries become their preferred places to be explored again and again. Syama Prasad Mookerjee was no exception. He too made the books his best buddies and spent with them quite a considerable time. His collection of books became so vast that it gradually acquired the shape of a rich library in itself. Apart from his library, he also got the membership of The Times Club, Oxford, London and the Presidency College Library. A voracious reader that he was, he came to terms with the intricacies of the Russian political and bureaucratic world of the 19th century through 'War and Peace' and 'Anna Karenina' of Count Leo Tolstoy. Back home he was highly influenced by Gurudev Rabindranath Tagore. Such literary readings made him fathom the most intriguing aspects of human life in its totality, comprising both positive and negative hues. 'Neel Darpan', the celebrated drama written by fellow Bengali Deen Bandhu Mitra made him understand the plight of the workers of indigo plantations owned by the supremacist British settled to satisfy their greed at all costs. Another interesting fact about his life was his choice of the subject he opted for his graduation. By opting English (Hons.), he had access to greats of English literature. Therefore, he got an opportunity to acquaint himself and understand the very Western ethos. The literary trend of Naturalism which was influenced by the principles of Equality, Liberty and Fraternity, which emanated from the French Revolution, had a significant influence on him. His excellent performance in graduation earned him felicitation with a gold medal given in memory of Bankim Chandra to students of the University for their academic brilliance.

A careful analysis of Dr. Syama Prasad Mookerjee's formative years both in the school and the University bring forth his growth aligned to the time he lived in. By then, Bengal had already established as a land thronged by great scholars who had a cosmopolitan outlook, but at the same time, they never hesitated in upholding nationalist ideas, which to them were essential for the emancipation of the Motherland. As a result of this peculiar milieu, Syama Prasad acquired a mental framework that enabled him to grow as a good citizen of the globe who never compromised his love and patriotism for the country. Mastering such a delicate balancing act between the two was not an easy task for his was a country subjugated and servile. One can wonder that there was not any internal malice towards intruding white population despite a steely resolve to oust them from the land. The answer lies in the teachings of the Bhagavad Gita, which had a profound impact on Syama Prasad Mookerjee. It is interesting to note that during his post-graduation, he took up the research topic on social dramas of the playwright Girish Chandra Ghosh and to understand Ghosh, it was necessary for him to understand both Swami Ramakrishna Paramhansa and his illustrious disciple Swami Vivekananda. Perhaps this academic necessity provided Syama Prasad Mookerjee with an opportunity to peep into the domain of Indian philosophical wisdom which eventually could quench his thirst for the most profound meanings of life.

As we all know, that a wide range of nationalists including Bankim Chandra Chatterjee, the author of 'the Anand Math', Vivekananda, Tilak, Gandhi and Aurobindo, to name a few, drew both solaces in colonial despair and inspiration for their struggle for independence from the Bhagavad Gita.

The sacred teachings instilled in them a kind of stoicism towards pain inflicted by the imperialist greed without losing sight of the righteous behaviour to be extended even towards the enemy. Taking up the cudgel against the British but without any racial malice must have come from these eternal words of wisdom. Syama Prasad too was no exception to this influence as proved by the testimony one can glean out from the pages of his diary penned during his Madhupur sojourn: 'Oh merciful God, let me glimpse you within me. I do not ask anything for myself. Only give me a place at your feet. Lift me up and take me in your fold; give me the strength and the yearning to invoke you... Forgive me in your infinite understanding and give me the inspiration not to be led astray again. Deliver me from vanity and my ego. Help me devote myself to the service of others and carry out Your will to the best of my ability for the rest of my life. It will not grieve me if You do not wish me to serve any particular purpose. I am not after fame and glory. Let me abide near you. Give me shelter at Your feet, take me to that unknown land and fill my mind with Your peace. You know whom I still love and care for. I do not claim anything from them. I just wish them the best. My mind yearns to see you, but I am trying my best to restrain it. I have realised the futility of this world. Here today, gone tomorrow—this is the process of life. Then why fuss over such trivial things? We are only travellers in transit. What is the difference between us and beasts if we spend the little time we have on this earth, steeped in a mire of lust and greed? I have often observed the instinctual behaviour of animals. If men, who have a soul and can recognise God, forget everything and indulge in these base pursuits, what can be more tragic?" He asked God to make his heart free from hatred and fill it with love for humanity and Him. He wanted to be fully surrendered unto God. Srimad Bhagavad Gita's 18th chapter, verse 66 has a similar connotation:

सर्व धर्मान्परित्यज्य मामेकं शरणं व्रज
अहं त्वां सर्वपापेभ्योमोक्षयिष्यामि मा शुचः ।।

The ultimate goal of *jiva* is to surrender completely and whole-heartedly before the Almighty. The pupil of literature was transformed into a philosopher gradually.

Lessons from William Carey

Scholarly reading aptitude and interest in literature never allowed Syama Prasad to sit idle or to waste his time. He had a penchant for contemplating the thoughts of the great intellectuals. Bangla language could not flourish without the contribution of William Carey. For this reason, Syama Prasad had deep regard for him. He served our nation for 41 years (1793-1834). He was one of the leaders of the Bengal Renaissance. He was the first to translate the Bible in Bangla. Though he would have done it as part of missionary work, he was soon well aware of the challenges of the Indian academic world. To read the Mahabharata, he acquired the proficiency in Sanskrit by 1796. He prepared the dictionary of Sanskrit-English and wrote Sanskrit grammar. He was a pioneer in the field of Indian education. Syama Prasad was influenced with him as William Carey sought to uplift the poor farmers of Bengal by opening the first vernacular school in Madnabati. Carey saw the importance of the Vernacular as the medium of instruction both for elementary and higher education. He thought that a precious amount of useful knowledge could be conveyed through the means of the Vernacular languages. At that time, before Macaulay, Public Instruction Committee also encouraged vernacular education.

William Carey was appointed in Presidency College to teach Bengali, Sanskrit and Marathi. He was wholly devoted to the poor men of Bengal, he assigned his salary for their upliftment, and himself lived and died as a poor man. Besides his Bengali grammar and dictionary, he wrote two textbooks, *Kathopakathanak* and *Itihasmala* for the students of the college. He also established a printing press in Serampore and Madnabati. He was the first to realise the potentialities of spoken Bengali and helped in the development of a new kind of prose. He also helped in the development of the language by encouraging Bengali writers, and printing their works as well as the older Bengali classics like *Ramayan* and *Anandmangal* in his press at Serampore.

In one of his speeches, Syama Prasad said, "The necessity of recognising our Vernacular as the best and most suitable medium for instruction which in recent years was pointed out by my late father, was nearly a century ago realised by Carey..." Syama Prasad had already the devotion for his mother-tongue, the influence of different philosophers gave a strong base to his love for the vernaculars. He made the reference of English novelist Hodgson with sincere regards in his speech. Hodgson wrote in 1837, "...I have no hesitation in saying that to found a college for the rearing of a competent body of translators and schoolmasters—in other words, for the systematic supply of good vernacular books and good vernacular teachers would be an infinitely better disposal of the parliamentary grant than the present application of it to the training of a promiscuous crowd of English."

Approximately, in his every lecture, Syama Prasad had presented his philosophical thoughts on teaching via the medium of vernaculars and the availability of competent teachers. He studied the education report of an American educationist, W. Adams, intensely. Adams spoke of the importance of having suitable vernacular textbooks. After joining the administration of Calcutta University, Syama Prasad executed this work promptly.

It was extraordinary about Syama Prasad that he always felt happy to remember the great personalities and their contribution towards society. Carey Centenary celebration was held on

17 August 1933 at Serampore. Syama Prasad participated in the programme and talked about his significant contributions.

Wonderful Reader and a Bibliophile

The variety and quality of the books in the library of Mookerjee house give an idea of the versatility and deep understanding of sciences and humanities alike. Syama Prasad got the love for the books in heritage. We already mentioned in the second chapter of the book that Dr. Ganga Prasad had built a library in his house, and used to spend a good portion of his income on it. Dr. Syama Prasad, just like his father, used to spend his scholarship on the collection of books. Three generations filled this library with books on all subjects. The books were their one obsession. Books were the everlasting friends of Syama Prasad. Every room, every corridor had shelves of books piled up to the ceiling along the walls. Cicero, the great philosopher of Greece, said it right that "the room without books is like a body without a soul". The philosophers from every corner of the world give considerable weightage to the importance of books. Dr. Mookerjee worshipped the books. He imbibed knowledge. It is perfectly all right that the worshipper of goddess Saraswati should have all the material to be used in the worship of the goddess of learning.

Dr. Reena Bhaduri, the niece of Syama Prasad, told us that to save the books from any danger during the Second World War, Dr. Mookerjee got transported all the books to his house at Madhupur within a night. According to Dr. Bhaduri, more than half of the portion of his house was filled with the books. After that, the Mookerjee brothers decided to donate the books for the welfare of the Nation as the books are the heritage of a Nation.

He was a versatile scholar. Books were his constant companions. He needed them to quench his thirst for more and more knowledge. That his interests were varied is proved by the fact that he collected books on almost every subject.

Some of the books were printed on handmade paper and on material like vellum. Many of them were illustrated and decorated by hand. The library was enriched with Robert Browning's 'The

Flight of the Duchess', Gautier's 'King Candaules', Flaubert's 'Simple Heart' and a copy of the famous story of 'Daphnis and Chloe' of Longus. Other such unique books in the collection are 'The English Bible' of the Dover Press, described as 'one of the noblest printed books ever made', the book of Common Prayer printed on hand-made paper and bound with oak covers with a leather spine and clasps to hold both sides of its covers, an illustrated edition of Goethe's Faust (1874) in original German, remarkable for its binding and decorations, a set of eight volumes of the works of William Shakespeare (1893) containing 1243 engravings and two significant volumes of the American editions of Boydell's 'Illustrations of the Dramatic Work of Shakespeare' (1852) containing engravings of pictures by eminent English artists well-bound editions of the individual plays of Shakespeare, specially illustrated and printed in limited editions, are also in the collections. Other such treasures were Milton's poetical works published in 1794-97 (3 Volumes), the library edition of John Ruskin in thirty-nine volumes and the Oxford edition of Samuel Johnson's works in eleven volumes. Books rare from the point of view of their date of publication include 'Aesop's Fables' with illustrations and annotations, first edition, 1668; Euclid's Elements of Geometry, first translated into English by H. Billingsley and printed (1570) by John Daye, London, Orations of Demosthenes, printed in 1599 in Greek and Latin on parallel pages, Fortescue's 'Laws of England' (1573) in English and Latin on opposite columns, first edition of Samuel Johnson's Dictionary of English Language (1755), a French dictionary by John Minshieu, Professor of Languages, London (1599), and an account of the Mughal Court by Thomas Coriate, printed in 1616. Large sets of works of Sir Walter Scott, Daniel Defoe, Charles Dickens, George Eliot, Rudyard Kipling, Robert Louis Stevenson, W.M. Thackeray, Charles & Mary Lamb and others grace his collection. The American Literature section is represented by H.W. Longfellow, E.A. Boe, Walt Whitman, Nathaniel Hawthorne, Henry James, R.W. Emerson and Washington Irving. Most of the classics in other European languages can be found in the collection. Besides Faust,

Goethe's works in fourteen volumes were available. The works of Moliere, Balzac, Gautier, Flaubert and Voltaire were also part of the library. It seems he had a particular liking for the adventures of Don Quixote. There are more than 20 translations of the book. All the famous Latin and Greek authors are represented in the library. The works of Ovid, Virgil, Cicero, Levy, Tacitus, the tragedies of Aeschylus, Sophocles, Euripides and the comedies of Aristophanes are there. Also, there are different editions of the works of Homer, the works of Thucydides, Dialogues of Plato, Metaphysics and Politics of Aristotle and Plutarch's Lives. The Oriental classics were well represented in Mookerjee's collection. The 'Sacred Books of the East' edited by Max Muller and different editions of the Ramayana were in Mookerjee family's library. The ten-volume edition of the Ramayana by Gorressio published at the expense of Charles Albert, King of Sardinia, is magnificent. William Carey and Joshua Marshman undertook the project of editing the original Sanskrit texts of the Ramayana with a prose translation in English and explanatory notes. The Vedas, Puranas, Upanishads and all standard works of Sanskrit literature with their commentaries were in the library. Boebtlink's Sanskrit dictionary in seven volumes and Radha Kanta Deb's 'Sabda Kalpadrum' were also there in the library. There is a scarce edition of Kalhana's 'Rajatarangini' which contains a French translation along with the Sanskrit text. Books on Education, Political Science, History and Anthropology are numerous and were in constant use by him as his books on Law. The works of Confucius, Kant, Hobbes, Voltaire and Emerson are to be found in his collection. Various editions of the Vedas and the Hindu Shastras, the Bible, the Koran and works on Buddhism were also available. Most of the books were purchased by the father and grandfather of Syama Prasad Mookerjee.

Syama Prasad loved to read life sketches of great people for self-education. He was of the opinion that reading biographies gives a lot of experience and learning.

Gurudev Rabindranath Tagore and Syama Prasad Mookerjee

Where the mind is without fear and the head is held high
Where knowledge is free;
Where the world has not been broken up into fragments
By narrow domestic walls;
Where words come out from the depth of truth;
Where tireless striving stretches its arms towards perfection;
Where the clear stream of reason has not lost its way
Into the dreary desert sand of dead habit;
Where the mind is led forward by Thee into ever—
Widening thought and action—
Into that heaven of freedom, my father, let
My country awake!

—Rabindranath Tagore

The above verse was the nucleus of the philosophy of Sir Asutosh Mookerjee and Dr. Syama Prasad Mookerjee. Both of them made references to the thoughts of the great poet and philosopher, Gurudev Rabindranath in their speeches.

Tagore was the symbol of the Bengal Renaissance. He was the height of intellectual awakening. He was the leader of this period and had a particular interest in educational reform. His contribution to the Bengal Renaissance was multi-faceted. In many ways, Rabindranath Tagore's writings (especially poems and songs) can be seen as imbued with the spirit of the Upanishads. His works repeatedly allude to Upanishadic ideas regarding soul, liberation, transmigration and—perhaps most essentially—about a spirit that imbues all creation, not unlike the Upanishadic Brahman. Tagore's English translation of a set of poems titled 'the Gitanjali' won him the Nobel Prize for literature in 1913. He was the first Asian to win this award. In fact, his fame attained a luminous height, taking him across continents on lecture tours and tours of friendship. For the world, he became the voice of India's spiritual heritage; and for India, especially for Bengal, he became a great living institution. Whosoever took an interest in the literature couldn't help getting influenced by the thoughts of Rabindranath Tagore. Syama Prasad was also the upshot of that soil of Bengal, in which Gurudev was getting new dimensions for his creative world. Syama Prasad's personality formation was taking place simultaneously at the time when the creative world of Gurudev was reaching the heights. Gurudev was the family friend of Mookerjees. He used to visit them frequently. He was a friend of Sir Asutosh and guide of Syama Prasad. Sir Asutosh and Gurudev were fond of discussing different philosophical and educational topics. Syama Prasad was accustomed to listen to them with great interest.

Sir Asutosh was accustomed to organise the lectures of great scholars in Calcutta University. He used to call scholars of Tagore's choice. But after the death of Sir Asutosh, the new university administration was in no mood to pursue his worship of excellence and spend money in order to invite eminent professors to serve in or to deliver lecture at the university. By 1928, Syama Prasad became influential in the syndicate of the University. He was also in the position to give suggestions to the Vice Chancellor on such matters. During the tenure of Dr. Suhrawardy, Syama Prasad could get the university to invite Dr. Anna Selig at the request of Gurudev. Dr. Selig was the Executive Secretary of the International University Service of Germany, and the university offered her a Readership for delivering specific lectures after she finished a similar series of lectures in Vishwa-Bharti.[5] To make the relationship stronger between Gurudev and the university, in 1932, Syama Prasad got the university senate to pass a resolution to invite the poet to design and deliver lectures on Bengali language and literature at the Masters level. Tagore had different views on formal education. He was one of the most progressive educators of his time. He considered education free from any bond. He particularly criticised colonial schools and colleges for teaching knowledge unrelated to students' regional, historical and lingual context, which often led to mechanical rote-learning instead of real comprehension. Syama Prasad too was against the rote learning, and during his Vice Chancellorship, he worked hard to remove this from the education system. Gurudev never agreed to be part of any formal institute. 31-year-old Syama Prasad tried his best to convince the 71-year-old Scholar. Gurudev couldn't refuse the request of Syama Prasad which shows the level of confidence that Syama Prasad had formed in Gurudev. It was decided that Gurudev would be given the status of a professor, but the ordinary rules of the university would not be applicable to him. This was unconventional, Gurudev was also an extraordinary scholar. Dr. Mookerjee gave reference to this incident in his convocation address at Vishwa Bharti in 1950. He told how eventually he became successful to get Gurudev and Vishwa Bharti close to the Calcutta University.

After 1932, the relationship between Syama Prasad and Gurudev Rabindranath Tagore became more enduring. Their ideology was similar to each other. Gurudev began to take an active interest in the university. In 1934, he inaugurated an 'International Club' established in the university out of funds donated by the American philanthropist Andrew Carnegie for promoting world peace. The University Cultural Association gave a felicitation to Gurudev on this occasion. Gurudev delivered a lecture on human values across national divides. Gurudev used to send his poems on different occasions of the university. The university established the bust of Sir Asutosh in its campus in his memory. On that occasion, Gurudev composed the following poem in honour of Sir Asutosh.

"Goddess of wisdom has left her signature in your name
and you have honoured her pride.
Your name will always be called in her victory saga.
Your memories will be added, in her worship,
in the temple of education."

Tagore delivered the inaugural address on the launching of a scheme of 'Education Week' in 1936. In his lecture, Gurudev proposed publishing a set of books to popularise education.

Gurudev showered his blessings and affection on Syama

Prasad throughout his lifetime. Syama Prasad and Gurudev's last meeting was held at Shantiniketan in August 1940 when the latter was being honoured with the D. Litt. Degree by the Oxford University. Gurudev took his last breath in August 1941.

His poem 'A Farewell' speaks poignantly to the themes of death and departure:

Look out once more with tired eyes, and see
How, where the sun has set, the sea and sky
Merge in the darkness, then will you see the trace
Of shining light left by my parting gaze.[6]

Though Gurudev left his physical body, his thoughts remained live in the ideas of Syama Prasad. How the thoughts of Gurudev influenced Syama Prasad can be easily understood in the following excerpt from Dr. Mookerjee's Diary:

"Oh God! Give me faith, strength, courage and peace of mind. Give me the will and the power to do good to others. Give me your blessings that I may think of You in times of prosperity and woe and merge myself in Your boundless affection. Forgive me for all the wrongs that I have done and lead me on to You and You alone. (7.1.39)...I thank God for whatever He has given me, and I pray to Him to give me strength and devotion to dedicate myself to Him." (27.1.1946)...I want to be merged in You by working for You. (16.1.1946)

Gurudev writes in the 'Gitanjali':

This is my prayer to thee, my Lord-strike, strike at the root of penury in my heart.

Give me the strength lightly to bear my joys and sorrows.

Give me the strength to make my love fruitful in service.

Give me the strength never to disown the poor or bend my knees before insolent might.

Give me the strength to raise my mind high above daily trifles.

And give me the strength to surrender my strength to thy will with love.

Dr. Mookerjee writes in his diary on 16 January 1946:

"Deliver me from the consciousness of 'me' and 'mine'...You are mine, and I am Yours. Let me find comfort in this belief. Give me strength, devotion and faith. Lead me away from deception and all evil thoughts. Oh God, reside in my soul and banish all bitterness from my mind. Let me realise that I can depend on no one else but You."

Gurudev writes:

Life of My life, I shall ever try to keep my body pure, knowing that thy living touch is upon all my limbs.

I shall ever try to keep all untruths out from my thoughts, knowing that thou art that truth which has kindled the light of reason in my mind.

I shall ever try to drive all evils away from my heart and keep my love in flower, knowing that thou hast thy seat in the inmost shrine of my heart.

And it shall be my endeavour to reveal thee in my actions, knowing it is thy power gives me the strength to act.

Syama Prasad at a Condolence Meeting of Gurudev Rabindranath Tagore

Dr. Mookerjee writes:

"Dear God, give me shelter at your feet...Never let me forget how insignificant I am, not in order to feel small and despise myself, but to be proud that I have been created by You and to live up to Your image. However insignificant I may be, I want to be merged in You by working for You. I don't want anything else."

Gurudev says:

My poet's vanity dies in shame before thy sight. O master poet, I have sat down at thy feet. Only let me make my life simple and straight, like a flute of reed for thee to fill with music...

If it is not my portion to meet thee in this my life, then let me ever feel that I have missed thy sight—let me not forget for a moment, let me carry the pangs of this sorrow in my dreams and in my wakeful hours.

Sir Vishveshwaraiah and Syama Prasad

Syama Prasad, as we know, was throughout a student of humanities during his days at the university; however, this fact did not mar his understanding about sciences. Better he became in his understanding about sciences in the influencing company of India's great scientist Bharat Ratna Sir Vishveshwaraiah. Himself an outstanding educationist, Syama Prasad had the privilege of regular correspondence with the illustrious brain engaged not only in a variety of scientific projects, but was also shaping the scientific temperament of the Indian masses which had forgotten the ancient marvels of Indian education in general and sciences in particular.

Sir Vishveshwaraiah also helped Syama Prasad in inculcating an understanding about the needs concerning the importance of sciences as subjects and of the research institutes and their role in making the country better equipped for growth in future. For this end, he sent Syama Prasad a number of documents which also included a report prepared by Bombay Technical and Educational Institution sent in 1922 and a host of convocation speeches of Mysore University which also included Sir Asutosh's address delivered in 1918.

When Syama Prasad got the responsibility of editing the 'Calcutta Review' in 1933, Sir Vishveshwaraiah sent him his speech 'Industrialising India' to get that published in the 'Calcutta Review'. On the request of Syama Prasad, he became the member of the five-year evaluation committee of Indian Institute of Science, Bangalore.

Promoting Medical Education

Belgachhia Medical College, established in 1903, occupied the unique position of the only non-official Medical College in India, run entirely by Indians. On 16.7.1921, Syama Prasad addressed the annual function of the college. He made the reference of post-war conditions, and financial stringency faced those days. He assured the audience that "any application made by the authorities of this college will meet with the most sympathetic treatment. I really fully understand your struggles and difficulties. We require not one, but several medical colleges in this Presidency and we want them all to be the highest type." From the stage, he paid tribute to the brilliant surgeon Lt. Col. Sureshprasad Sarvadhikari and Ras Bihari Ghosh, a great social servant who, if alive, could have taken out the college from financial problems.

Syama Prasad ignited inspiration in all the audience to do great for society. He said, "The physicians can never deceive Nature... Let your ideas be high and forget not that the noble mission of the profession you have chosen is to do good to others. The poor and the rich, the weak and the strong, will alike require your assistance. Be it for you to serve not alone the wealthy and the influential, but all who may seek your assistance in distress. Be it for you to act as the faithful servants to humanity, ever ready and willing to alleviate the sufferings of all who in distress summon you for help." In later years, Syama Prasad became trusty of Medical Education Society of Bengal.

Interest in Journalism

Syama Prasad wanted to be a journalist. His father encouraged all his worthy pursuits and sent him to Pat Lovett, a famed journalist and editor of a famous weekly 'Capital'. They had a pleasant conversation, and Lovett wrote back to Sir Asutosh and complimented Syama Prasad as a "charming young fellow who immediately conquered my sympathy. He has a worthy journalistic ambition which I shall do my best to encourage... He has the makings of a man".When he was in the M.A. class, Syama Prasad along with Ramaprasad, started writing a Bengali monthly journal called Bangabani, which continued successfully for six years to come. Quite a few poems and prose compositions of Tagore were published here for the first time.

Many reputed personalities contributed to this journal, such as Jyotirindranath Tagore, Surendra Nath Sen, Kabishekhar Kalidas Ray, Chapala Bala Basu, Kumud Ranjan Mollik, and many other eminent personalities. Prof. Binoy Kumar Sarkar (an economist) got his article 'the Making of Hindu Nation' published. But the best part of this journal was that it published controversial novel 'Pather Dabi' in serials written by the famous novelist Sarat Chandra Chatterjee. But by this time, Syama Prasad and Ramaprasad became too busy with other works, and the journal had to be discontinued from 1928. Much later, Syama Prasad himself founded an English daily called 'Nationalist' and 'Hindustan' in Bengali in 1944. We found a deed of the partnership (Printing of Newspaper, Magazine and Periodicals) between Hemendra Nath Dutta and Syama Prasad Mookerjee in the private papers of Dr. Mookerjee.

Married Life of Syama Prasad

On 16th April 1922, Syama Prasad entered into wedlock while he was pursuing M.A. He got married to Sudha Debi (Chakraborty), daughter of Beni Madhab Chakraborty and grand daughter of Bihari Lal Chakraborty, the famed poet in Bengali. It may hereby be mentioned that another son of Bihari Lal Chakraborty, with the name Saral Kumar Chakraborty, married the eldest daughter of Rabindranath Tagore. Dr. Beni Madhab was very gentle and a non-snarled person. He gave all Indian sacraments to his daughter in legacy. Dr. Beni Madhab was very happy to get Syama Prasad as his son-in-law. He was in regular correspondence with him. Sudha Debi was a very diligent and dedicated woman. She had never made any complaint about the busy schedule of

Syama Prasad with his wife Sudha Debi

Syama Prasad. They had five children. But the youngest son lived only for four months, who died of diphtheria. Sudha Debi was profoundly disturbed and depressed over this loss. She never came out of this depression and contracted double pneumonia shortly afterwards.

Sudha Debi died an untimely death in 1933, eleven years after her marriage. At the time of Sudha Debi's death, Syama Prasad could only say, "What a terrible, terrible disaster!"

Giving condolence to Syama Prasad, Rabindranath Tagore said, "I know you have a very strong mind. You will get out of this sorrow and distress with the passing of time. I pray that you receive that message of renunciation, which serves as the bridge between this world and the next."

The truth is that while all of us can stay on this earth for some time, no one can stay forever. The end of life's journey is inevitable

Syama Prasad with Monotosh Mookerjee (rear row left), Subendu Kumar Banerjee (rear row right), Anutosh Mookerjee (middle row left), Sabita Banerjee (middle row right), Arati Bhattacharjee (front row left), Chittatosh Mookerjee (front row middle), Sivatosh Mookerjee (front row middle), Debatosh Mookerjee (front row left)

and similar for each and every one of us. According to Tagore, both the origin and the end of life lie in God. Life originates from God, and ultimately with Death, unites with God. After completing life's journey, death comes as redemption for human beings. He describes the cycle of life and birth in great detail in his literature. Syama Prasad had a significant influence of Tagore and the philosophy of *Bhagavad Gita* on him. So, it is not a surprise that he was able to get out of this sorrow soon. He indulged himself more in University affairs.

He took the death of his wife as a signal for renunciation of his personal life and dedication of his time and energies for the betterment of the society as a whole.

Syama Prasad's children Anutosh, Debtosh, Sabita and Arti were tiny at that time. He recalled in his diary how his children were brought up by their aunt, Tara Devi: "*Boudi* (Tara Devi) took my children to her bosom and gave them a lot of affection...When the tragedy struck, she willingly took charge of my children, and I was grateful to her." She parented them as her own children. Syama Prasad's children had very few occasions to miss the love of their mother.

Barrister Syama Prasad Mookerjee

As per the guidelines of Justice father Sir Asutosh, Syama Prasad took admission in the Law department of the University. Brilliant Syama Prasad passed the Bachelor of Law examination in 1924 with first position and first division and became eligible to practise in the High Court as an advocate in the Calcutta High Court. However it is in 'English Bar', it was necessary to pursue the degree course of Barrister from England. Syama Prasad wanted to understand the Law deeply. Syama Prasad took admission in Lincoln's Inn, London on 14th April,

Barrister Syama Prasad in London

1926. The main objective of Syama Prasad's visit to England was not a legal distinction. He wanted to acquire an in-depth knowledge of British and French Universities. He was devoting most of his time to understand the current educational policies of the West. He did not indulge in any other pastimes. He obtained his Barrister's degree on 11th May, 1927. He represented Calcutta University in the British Government's Conferences of the Universities in London in 1926.

Friends in London

Syama Prasad lived at 112, Gower Street in London with historian Surendranath Sen and Jatindra Mohan Majumdar. During his Britain stay, Syama Prasad had developed a great friendship with Sir Iwans Greeves, R.O. Raha (Rudolph Ogalis Raha) and Dr. Sarvepalli Radhakrishnan. It is noticeable that R.O. Raha took great care of Syama Prasad during his London stay. On the death of R.O. Raha, Syama Prasad wrote on 16 January 1939 in his diary, "He was one of the best souls. I have come across a most loyal friend. My indebtedness to him, while I was in England, cannot be repaid. I was glad to have helped him in getting the post of Residence Inspector, which he held with undoubted efficiency till the time of his death. He was a staunch nationalist. He liked to call himself Ramen Raha... His last wish was that he should be cremated at Nimotallah according to Hindu rites, his ashes only to be entombed in the Christian burial ground."

Dr. Syama Prasad, Dr. Radhakrishnan, Jatindra Mohan Majumdar—in London in 1926 when Syama Prasad & Dr. S. Radhakrishnan attended Commonwealth University Conference as CU delegates in Cambridge

Though Syama Prasad and Radhakrishnan knew each other before leaving for England, their stay in London was remarkable for their friendship to grow. Most often, they shared their thoughts on different subjects with each other, and their views were identical on most of the essential topics like religion. The impact of Indian Vedantic philosophy and Swami Vivekananda's philosophical thoughts was very much reflected in their thoughts. In the biography of Syama Prasad, Tathagata Roy has observed that although Syama Prasad's public duties did not permit him to practise seriously at the bar, once he represented Radhakrishnan free of cost in a libel suit. Tathagat Roy also observed that Radhakrishnan found himself in sympathy with Gandhi and Syama Prasad Mookerjee. Though Syama Prasad was much younger than Radhakrishnan, it was Syama Prasad's quality that people like Sir Vishveshwaraiah, Acharya P.C. Ray, Rabindranath Tagore, Gandhi, Dr. Radhakrishnan, etc., much older in years to him, were all attracted towards the personality of Syama Prasad.

In the foreword to 'Educational Speeches of Dr. Syama Prasad Mookerjee', Radhakrishnan wrote: "His religion was not of the narrow kind. He was catholic in his sympathies and broad-minded in his outlook. Patriotism is not merely loving of the land in which we are born; it is respect for the ideals by which we are sustained. That man has a spiritual dimension that its development can take place in various ways, that we should have respect for all these ways are some of the cardinal features of Indian tradition. It is Indian and not merely Hindu. Syama Prasad Mookerjee was an ardent advocate of these great ideals."

Father as Mentor and Guide

Like any father vigilant and prudent for his progeny, Sir Asutosh too was keen to inculcate in his son everything that would have equipped Syama Prasad with attributes which eventually defined his persona as a learned patriot with an acute understanding of not only the existing lacunae in the sphere of education, but also its needs to usher in a better future. As a consequence of this mentoring by Sir Asutosh, Syama Prasad was elected as a member of the Senate of his Alma Mater immediately after completing post-graduation. His election was an index of his abilities as a scholar who had the calibre to make a difference in the academic milieu of the time he lived in. In other words, the guidance of his father ensured that the University was not going to face any dearth of able and adroit human resource as Syama Prasad was cast in the dye of an educationist ready to step in his father's shoes. As it can be gleaned from one of the letters exchanged between Syama Prasad and Bankda, the British Government was planning to engage Sir Asutosh Mookerjee in an ostensibly high rank and reputed work back in England itself. But the ulterior motive was to ward off any situation that would have allowed Mookerjee to join India's Struggle for Independence after his retirement which was due on 31 December 1924. The colonial Government was fearful that such an association would strengthen the rank and file of the freedom fighters. But the Government did know little that Sir Mookerjee, who held the love for motherland as supreme was not only himself, but has prepared his son too for the cause of betterment of the motherland through taking up education, the most potent weapon to fight for freedom.

In many ways, the relationship between the father and the son emulated the ancient bond between the Guru and his disciple. The best testimonial of this fact can be sighted on one occasion when in May 1924, Syama Prasad Mookerjee was entrusted with the responsibility of representing Calcutta University at the Shimla Conference. On the eve of the journey, Sir Asutosh Mookerjee sat with Syama Prasad for a considerable time to discuss his point of view on the educational landscape of the day. He also shared his own experiences pertinent to such an event. This incident was one of many such mentoring sessions Syama was to be benefited with immensely in the years to follow.

In fact, Syama Prasad imbibed the ideas of Sir Asutosh Mookerjee about the University as an instrument to exercise a beneficent influence upon the life of a nation. According to Sir Mookerjee, university was a must because its teachings dominate the actions of men and produce a profound but subtle influence upon the course of civilisation. He used to discuss his ambition of an intellectual regeneration through nation-wide progress of education with him. Consequently, this constant scholarly nurturing by his father made Syama Prasad ready to take up the mantle successfully as an educationist and academic administrator.

Ironically, the lessons of the father to his beloved son imparted before Shimla Conference was to be the last as Syama Prasad was never to meet his father again. The son got a telegram about his father's illness in the midst of the Conference, but before he could reach to be by the side of his father, only mortal remains of Sir Asutosh were there to greet the bereaved son Syama Prasad.

Excerpts from the writings of Rabindranath Tagore and Michael Sadler on the untimely death of Asutosh in 1924 summarise his great vision and abilities succinctly.

Tagore wrote: 'Men are always rare in all countries through whom the aspiration of their people can hope to find its fulfilment, who have the thundering voices to say that what is needed shall be done; Asutosh had the magic voice of assurance. He had the courage to dream because he had the power to fight and the confidence to win—his will itself was the path to the goal'.

Michael Sadler who was the Chairman of the Calcutta University Commission (1917-1919) of which Asutosh was a member, wrote, "In Asutosh Mookerjee, India has lost one of her greatest men; the world one of its commanding personalities. He was mighty in battle. He could have ruled an empire. But he gave the best of his powers to education because he believed that in education rightly lies the secret of human welfare and the key to every empire's moral strength."

Young Blood in the University Syndicate

As we all know that running huge educational establishments like universities need an adroit and robust system of administrative governance and academic excellence. To that end was devised the system of the Syndicate for smooth running of universities. A syndicate of a university is expected to have an all-round approach to manage the institution. In other words, it is likely to look after almost every conceivable work of a university. Therefore, the members of such a significant body are chosen on the basis of their administrative and scholarly merit.

In 1924, the Syndicate of the Calcutta University lost one of its most prolific members in Sir Asutosh Mookerjee, and the University was in search of someone who could step in the shoes of Sir Mookerjee. The decision-makers of the University found that no one else but young Syama Prasad Mookerjee was the best resource to step in the shoes of his father in the all-powerful Syndicate of the University. Syama Prasad was 23, but he had a wise head on young shoulders.

Syama Prasad proved himself a befitting member of the body, and he not only understood the new responsibilities, but devoted himself for the task of the betterment of his alma mater now as a member of the Syndicate. In fact, his transition from a student of the University to a member of the Syndicate was all too smooth because of the masterly guidance of his father to take up challenges of future and come out brighter. In a short span of time, he was liked and appreciated by everyone in the organisation. The praise he received from India's pioneering scientist and an elder statesman of education, Acharya Prafulla Chandra Roy is an index of his merit and abilities helping him perform his duties as an educationist and administrator.

In the words of Acharya P.C. Ray, "You seem to have emerged as a real *bap ka beta in* the University! No one is prepared to work hard and so selflessly as you are now doing." Acharya was elder to him by 40 years, yet Syama Prasad found in him a friend to whom he could look up to when in need of a competent counsel. Above all, Acharya too listened to him with the alacrity of a youth. On one such occasion, Acharya did listen to him and agreed to render his services for the University even after his retirement.

As a member of the University syndicate, Syama Prasad continued the work of organising lectures for the benefit of the students. It is noteworthy that the foundation of the 'Kamla Lectures' was laid by his father after Kamla, Syama Prasad

Mookerjee's sister, died at a young age. Syama Prasad's influence and stature grew leaps and bounds, and he could bring to the dias the most prominent names of the time. And, therefore, scholars like Sarojini Naidu, Annie Besant and even Gurudev Rabindranath Tagore, who came to deliver his famous lectures on 'Manusher Dharma' in 1933. Undoubtedly, through such initiatives, Syama Prasad Mookerjee was not only serving the academia of his times and modelling education system for the future, but, at the same time, bringing accolades to the University which remained the country's most sought-after Institute for higher education.

There is a reference of an institute which played an important and useful part in moulding student life in Calcutta.[7] At the annual function of the Institute, Syama Prasad delivered the key speech and in that, he made reference to the literary meetings of the Institute. Thirty-six meetings held in the whole year and at each meeting, some instructive subject was discussed by a competent speaker. It helped widen the outlook, to elevate the moral and intellectual character of students. Syama Prasad also showed his gratitude to the late Sec. Dewan Bahadur Hiralal who raised donations to ₹12,000/- to the furniture fund of the Institute. The time period of this speech is around 1928. He was totally engrossed in the upliftment of the education system.

His stint as a member of the Syndicate also provided Syama Prasad with the first-hand experience of the education system of the time with all its inherent lacunae that made him strive for its betterment for all his life. He thoroughly understood the processes and the policies meant to run the education system of the country. As a result of his keen interest and an acute understanding, his ideas and suggestions began to find multiple ears and brains involved in running the education system in India. Along with its more obvious functions, Syama Prasad understood the role of education in making the countrymen strive for the independence of the country. At the same time, he also realised how the colonial Government is using education merely as an instrument for the subversion of the system for an end not suited to what education embodies, intellectual interests and above all humanity. His fears were not unfounded as corroborated by Mr. Sadler, who said, "I feel grave concern at the injury which may be done to higher education in India and to the intellectual interests of Bengal by the Calcutta University Amendment Bill which has been submitted by the Bengal Government for the Viceroy's sanction." Therefore, Syama Prasad took the decision to fight the Bengal Legislative Assembly election from the university constituency so that he might influence the state education policy and be aware of all the activities related to education.

The Young Legislature

Syama Prasad became the youngest legislature in 1929. He entered the Bengal Legislative Council as the Congress candidate. In 1930, Congress staged the walkout from the Council. Syama Prasad resigned from Congress and again fought the election as an independent candidate. And his stature was such that he won the election. He took oath as the member of Bengal Legislative Council on 17 March 1930. Syama Prasad's biographer Balraj Madhok says that Dr. Mookerjee's entry into politics should be dated from 1937 when he was elected to the Bengal Legislative assembly. However, Dr. Naba Kumar Adak, who did extensive research on Syama Prasad's role in Bengal politics, found that he was extremely active in Bengal Legislative Council and he not only defended and extended the cause of education, his prime concern, but also showed his keen interest in other spheres of public life. His involvement in politics was not at all unexpected as he always had an interest in serving people and considered it as his highest duty.

Praphulla C. Ghosh, the teacher of Dr. Mookerjee in Presidency college, said five years before his entering into politics, "He has the making of a public man. He has tact, common sense, organising capacity, readiness in the debate, robust sense of humour." His teacher's belief was manifested word for word in the coming years. Syama Prasad believed that one couldn't bring change in the system while standing outside. In the meetings and debates of Bengal Legislative Council, he fearlessly supported the cause of truth and worked relentlessly for the interests of the academic world along with the national cause and concern. He was not elected as a Congress candidate, but he supported the party actively throughout his tenure. However, the neutral response of Congress party on Communal Award (1932) made him upset, and his trust in this political organisation was broken.

During this period, Syama Prasad Mookerjee was actively involved in the decision-making of the University and correspondences between the University and the Government.

Syama Prasad had high regard and admiration for the Satyagrahis. He remarked, "The political prisoners are not persons who have committed heinous acts which violently offend our moral feelings. Call them misguided, if you like, disapprove of the consequences of their action, if you choose, but unless you are untrue to yourself, you cannot doubt their sincerity or question their capacity for suffering and their spirit of sacrifice. One ideal and one alone has impelled their action, and that is a fervent zeal to free their motherland from foreign domination. You say they have broken the provisions of your lawless ordinances. If they have done so, the remedy open to the Government is prosecution, conviction and imprisonment. That has been done and done with a vengeance. The area of jail is sought to be widened, and it will soon have to be made as wide as the province itself. But what laws, God-made or human-made, do empower Government to persecute and commit violence on prisoners mercilessly."[8] He could not bear the maltreatment forced upon the political prisoners by the jail authorities violating their own code of conduct.

Syama Prasad Mookerjee outcried in the Council on the cases of repression made by the Government or the Police. Though Government did not declare wearing of Khaddar and Gandhi cap illegal, yet the police in Contai, a city in West Bengal, had issued notices to bus owners not to allow persons who were wearing Khaddar and Gandhi cap to board the buses. He condemned the action of the police. He protested in the Council against "several cases where the police entered into the compound of different colleges unasked for and assaulted the loyal students of those colleges."

It looks as though he was all the time ready to fight for the cause of liberty. He played the role of a guard of peoples' liberty and freedom. He criticised the British Government for their high expenditure in Budget on police and jails by saying, "If you spend half of that sum towards the solution of the question of unemployment, it will be eradicating the rising unrest among the youth." He was against the biased policy of the Government. The Government was pursuing the policy of appointing only Europeans, not any Indian, in different Government services including the medical services. Therefore, on 22 August 1930, he wanted to know how many successful medical students were appointed in the Bengal Medical Service between 1922 and 1930, and the provision of the appointment under Provincial Service Recruitment Rules.[9]

The Government of Bengal produced a 'black bill', under which it demanded the extra power for the police so that the police might arrest any suspect any time. Syama Prasad stringently said, "This bill is perfect in its imperfection". Syama Prasad's indomitable courage to admonish the members in the Council was not new. He always supported truthfulness and never hesitated to oppose the falsehood.

This matter is of that time when Syama Prasad was just eighteen years old. In a meeting of some agitated students, J. Chaudhary (III Division, M.Sc. in Chemistry) abused and criticised the University teachers in his presidential address. Syama Prasad got furious at his remarks and said, "What right has a person, who himself is a Third Class M.A. in Chemistry to judge the capacities of almost all lecturers in all the subjects?" He said that the atmosphere of the University is sacred. The teachers of the University are able and worthy. The University is a temple of learning.

Syama Prasad made a scorching attack on 26 March 1930, against Mr. H.E. Stapleton, the then officiating Director of Public Instruction for his anti-student attitude. He told the Council that this man in 1925 when he was the Principal of the Presidency College gave punishment to the students for hoisting the national flag, celebrating the Jatin Das Day and boycotting of an academic function. Though it was announced that 3 February 1928 would be observed as a general hartal day and on that day, most of the colleges were closed. Mr. Stapleton, the then Principal, kept the Presidency College open and let loose assault and bloodshed. At the instance of Mr. Stapleton, police assaulted a student so much that he had to be removed to a hospital, and, ultimately he died. Syama Prasad Mookerjee observed Mr. Stapleton as 'short-sighted and reactionary' and 'tactless and inefficient'. He advocated that the reign of terror must be brought to an end and the Government should take fairly reasonable measures against such haughty and arrogant officers.

Syama Prasad Mookerjee was extremely concerned for implementing a policy of compulsory physical training and military drill in schools, colleges and universities. However, the Director of Public Instruction, Mr. Stapleton was unnecessarily delaying this demand. Syama Prasad Mookerjee sharply criticised Mr. Stapleton for this and put before the House his views on a physical training course for students and said that it is "a matter of national importance and of national interest". He emphasised, "We cannot hope to advance unless we can turn men capable of shouldering the burdens of self-government and of defence properly." He demanded, "A declaration of policy on this question which will introduce a new era in the history of education in this province." On the same date, 8 August 1929, the Council passed the resolution. "It recommends to the government the urgent necessity of promulgating rules and regulations for making compulsory in all schools for boys to take a lesson in physical training and military drill, and all colleges for students to receive military training."[10]

Dr. Mookerjee had to fight for the disbursal of financial aid to the Calcutta University. He wanted an assurance from the Government that necessary funds would be provided for in the Supplementary Budget in July 1930, enabling the University to carry on its existence until the end of the financial year of 1930. The British Government was least bothered for the higher education institutes. With deep emotions, he urged, "It (the

Calcutta University, the oldest and largest among the Indian Universities) is a national asset of which every Indian ought to be proud. If there are defects, let us, by all means, cooperate in removing them; but it must, at any rate, be given sufficient funds so that it might live and not die a premature death."[11]

On the other hand, the House instituted a retrenchment committee to find out how the Government could reduce its expenditure in different departments. The Committee recommended curtailment of activities of School Hygiene Department, the abolition of the Calcutta Technical School and reduction of expenditure in the Education Department. Syama Prasad Mookerjee said, that it will retard the progress of the province. He also reminded the Education Minister that earlier a conference had been held in the residence of the Minister for Education to consider the question of de-provincialisation of Government schools and colleges. Syama Prasad Mookerjee demanded that savings, which might occur from such de-provincialisation, must be spent on education. He also opposed the recommendation for reduction of grants to the Calcutta University citing that only the previous year, Government, after a prolonged discussion, had given a grant carefully scrutinising the University's expenditure which in no way could be reduced again. The Retrenchment Committee recommended five per cent cut in the expenditure of Calcutta University. He reaffirmed his demand, "No reduction in the grant is at all feasible or justifiable."

Opposing the recommendation for closing a training college, Dr. Mookerjee spoke if that proposal were accepted, it would be disastrous to the cause of secondary education in the province. He also opposed the proposal of abolishing the Government Commercial Institute. However, the Retrenchment Committee did not recommend any reduction of the grant to the Police Department, which used to get a grant to the extent of 25% of the total Budget. He expressed his dissatisfaction in these words, "I must say—to use a hackneyed expression—that the nation-building departments, already badly financed, should not suffer any more, for the purpose of enabling the Hon'ble Mr. Prentice and his department to flourish."

Coming to the issue of the necessity of spreading primary education, Syama Prasad Mookerjee spoke that neglecting primary education was one of the drawbacks of educational system. He asked, "But...who is responsible for the fact that primary education has not made any advance in this country?...For the last 150 years, who have ruled this country? It was the bureaucracy consisting of representatives of the country, from which Mr. Dain comes...What explanation can Mr. Dain offer?"

Syama Prasad Mookerjee argued that Mr. Dain might ask for diversion of funds from other departments, which used to get fabulous grants if he was at all eager to advance primary education. He spoke, "Let me again put Mr. Dain's sincerity to the test. Mr. Dain is anxious that money should be diverted from other heads to primary education. Would Mr. Dain come forward and support me when I say that a portion of the police grant, amounting to ₹2 crores and 27 lakhs per year. He stated that this grant involves the payment of salaries at a stupendous scale unparalleled in the history of the civilised world. He also suggested that diversion of funds could be made from the expenditure of crores of rupees for checking the civil disobedience movement" on the ground that the Europeans in Bengal are rich enough to bear its cost and that a portion of it should be diverted to primary education." He asserted that Mr. Dain would not venture to curtail the expenditure of all these departments because he belonged to that class who hated university education had aroused the national consciousness of this vast country. Syama Prasad Mookerjee suggested that the different stages of education must be looked upon as component parts of one living organism and that the only remedy was to pursue an educational equally and beneficially. Mr. W.C. Wordsworth congratulated and supported the contents of the speech of Syama Prasad Mookerjee. He gave his full support to Syama Prasad Mookerjee's tribute to what university education had done for Bengal.[12]

Syama Prasad Mookerjee took extra burden in this sphere as a representative of the Calcutta University to see that justice was being done in the field of education and educational services and systems of Bengal.

Regarding the administration and appointment of the Calcutta University, Muslim members, especially Khan Bahadur Azizul Haque, raised the issue that their community was not sufficiently represented in Calcutta University according to the numerical strength of their population. Dr. Mookerjee took pains to make them understand that the Calcutta University did not deliberately bar any Muslim from entering into the services and being a member of the Senate and the Syndicate and other bodies of the Calcutta University. He answered that he was hurt by these grievances and complaints of the Muslim members regarding the education system of Calcutta University. He stated that in case of appointment of the Registrar, the Syndicate of the Calcutta University had excluded the name of a Muhammadan because it thought he was inferior to the other two. The Syndicate decided the question entirely on merits. It proceeded in such cases not on communal grounds, but based on merits. Referring to Khan Bahadur Azizul Haque's grievance that a certain Muhammadan gentleman had not been elected a member of the Syndicate, he told the House that Khan Bhadur Azizul Haque knew that two very distinguished educationists had also been defeated. They were Dr. Radha Krishnan and Dr. Urquhart. He questioned, "Was that for any communal reason? Was Dr. Urquhart defeated because he happened to be a Christian? Or, Dr. Radha Krishnan because he was a Hindu?...to suggest that when a Muhammadan gentleman was defeated, he was defeated because he was a Muhammadan is certainly doing us less than justice."

Muslim members alleged that no Muhammadan except Mr. Asanullah had been elected to the Syndicate except for a very short period. Refuting this allegation, Syama Prasad Mookerjee mentioned that Dr. A. Suhrawardy had been elected a member of the Syndicate by the entire body of the Senate a few years back and had been there for a full term. Dr. H. Suhrawardy, the then Vice Chancellor, had also been elected on P.R.S. and Ph.D., D.Sc. Boards. He stated, "he must be a competent examiner, able to examine a thesis for your highest examinations before you can offer it to him," and there was none among the Muslims.

Nazimuddin had spoken highly about Syama Prasad Mookerjee's contribution in settling the communal demand of the Muslims while not allowing the academic interests of the University to be affected. Nazimuddin also accepted that the University had no communal bias.

Mr. W.C. Wordsworth, who at that time was also a member of the Senate of the University, spoke, "The University serves all classes, young men and young women, Hindus, Muhammadans, Europeans...it does not matter a straw whether the majority of men of University are Hindus, or Muhammadans, or Europeans, or whoever else they may be. The University wants scholars to serve it. It wants their scholarship, their enthusiasm, their knowledge of education...when we work together at the University; we seldom trouble to think whether the men round the table are Hindus or Muhammadans or Europeans. I wish that communalism were never likely to enter the University may never be marred by communal bitterness." Syama Prasad Mookerjee established with facts and figures that University was not communal in its outlook. However, certain members were not prepared to look into facts, but would go on placing their biased opinions. Syama Prasad Mookerjee requested those members not to make the University a game of communal politics. He argued, "The University must be a national organisation, looking at educational problems not from the narrow outlook of any particular community, but solely from the standpoint of national advancement and must cater to the needs of all communities and sects..."There is no reason why there should be any such misunderstanding. Let us work together in the best interest of the province, in the interest of both the great communities, and I am sure that my Muhammadan friends will find ample support from every shade of opinion so far as the University is concerned." This we will discuss in details in the sixth chapter.

Syama Prasad Mookerjee was all set to reach the pinnacle of an unfading brilliance which to his adversaries was a shining scimitar and a flame for masses groping in the dark alleys of distressing times. His roaring exhortations in the Legislative Council to make education free from the clutches of Government were taken verbatim by the fellow Indians even though the British nerves were not calm on the same. But he was firm in his belief that the University in itself had capable mechanism to address all the circumstantial challenges thrown at her by the time he lived in. This stance he maintained and worked for even when most of his time was being consumed by politics.

Support to Dr. Hassan Suhrawardy and Prof. Hasan Shaheed Suhrawardy

Dr. Hassan Suhrawardy served Calcutta University from 1930 to 1934 as the Vice Chancellor though he knew little about educational administration. He was also the first Muslim Vice Chancellor of the Calcutta University. However, Syama Prasad liberally cooperated the new Vice Chancellor. In return, Dr. Suhrawardy always submitted to the better judgement and suggestions of Syama Prasad. Syama Prasad was said to be his chief counsel. Prof. Hasan Shaheed Suhrawardy, the cousin of Dr. Hassan Suhrawardy, was appointed as the Vageshwari Professor of Comparative Arts in 1932. On his appointment, there was a lot of objections. Though he was a deserving candidate, he was Nizam Professor of Iranian Art in the Vishwa Bharati. He had studied in Oxford, Russia and France. He taught English at the University of St. Petersburg. His kinship with the Vice Chancellor was the reason for opposition. People like Sir Manmatha Nath Mukherjee and Rama Prasad were opposing his candidature. However, Syama Prasad along with Rabindra Nath Tagore endorsed his appointment. Syama Prasad proclaimed that through the appointment of a Muslim, 'the university is entering a new phase and is telling everyone in the world that the statement which is sometimes made that this university is confined to a class is not correct; and that it is the university of Bengal, the university of India'.

Syama Prasad was working hard to make the University better. He whole-heartedly devoted himself in the administration work of the University. His thoughts were clear on the educational policy and the demand of the time. He was very much vocal about the education policy in the Bengal Legislative Council. He wanted to develop national education policy. At All Bengal University and College Teachers' Conference on 22 February 1933, just eight months before his Vice Chancellorship, he said, "The students that we are turning out do not have the capacity to fight life's struggle... we have to bear in mind that following the education that we give them, they should be made able to earn a living through a profession or business. The system of education that we have right now is singularly unsuitable for this purpose." At another place, he stated, "...It is also for you not only to inculcate in the minds of youth the passion for knowledge and truth and spirit or reverence, but also to foster in them the love of their motherland—that real patriotism—which impels one to sacrifice everything for the good of one's country."

He commented this against the education policy of Macaulay. According to Tathagata Roy, "Macaulay wanted to produce such class of persons, which was Indian in blood and colour, but English in taste, in opinions, in morals, and in intellect." Syama Prasad wanted to make people free from such mentality. He aspired political, educational, cultural and social freedom. His thoughts were always in consonance with what Sir Asutosh had declared, referring, of course, to the field of education, "Freedom first, freedom second, freedom always."

The people who were well aware of the talent of Syama Prasad didn't get surprised at his selection on the post of Vice Chancellor of Calcutta university. However, getting a paramount and key position at a very young age was a prodigious episode. His precursor, Dr. Hassan Suhrawardy said, "Nobody knows more than I personally do of the great help that as Vice Chancellor I got from you and the great difficulty I would have been in without your cooperation. Your hard work, your arduous labour in connection with the reorganisation of the University, has been well recognised and rewarded." The former Dean of Arts Faculty, Sir Z.R. Zahid Suhrawardy joined him by saying, "We congratulate you that at this early age, you have been able to become the head of this institution, but we have reason to congratulate the University more than yourself. In supporting the vote of condolence which was proposed after the death of your illustrious father, I had the honour of observing that whenever mention was made of the Calcutta University, one could not but think of Sir Asutosh as Vice Chancellor. As a colleague of your illustrious father, I had occasion to value the intellectual capacity of that great man, and I have since found that you, his worthy son, have very much inherited his greatness and undoubted worth. I have a very high opinion of your ability." Almost everybody was pleased with his selection. Dr. M. Ishaque, a noted scholar of Persian and the founder of the Iran Society in Calcutta, and a member of the Senate threw a party in his honour at the zoological gardens.

Mr. Syama Prasad Mookerjee, M.A., B.L., Bar-At Law. M.L.C. Vice Chancellor, Calcutta University

Syama Prasad's selection as the Vice Chancellor was the first major manifestation of his contributions towards nation-building. It was just the beginning of the indispensable contributions of Syama Prasad in the direction of national solidarity.

Endnotes

1. Roy, 2008, p. 13.
2. This house was built in the memory of his grandfather Ganga Prasad. He had a great attraction for 'Ganga Prasad House'. Mookerjee family was used to celebrate *Durga Pooja* in 'Ganga Prasad House'. They used to spend the Christmas holidays there.
3. Leaves from a Diary, p. 166.
4. II-IV instalment, private papers of Syama Prasad, Correspondence with Sadler, M.E.

5. Tathagata Roy, p. 59.
6. *'Rabindranath Tagore: selected poems', New Delhi: Oxford University Press, 2004.*
7. II-IV instalment, S.No. 25, Speeches by him, private papers of Syama Prasad; on the Annual Report of the Institute. The name of the Institute is not mentioned in the documents.
8. BLCP, Vol. 35, 11.08.30, p.77.
9. BLCP, Vol.35, 20.03.30, pp. 679-681.
10. BLCP, Vol. 33, 8.4.29, p. 229.
11. BLCP. Vol.36, No.3, 27.03.31, p. 619.
12. Adak p. 86-89,

□

5
The Young Vice Chancellor

If thou canst plan a noble deed,
And never flag till it succeeds,
Though in the strife thy heart must bleed;
Whatever obstacles control,
Thine hour will come. Go on, true, soul,
Thou' lt win the prize, thou'lt reach the goal.

(From a poem referred by Sir Asutosh Mookerjee in his Convocation address, Calcutta University, 18 May 1922.)

Our present Vice Chancellor (Dr. Syama Prasad Mookerjee) deserves the blessings of the motherland.

—**Rabindranath Tagore** (Excerpt from Calcutta University Convocation address delivered on 17 February 1937)

In the past, the higher education system of our country has seen an unprecedented evolution and gave to the world premiere universities like Taxila and Nalanda. These ancient institutions ceased to exist for various reasons including wilful destruction and burning of some of them as a consequence of conquests and military raids by invading outsiders. However, the spirit of learning did not wane even when such formal institutions became rare to find for many centuries. By the time the west had come up with some renowned universities like Oxford and Cambridge beginning to have an impact on the map of the education world.

With the coming of the British as the new masters of the fate of the servile Indians came the requirements of people who could man the machine of imperialism. Thus, the British established a few universities, but with a primary aim to produce human resource suitable for the colonial interests. However, it is a different story about how these institutions became a breeding ground of nationalism. Calcutta University was then the finest of all the existing institutions meant for higher education. It gradually grew as the virtual epicentre of the Indian education surprisingly under the guidance of Indians like Sir Asutosh Mookerjee and attracted the best brains of India both in humanities and sciences. Some of the illustrious names that added to the luster of the university have already been discussed in the earlier chapters.

In 1934, something unprecedented was witnessed in the history of the university. Syama Prasad became the Vice Chancellor of the university at the age of 33. He was the youngest to sport the robes of the head of such an immensely prestigious university. But with great power come greater challenges to address. It was true also in the case of Syama Prasad. Challenges were present in all forms and shapes. Apart from running the day-to-day administration of the university, he was expected to shape up the academic landscape. He also had an arduous task to fight for the educational rights of the teeming millions of Indians and garner as much as he could from a colonial government which was bent more upon beefing up police and military establishments rather than spending on matters like education. The people were looking at him with high expectations also to carry on the work of educational reconstruction and implementation of the policies initiated by Sir Asutosh when he was Vice Chancellor of Calcutta University. These new initiatives were aimed at educating more and more Indians. Syama Prasad's stint as a member of the university senate and syndicate proved helpful in equipping him with the experience which eventually proved handy in addressing challenges which

Vice Chancellor Syama Prasad Mookerjee

could have mired any Vice Chancellor of the university.

Nonetheless, the biggest challenge before Syama Prasad was thrown almost a century ago in 1835, by Thomas Babington Macaulay who proposed his historical 'minute' aimed at an unprecedented subversion of all sorts to create a class of Indians to serve as serfs in perpetuity. Macaulay wrote in 'Minute on Indian education':

"...a single shelf of a good European library was worth the whole native literature of India and Arabia...I certainly never met with any orientalist who ventured to maintain that the Arabic and Sanskrit poetry could be compared to that of the great European nations. But when we pass from works of imagination to works in which facts are recorded and general principles investigated, the superiority of the Europeans becomes immeasurable. It is, I believe, no exaggeration to say that all the historical information which has been collected from all the books written in the Sanskrit language is less valuable than what may be found in the most paltry abridgements used at preparatory schools in England...We must at present do our best to form a class who may be interpreters between us and the millions whom we govern, a class of persons Indian in blood and colour, but English in taste, in opinions, in morals and intellect."

In those early days, two courses were open to those officially responsible for the education of the people. They might have utilised the widespread indigenous system after infusing new life into it, reconstructing and reorganising it wherever necessary and making it the vehicle of new ideas and ideals; or they might have created an altogether new system, unconnected with the indigenous one, and used it for the education of the people of this country. By an irony of fate, they adopted the latter course. Thus, was evolved a system which was primarily dissociated from the cultural and educational traditions of the people and which made an alien language the vehicle of new ideas that were expected to regenerate the people of India. And the foreign government lost a splendid opportunity to build what might have been a genuinely national system of education—a system democratic in its foundation and based on the language and culture of the people. It is well known that the fateful decision to introduce an altogether new system of education was strengthened by the fact that the Government wanted to train a set of Indians who could occupy subordinate offices under the Government and help in the administration of the country, thereby keeping down the cost of administration. Thus, it was that the present system of education came to be prized not for its cultural values, but for the economic return it brought.

Syama Prasad intensely studied the system of education in British India and prepared a well-researched paper on it. (Mookerjee, Syama Prasad. "Education in British India." *The Annals of the American Academy of Political and Social Science*, Vol. 233, 1944, pp. 30–38. *JSTOR*, www.jstor.org/stable/1025819.)

Some of the new initiatives taken by Dr. Syama Prasad Mookerjee were:

The Revival of the Glory and Richness of the Indian Languages

The greatest challenge was to conduct classes and examination in a foreign language. Generally, if the medium of education is not the mother-tongue, the speed of learning is adversely affected. One of the negative consequences of learning through foreign language was that the ordinary student found the English language difficult and that he was somehow passing away without understanding the subject. The second fatal result was that the gap between the masses and the English-educated people was widening and this difference was a byproduct of Macaulay's biased attitude. Renowned Bengali writer Bankim Chandra Chatterjee repeatedly mentioned the growing gulf between English-educated *Babu* and the masses, in '*Banga Darshan*'.[1] The young Vice Chancellor fought against Macaulay's ill-willary policy and tried hard to bring back the respect to Indian languages by abolishing the English-language monopoly. It was very tough to bring back the glory of Indian languages. The education imparted through the medium of a foreign language had produced a class of men who were so denationalised that any proposal for recognition of the Indian languages as the vehicle of teaching and examination up to the highest university stage was either ridiculed as impossible or branded as reactionary. It seemed as if Syama Prasad Mookerjee had decided to give shape to the ideas of Bharatendu Harishchandra, the father of modern Hindi.

निज भाषा उन्नति अहै, सब उन्नति को मूल।
बिन निज भाषा-ज्ञान के, मिटत न हिय को सूल।।
विविध कला शिक्षा अमित, ज्ञान अनेक प्रकार।
सब देसन से लै करहू, भाषा माहि प्रचार।।

(Progress is made in one's language (the mother-tongue), as it is the foundation of all progress. Without the knowledge of the mother-tongue, there is no cure for the pain of the heart. Many arts and education infinite, knowledge of various kinds should be taken from all countries, but be propagated in one's mother-tongue.)

Syama Prasad introduced Bengali and other regional languages, in the educational system, whether it be medium of instruction or the examination. He felt that without this provision, people would have continued to have an aversion to taking up higher studies. Syama Prasad in the Bengal Legislative Council had reminded the Government that in 1921, a proposal was moved to restructure the entire matriculation examination, the most important issue of which was the mother-tongue in the teaching medium of the teaching of all subjects except English. Remember that Sir Asutosh Mookerjee brought the proposal. Syama Prasad told the council that it would be tough to get the best results if the training in the school was given in foreign language, he asked the British Government that if the story of 'Spanish Armada'[2] had been ended in some other way and the British were sitting under some additional foreign power, they would have faced the difficulties that we Indians were facing. He spoke strongly why not let our students receive basic training in subjects like History, Geography, Mathematics in schools in their mother-tongue. In this manner only, they would take a genuine and vibrant interest in their work which is essential in the early period of their educational life.[3]

Syama Prasad Mookerjee first made mother-tongue a medium for primary and secondary level teaching and examination. Subsequently, the mother-tongue was made the medium of instruction and examination up to graduation level. He started Honours courses in Bengali, Urdu and Hindi. A dictionary was created by collecting technical words of various subjects and their Bengali synonyms to facilitate the creation of textbooks in Bengali. The preparation and compilation of official, scientific and technical terminology in Bengali was a very important service for Bengali language. Vice Chancellor Syama Prasad appointed Rajasekhar Bose, a chemist and high-grade writer, as chairman of the committee set up for this job. Tagore also made an unprecedented contribution to the work, and it is the result of the committee's hard work that technical and scientific textbooks are available in Bengali.

Syama Prasad had imagined, "When in this manner the university will be able to prepare a complete glossary of words in all subjects and for all standards. This will enrich Bengali language and literature and also make it possible for us to take steps for extending the use of vernaculars for the higher examinations of the University." He also gave permission to write research thesis in the mother-tongue. He initiated the practise of carrying on a lot of educational and scientific research work, through the medium of Bengali. In fact, in 1935, he brought about a radical change in secondary education, by the revised Matriculation Regulations, where instruction was to be imparted through the medium of mother-tongue. The Calcutta University, for the very first time, had awarded the degree of Doctor of Philosophy to a successful candidate, who had written his thesis in Bengali language. Inspired by Syama Prasad, the university started publishing book series in Bengali on various branches of knowledge to enhance Bengali literature and people's interest in Bengali language. He published books in general colloquial language on numerous subjects of literary and scientific interest to educate the masses and familiarise themselves with the truth and facts of science.

The task of standardising the spelling of Bengali language also started during his Vice Chancellorship. For this, he constituted a sub-committee. The sub-committee collected the views of various Bengali scholars to give a scientific basis to Bengali language. Top litterateurs like Rabindranath and Sarat Chandra Chatterjee agreed to the work of the sub-committee. To further enrich Bengali language, Syama Prasad gave permission to conduct research in Bengali language and literature. In 1935, the university also published a booklet on the scientific use of Bengali whose introduction was written by Syama Prasad himself.

"Ila Saraswati Mahi Tisro Devirmayo Bhuvaha Barhih Seedantva Sridhah."

—(13/9, Rigveda)

The three goddesses—'Earth', 'Saraswati' and 'Vani' (mother-tongue) are the givers of joy, and never lose their abundance. One should respect his Motherland, his culture and his mother-tongue because they are givers of happiness. A person who is respectful towards his land, civilisation and language attains greatness, and he acquires all of life's happiness. His deeds should be such that makes the Motherland, the culture and language proud of him.

In the *Atharva Veda*, it is said, "Let us not turn away from our mother-tongue. May we always look upon our mother-tongue with favour. Those who are desirous of pleasing the gods 'chant prayers' to them in the mother-tongue. It is the mother-tongue which performs the function of purification. Each word of the mother-tongue is bound to us with ties of blood. Clarified butter flows through each word of the mother-tongue. All the 'sacred arts' find expression in our mother-tongue. May we use our mother-tongue to describe the glory of the gods."

When Syama Prasad broke the tradition of the university for the betterment of the mother-tongue:

The need to make mother-tongue medium of education was accepted in the National Education Movement of the Swadeshi Movement. The efforts were made primarily by Rabindranath Tagore, Sir Akbar Hydari, Sir Asutosh Mookerjee, and a few others who for many years had been advocating the case of Indian languages. However, nothing could be done until some among them were so placed as to be able to translate these ideas into action. Syama Prasad Mookerjee, Pandit Madan Mohan Malviya and Sir Akbar Hydari need special mention in introducing the mother-tongue as the medium of education. In a research paper published in the Annals of the American Academy, Syama Prasad presented India's plight in the following words, "India is the only country in the world which presents the curious spectacle of young pupils learning in school through a foreign tongue which they can only imperfectly understand."

Rabindranath always emphasised that education should be imparted through the mother-tongue. He believed that the medium of English was a significant obstacle to Indian students. *'Shikshar Herfer'*, published in 1892, was the first article in which Rabindranath discussed the English teaching system of the country elaborately. He never believed that English should be the only language of instruction, though; we should not forget that he never denied the importance of learning English. He observed, "...English is a very foreign language. There is no similarity with our language regarding spelling designation. After that, the imagery and subject matter are also foreign. Nothing is known, so the idea is to start before it is born. Do not chew and swallow it. May be there is a story about a haymaking in a children's reader, that is particularly familiar to an English boy, so it is especially pleasing ...but when our boys read them in a foreign language, they do not have any memories, do not see anything like a picture in front of their minds, move blindly in the dark...the destitute children are chained to a foreign prison... in the grammar and dictionary of foreign languages. There is no life, no joy, no respite, no freshness; there is no place to sit in the river; it is in the very dry, narrow jungle. Does it mean that he or she can ever get mental nutrition, an outgrowth of heart, sacrificing character? Can he, at his adulthood, work out his wisdom. He can overcome his obstacles, improve his head at his natural brilliance. Does he learn to memorise, duplicate and enslave?"[4]

There is no doubt that thinking and imagination are two

vital forces for living. That is, if one were to be human-like human beings, then those two substances would not be eliminated from life. Therefore, it is for sure that if he has not practised thought and imagination since childhood, he would not be available to him at work.

But in our current education, that path is blocked. For a long time, we had to engage in pure language learning. As Tagore said it earlier, "English is such a foreign language, and our teachers are usually so well-educated that it is not easy to enter into our minds immediately with language. That is why, we have to wait a long time to become familiar with the English spirit, and then our thoughts are restless without finding any suitable work. Big classes and serious thought topics are put before us in class—then they have no power even when they are well mastered—all of them have to be swallowed together in one swallow."[5]

Rabindranath deeply felt the agony for the impartial behaviour with the mother-tongue. Tagore said in one of his articles that the birthright of education in his mother-tongue was also a matter of argument and debate in this unfortunate country.

In 1936, Syama Prasad as Vice Chancellor wrote to the poet requesting him to deliver the address at the annual convocation of the university. This was unprecedented for so far; no 'outsider' had been invited to address the convocation. Rabindranath accepted his invitation in 1937 with the words, "...but I would accept the honour (to deliver the address at the convocation) only on a particular condition. You know of my life's great desire of seeing our language firmly and finally established as the medium of instruction in the university...If you are going to break a tradition by asking me, an outsider, to address the convocation, you will have to break yet another convention and permit me to address in Bengali. Syama Prasad was glad at this and readily accepted the condition put by Gurudev. Syama Prasad persuaded Sir John Anderson, the Governor of Bengal and the Chancellor of the University to give consent for the convocation address to be delivered in Bengali by Rabindranath Tagore. The Chancellor agreed. This was the first time that the Convocation address

(Chhatrasambhashan) was delivered in Bengali. This was also the first time that a non-official delivers the address. Rabindranath showed his gratitude by mentioning, "With the considerable courage, Sir Asutosh violated the first ritual when he dared to give a Bengali-speaking author like me the title of university doctor. Today, his son invited me to read the speech in Bangla on this occasion. University is blessed by his right son, Mr. Syama Prasad...I have had the opportunity to express the hope that the University of Bengal will be glorified in the mother-tongue of its people."

Rabindranath ended this historical address with a striking prayer—

O lord!
Give us the pride that lies
In courting the impossible
And unbearable sorrow.
Lift us up and out of the enchanted
trance of emotionalism.
Sternly upbraid this wallowing in the
dust of meanness.
Remove the bondage of the slavery of the mind,
the perennial disability of fate,
put an end to the stupid sacrifice of
human dignity at the feet of the unworthy,
ruthlessly pulverise the shameful follies
piled up over the ages.
Let us lift our heads high
without fear
under the endless sky
in the magnificent light,
in the wind of freedom.

This address was the slap in the face of Macaulay's successors. This was the beginning of the end of the supremacy of English on the Indian languages.

The Reorganisation of Matriculation Course

Most of the unsatisfactory features of undergraduate and postgraduate education had their origin in a defective system of secondary education. The future of university education depended vitally on the reorganisation of secondary education. Dr. Mookerjee observed that remodelling of the secondary education system was necessary, and Calcutta University was firm to bring these changes. He said that they would not succumb before the government of Bengal.

Sir Asutosh Mookerjee organised various conferences of Principals in 1921, in which the members of the management committee also took part. Multiple changes were discussed in the conferences, and based on that, a bill was formed and sent in September 1921 for the approval of the Government. It took nearly two years to make the Government's opinion somewhat positive on the bill. Obviously, during that movement, nothing was quickly found.

Syama Prasad again raised the issue of restructuring of secondary education as Vice Chancellor and brought a Bill which decided that the mother-tongue would be the medium of instruction and examination. The pivot of the bill was undoubtedly the vernacularisation of secondary education. This change was long overdue and which was justly regarded as of far-reaching significance. The list of subjects had also been revised to render the entire course more up-to-date, useful and practical. History and Geography were to be made compulsory and Elementary Science was included in the list of optional subjects with the condition that it would be made mandatory after five years. Certain new subjects like Domestic Science and Music were added, some practical subjects were added to the list of subjects. It was made compulsory for the students to read at least one vocational subject and get a certificate from a qualified teacher and only then his tenth certificate would be valid. This would stimulate young people to train themselves in some skill, and it would make them more earnest and self-reliant.[6] Syama Prasad faced a lot of difficulties in implementing the above Bill of

Calcutta University. The Government refused to accept the Bill as the British Government felt that it would reduce the knowledge of English language among the students. Though Syama Prasad said that in this manner they would save students' time because the students read some subjects in his mother-tongue at the primary level and again, they had to learn those subjects in English. This is just the wastage of time.

Calcutta University and Syama Prasad were adamant on their decision, saying that every Indian had been waiting for a very long time. He said, "This is a change which every responsible citizen will admit, is overdue. This is a change which does not require concealment, which is calculated to sow the seeds of national education. An Indian student has as much right to be taught through the medium of his vernaculars as an English student has." Finally, Syama Prasad succeeded in implementing the Bill.[7]

The Establishment of Information and Employment Board

Why was the British Government not spending some part of the budget to generate jobs and improving the education policy? The problems of educated unemployment were distressing Syama Prasad. It was constantly forcing him to roar in the Bengal Legislative Council on the question of joblessness of educated youth? It's known that in a famous letter to Lord Amherst (11 December 1823), Ram Mohan Roy sought English education primarily for a more liberal and enlightened system of instruction, embracing Mathematics, Natural Philosophy, Chemistry, Anatomy, with other useful sciences. However, Macaulay and Wood didn't give special place to these subjects in the education policy of India. The Bachelor of Science degree at the Calcutta University was introduced in the ninth decade of the 19th century, and in 1908, only 38 students appeared in the B.Sc. examination, whereas, 1,200 students appeared in the B.A. exam. The inevitable result was that the numbers of graduates who could work as clerks in Government offices increased. The young Vice Chancellor took steps towards rebuilding the curriculum and included practical and professional subjects in the curriculum to address this problem. He stressed on the diversification of education to enable educated youth to be fit for the different jobs.

He had, therefore, set up an Appointments Board in the Calcutta University with the object of finding suitable employment for its products. Our alien rulers of the time were seeking to lower the pressure on the employment market by attempts to restrict educational facilities. Syama Prasad raised everywhere his loud voice of protest against such a policy. He pointed out that the remedy lay in the establishment of particular types of institutions for scientific and technical training and the opening out of new avenues of employment. In dealing with this problem, he sought the co-operation of government and various commercial and industrial interests with the University. He delivered a speech on 'Education and Unemployment' at the Scottish Church College on 7 December 1935 and observed that the state requires specialised institutions to train students in various professions.

Change in Examination System

In September 1934, Syama Prasad took some significant decisions related to the teachers, time table, and the examination system. The purpose behind these changes was that the teachers should excellently teach the students so that all the students could well assimilate the knowledge and not just pass the exams by cramming. He made the viva voce examination necessary for the students and also ensured that they were given adequate training so that they could perform well in the oral exam. He also issued the guidelines for the examination board in this context. The viva-voce examination system can bring surprising changes in the students' oratory skills which can make them self-confident.

His second major decision in this sequence was that the number of lectures in the students' time table should be decreased and the number of tutorials should be increased. The teacher-student ratio is less in tutorials as comparative to lectures, and the teacher can give personal attention to every student. As students spend half their growing years in school and college, teachers have a significant role to play in shaping the personality of the students. A teacher who is in constant touch with the students can become the primary source of on-campus support for the students for their issues also. He made it compulsory for students to submit at least 20 assignments in their tutorials and for which they would be given marks as well. He prepared the teachers to play the role of a trained counsellor. Attendance was made compulsory in lectures and tutorials. He allowed talented meritorious students to spend more time in the library. He requested the teachers to select the best students and give them proper guidance. He divided the postgraduate examinations into two semesters so that the students would get more serious about the exam and studies.

The Fundamental Changes for Teachers

Syama Prasad Mookerjee ensured that the teachers get the time table of the next session before they go on summer vacation so that if teachers want some change as per their convenience, it could be modified and proper reconciliation can be done before the classes start. He made it mandatory for the heads of departments to appear in the university all day, and it was imperative for teachers that they should be present in the university at the time of their lectures and tutorials. If any teacher wanted to take leave, he should notify that to the time table in-charge so that his lectures would be adjusted. He instructed the teachers to complete their curriculum within a time frame, even if they had to take extra classes. It was requested to every teacher and the heads of departments to submit an account of the work done to the Executive Committee twice a year. Each department needed to submit its annual report. He also initiated the task of restructuring the methodology for the course of each paper. He aimed to implement the practical curriculum. He told the teachers that they have to give at least one public lecture in a year on the subject they are interested in. However, that would be the type of lecture that could address some of the major problems of the masses. In this context, he appealed to the teachers' community to work together and prepare lectures, which would also be published by the University in the form of small booklets. His opinion was to run an 'exchange programme' of university and college teachers so that students could be benefitted at the postgraduate level. He also emphasised on simplification of the administrative system so that the time of teachers and students might be saved and they could work smoothly.

Teacher Training Programme Initiative

The human being must always strive to achieve efficiency and perfection. He introduced specialised training courses for teachers so that their teaching art becomes even more palatable and skilful. He was of the view that the trained teacher is the focal point of the Institute's valuable property and the teaching art of teachers can judge the institution's quality.

He conducted inspirational lectures for teachers from time to time. He introduced refresher courses for various disciplines. He said that without proper training of the teachers, the quality of education might be affected. A good teacher should be able to create a keen interest in his students and also make his students confident. A teacher is an interpreter of our heritage. He stressed on the need for a large number of trained teachers.

Syama Prasad introduced Teacher's Training Department. Even today, the significance of such a department is highly appreciated. Recently, Govt. of India has initiated Teacher Training Programs for college and university teachers. In 1932, the Bengal Retrenchment Committee was formed and which subsequently recommended the abolition of the two training colleges, that of David Hare Training College and Dacca Training College, due to financial crisis. Herein, Syama Prasad took up the cause, wherein he pressed the Government, for the retention of both the above colleges as well as the establishment of new ones.

The Establishment of Applied Courses

Geography, related to both physical and social sciences, provides a specific background in determining public or private policies based on which analysis of problems is convenient. Syama prasad was of the view that Geography should be taught as a mandatory subject till matriculation; however, he introduced the subject from matriculation to the Master's degree. In this series, he also made History as a compulsory subject till matriculation and established it as a subject up to graduation. History is useful in examining and analysing a sequence of past events, and objectively determines the patterns of cause and effect that determine them. The study of History presents a way of providing 'perspective' on the current problems. He also introduced the curriculum of the history and culture of Islam; his aim was that students should understand the *Ganga Jamuni* culture and stay away from the communal hatred being spread by the British.

Recognising the importance of Agronomy, the Vice Chancellor introduced the diploma course in Agriculture. He started the study of practical Botany subjects from Ghosh Trust and Agriculture Science from Khaira Trust at the Dept of Chemistry in University College of Science and Technology in 1935. He requested the Royal Commission on Agriculture to assist the University of Calcutta to carry out research in Agriculture.[8] The scholarship for the popularisation of Agronomy in the students was also extended from the Khaira Trust to be supported by Dr. B.C. Roy, Pramathanath Banerjee, Dr. P.M. Banerjee and Nivaran Babu. Syama Prasad Mookerjee had a profound experience in the establishment of new subjects. So, the university always collaborated with him in this direction. It is to be remembered that in 1946, Syama Prasad played a significant role in the committee which was appointed to set up the Jute Technical Institute. Jute Association agreed upon the Committee's recommendations and became ready to fund the university-affiliated Jute Institute.

He also introduced the subjects of Sanitary Engineering and Communication Engineering at the University. Introduced a separate paper of Communication Engineering in the Physics curriculum, eventually which formed a separate Department in the name of Radio physics and Electronics. The curriculum was modified to increase the standard and usefulness of various disciplines of the Faculty of Art, Science, Drugs and Engineering. Students were sent abroad to study and pursue higher education in the subjects related to Braille system, Bank, Botany and Chemistry.

The Establishment of Social Welfare and Business Management

Syama Prasad believed that social welfare has a crucial role in education, so he founded the Social Welfare Institute. He made it mandatory for the students to do social service for three to four months. He also had the idea of establishing an all India Social Work Institution to impart training of social welfare to the youth. In the same order of social welfare, he wanted to make youth aware of labour law. In 1938, he invited Rajinikanth Das, an expert in labour law, to deliver a lecture on the problems and rules of the Indian Labor Law. He believed that learning Business Management could ensure the achievement of the organisation's objectives under limited resources. Given the demand of time, he started subjects such as 'Commerce' and 'Business Management'.

Education for Women

Syama Prasad considered it very necessary to educate women for the creation of any civilised society. He had a clear reflection on the subject of educating women even before he became the Vice Chancellor. He believed that the subjects of women's interest should be included in the curriculum and in this way, their parents would also like to educate them.

He introduced the curriculum of Home Science for women from Bihari Lal Mitra Kosh. The subject of Social Welfare was added to the curriculum along with the disciplines, like music, sewing, embroidery and weaving. Dr. Mookerjee insisted on vocational education for both the boys and the girls. He started building hostels for girl students as the number of girl students was increasing. He submitted a proposal in this regard to the Government that the university was willing to spend half the cost of construction of the hostel if the government pays the rest. He also gave his guidance to the Nari Shiksha Samiti, Calcutta from time to time. At his behest, the principal of Sunderwati Women's

College in Bhagalpur, Punjab, Sharadha Devi Vedalankar wrote a dissertation on 'Guru Nanak's Contribution to Culture and Literature'.

Dr. Mookerjee envisaged the education of women and adults. Today, we are still trying to take this aspect further and striving hard to educate adults. The critical importance of this field of education has been in no way diminished.

The Promotion of Foreign Languages

Under the Vice Chancellorship of Syama Prasad, provisions were made for the study of important foreign languages, both eastern and western. He pleaded that English should remain a compulsory second language and should be taught to all. He launched research facilities in Chinese and Tibetan languages and culture. He established the Department of Chinese and Tibetan language to help students understand the international relations and the society and culture of other countries. It is noticeable that Sir Asutosh introduced these languages in graduation as elective subjects. Syama Prasad established the relationship between the University of Calcutta and the Chinese Ministry of Education. Five outstanding students of the Chinese language had been given scholarships from China.

While at the post of the President of the Council of Postgraduate Teaching in Arts, he tried to expand the program further. He pleaded with the Chinese Minister of Education to send a Chinese-language scholar so that the students could be taught the Chinese language smoothly. China arranged a teacher for the university. He threw one more proposal to China. And, virtually, the Calcutta University had formulated a policy of inviting foreign scholars to propagate and disseminate Indian culture and civilisation. Whichever foreign scholar wanted to learn Sanskrit, Indian philosophy or Indian History and Culture, the proposal was made by the University of Calcutta for providing facilities and annual honoraria to that foreign scholar. First of all, this proposal was sent to China. Dr. Mookerjee prepared a skilled staff to carry research on these topics. The motive was to highlight a lot of unaltered parts of the ancient civilisation. He did so to enhance academic and cultural importance.

It is to be noted that Prof. Tan Yun Shan, director of the China House of Vishwa Bharati University, had a profound friendship with Syama Prasad Mookerjee, Professor Tan Yun Shan discussed in detail with the Chinese Minister of Education on the proposal of the University of Calcutta. China's then Education Minister, Shu Chia Hua wrote in a letter to Dr. Syama Prasad Mookerjee, "the University of Calcutta has earned an important place and the popularity on an international level which is appreciable." He indicated that he had to work with him positively.

In 1945, Dr. Mookerjee got prepared a scheme for the study of Russian language and literature. Shishir Kumar Mukherjee formulated the scheme. Dr. Mookerjee was of the view that the Russian language was one of the major languages of the world and was full of great literature. Various research papers and journals were available in the Russian language. It was challenging to take references from them as the English translation of them was not available. After some time, this scheme was implemented, and now the University of Calcutta offers a doctorate in the Russian language.

The knowledge of different languages and literature brings maturity in thinking as well as expand the field of learning. It also makes the friendly relation among the nations. Good ties with neighbouring countries give a sharp image. He also launched special refresher courses for teachers of English language. The young Vice Chancellor thought that while providing the status of primary language to the mother-tongue, establishing English as a second language and imparting knowledge of other ancient and modern languages brings firmness in political relations.

Military Training Planning

In the previous chapter, we have discussed how Syama Prasad implemented the military training scheme for students after so many debates with the British government in the Bengal Legislative Council. To start a smooth military training at the

University, a new University Training Course was created. He made every effort to empower the course so that all students could get training and the aspiring students could make the army their career. Military Training was his favourite subject. He also discussed with Major General G. Lindsay for successful implementation of the scheme. He also held camps for students.

The physical training was imparted to students in the camps. In his first convocation address of Calcutta University, Dr. Mookerjee expressed his concern, "What is education worth if our youths, in general, are physically weak or unfit, unable to stand the stress and stress of modern life?" Syama Prasad understood the importance of the strength of the nation, and that is why, he was always willing to provide military training for the students. He used to meet the military authorities for proper military training arrangements. It was the reason why he was invited to the selection board for the selection of suitable candidates in the Indian army. The Bengal home secretariat (Defence) specially wrote a letter on 6 January 1947 to invite him in a meeting to ascertain his views on NCC and its pattern. It is admirable that Syama Prasad at the very right time felt that Indians were not adequately trained to defend themselves from foreign invasions. He very rightfully said that an autonomous India was unthinkable without a National Army and a National Navy controlled and manned by Indians themselves.

Syama Prasad at Madhupur in a Camp

It was unfortunate that in the early years of India's independence, we lost a large part because of policies that were contrary to his views on strategic issues.

Organising University Foundation Day

One of the highly acclaimed contributions of Syama Prasad Mookerjee was the initiation of the University Foundation Day.

The foundation day celebrations were first held in February

1935 in the history of Calcutta University. Syama Prasad Mookerjee was of the view that the Foundation Day celebrations should be celebrated as an annual festival to assess year-round achievements. The university should be proud of its historic accomplishments and move on to the path of advancement. It was an excellent opportunity for participants to showcase talent in various cultural and sports programmes.

Syama Prasad as Vice Chancellor of Calcutta University taking salute from the students on the University Foundation Day – 1937 at Calcutta Maidan

On the same occasion, Syama Prasad said, " One of the great needs of the hour is to build up a healthy corporate life in this university, to provide for our students the amplest facilities for the full exercise of their powers, so that the great qualities which lie dormant in them may shine forth in perfection; to help in the establishment of student organisations with a view to equip them to face the battle of life; to develop them into men, strong and self-reliant, hard-working and fearless, proud of their national culture, but not narrow in their outlook, anxious to promote peace and happiness, filled with a lofty idealism, but not swayed by class hatred or unthinking emotion- men who will be the worthy leaders of a new Bengal, who will carry the torch of learning and freedom to the lasting glory of their beloved motherland."[9]

During the Foundation Day celebrations, thousands of students from the university and related colleges took a spectacular procession with the symbols and bands of their respective colleges. He requested Rabindranath to write two songs for the celebration. The march of students sung the song *Cholo Jai, Cholo Jai* written by Rabindranath. The second song of Rabindranath *Shubh Karma* was made the university song.

The students who led the procession took the flag in hand, which was designed by Syama Prasad. A stage was created outside the Presidency College on which the Vice Chancellor and the members of the Senate were present, and the procession of students used to salute them and reach the university after crossing various colleges. At the ceremony, students used to present multiple sports events and the Vice Chancellor used to address the students.

Emblem of Calcutta University before 1933 and the Emblem designed by Syama Prasad

The foundation day celebration was interrupted after his tenure. He wrote on 24 January 1939 in his diary, "How I wished that these celebrations would be regularly observed as annual functions and would introduce permanently a healthy atmosphere among the student's community. Though the memory of the three great functions remains, their continuity has not been maintained."[10]

The Establishment of the Asutosh Museum and the Fine Art Gallery

At the then time, archaeologists had discovered human-made objects of ancient civilisations that needed to be preserved. The research work on those antiques was also to be carried out. So, to serve this purpose, Dr. Mookerjee established the Asutosh Museum in 1937. It was the first public museum opened by any university in India. With the opening of the museum, a certificate course of

Art Appreciation was launched through the museum to conserve and exhibit the study of Indology, Indian art and archaeology at the university level. DP Ghosh was the museum's first curator.

It is to be noted that Professor Birbal Sahni, a well-known scholar of archaeological studies and ancient history, discovered some ancient coins from the Khokhra Kot fort in 1936. These coins belonged to the 100 BC. He presented them to the museum. Dr. Sahni was appointed by the Calcutta University for the Aadhaar Chandra Lecture series in 1938. In 1938 with the permission of the Government of India and in collaboration with the Department of Archaeology, the staff and students of Calcutta University started excavation work in Bangadh, Dinjapur.

Syama Prasad Mookerjee contacted many generous people and mobilised enough resources to maintain the museum. Currently, more than 25000 Indian art specimens are adorning the museum. Initially, the museum was established at the back of the old Senate Hall. In 1942, during World War II, to protect the museum objects from the threat of bombing, it was placed in the basement of Murshidabad Imamabad, and after five years, the museum was replaced in the back of the old Senate Hall. Eventually, the new building for the museum was built in the year 1960 and became a significant museum of national importance.

Old Senate Hall

The Establishment of Student Welfare Board and Various Clubs

Sports and cultural events are as essential as academics for the multifaceted development of the students. For this, Dr. Mookerjee set up a university Boating Club, Athletic Club and a gym for the students. The body must be healthy and strong with a sharp mind. The youth is the future of our country. So, it must be healthy and robust in the body with reverence. The students should be energetic in all respects, be it studies or sports. So, he acquired a playground for the University at the Presidency ground to organise sports events. He set up a board for the welfare of the students, which did a lot of good work. It had the objective of providing various facilities for the students such as providing coaches for physical training and free medical testing and treatment. This board worked as a central institution for the advancement of character and efficiency.

Given the growing number of students, the Board aimed to establish various hostels for students in each college and to arrange food facilities for students of all classes and sects.

The Expansion of Library and Reading Room

It is impossible to carry on higher studies without the library and reading room. During his time, the University library did not have sufficient accommodation, but the student strength was increasing at a swift pace. Syama Prasad took the task of expanding the Library by building the fourth storey in the Asutosh Building, where the University General Library and the Lending library is located. Today, the students are immensely benefited by it.

The library, as well as the area of the reading room, was also extended. He wanted that the best and the brilliant students spend more time in the library.

He got painted the murals on the walls of the library which depicted the story of India's development and also highlighted the contribution of the State of Bengal to India's growth and expressed confidence in how the reading room would inspire teachers and students. The special mention is that Sir Asutosh extended the books in this library, he had bought the entire library of Prof. R. Pishel of Berlin in 1909 with the then Government of India money. The library had almost all the important literature of North America and Europe along with the literature of Sanskrit, Prakrit, Pali and Philosophy. He created three permanent posts to see the work of the library. It was his attempt to set up a post-graduate lending library on the first floor of Darbhanga Hall (Asutosh

Asutosh Building

Building) which was extended by Syama Prasad Mookerjee in 1935 and shifted the library to the upper floors of the building.

The library was moved to the newly built building on 6 March 1967.

In the field of education, Syama Prasad Mookerjee made several innovations. The change done in the University of Calcutta, was just a small glimpse of what he had done in the entire education sector. This was only the beginning. His noble and original ideas would be discussed in the seventh chapter of the book.

Syama Prasad as Vice Chancellor of Calcutta University with Lord Brabourne—Chancellor and Governor

Calcutta University bestowed Syama Prasad Mookerjee with an honorary doctorate in 1938.

The value of his services could not be repaid in any way. He did not take the facilities or salary from the University. He was serving the nation. However, the University could express its gratitude towards him by honouring him with the degree of doctorate. In 1938, the Banaras Hindu University honoured him with another honorary doctorate. Though he never longed for recognition. He was always busy doing service for the upliftment of the society. He was soon identified by the world and given place in the Biographia Encyclopedia of the World's Eminent Socialites in 1944.

Endnotes

1. Sumit Sarkar, *Bengal mei Swadesh Aandolan*, p.126.
2. The Spanish Armada was an enormous 130-ship naval fleet dispatched by Spain in 1588 as part of a planned invasion of England. Following years of hostilities between Spain and England, King Philip II of Spain assembled the flotilla in the hope of removing Protestant Queen Elizabeth I from the throne and restoring the Roman Catholic faith in England. Spain's "Invincible Armada" set

sail that May, but it was outfoxed by the English, then battered by storms while limping back to Spain with at least a third of its ships sunk or damaged. The defeat of the Spanish Armada led to a surge of national pride in England and was one of the most significant chapters of the Anglo-Spanish War.

3. BLCP, Vol. 43, no. 5 19/3/34, p.416
4. www.tagoreweb.in
5. ibid.
6. Gandhi too proposed this in Wardha Scheme in 1937. The Central Advisory Board of Education recommended it. The motive of 'Kaushal Bharat', coined by our present Prime Minister Sh. Narendra Modi, is to make our youth eligible for employment.
7. II-IV instalment, Speeches by Syama Prasad Mookerjee, NMML, New Delhi.
8. I instalment, file no. 1, NMML, New Delhi.
9. V-VIII instalment, Speeches by Dr. Mookerjee, Sr. no. 5, p.3.
10. Leaves from a Diary, p.14.

□

6

Dr. Syama Prasad Mookerjee: Beyond the Communalisation of Education

That Hindu-Muslim unity will come, not by one placating the other in an irrational manner, not by one dominating over the other in a wicked way, but by an open recognition of the fact that both occupy the position of India's children and though there are some important spheres of their lives where differences may be manifest, there is a fundamental unity between both, and by the maintenance of their combined welfare will India's lasting prosperity be achieved.

—Dr. Syama Prasad Mookerjee

"His (Dr. Mookerjee's) religion was not of narrow kind. He was catholic in his sympathies and broad-minded in his outlook. That man (Dr. Mookerjee) has a spiritual dimension. It is Indian and not merely Hindu."

—Dr. Sarvpalli Radhakrishnan

The Act of 1935 came into force on 1 April 1937. Election to the Bengal Legislative Assembly was held on the basis of Communal Award.[1] It was a conspiracy to divide India. The polls did not produce a single-party majority in the Assembly. Fazlul Haq's Krishak Praja Party emerged as the single largest party. In coalition with Muslim League led by Sir Nazimuddin, Krishak Praja Party led by Fazlul Haq formed the government. The registered graduates of Calcutta University elected Dr. Mookerjee as an independent candidate to the Bengal Legislative Assembly. Dr. Mookerjee wrote: "The Praja Party was a non-communal organisation with an economic programme while the League was the political body of the Muslims."[2] Dr. Mookerjee explained the political situation in his diary: "Fazlul Haq, lovable and emotional as he is, was dying for power...He did not wish to fall into the arms of the League. He implored the Congress to form a Coalition ministry with himself as Prime Minister." However, the Congress High Command did not allow any Coalition. If this had been done, Bengal would never have gone under the heels of League-cum-British conspiracy. The province would have developed into a healthy and robust region with the joint efforts of representative Hindus and Muslims. The High Command of the Congress did not allow this to be done. Congress policy regarding acceptance of office was still uncertain. Sarat Bose himself was even then deluding himself with such a declaration, 'The Congress has come to the Legislature to end the Constitution and not to work it.'

Fazlul Haq could not wait indefinitely. He joined the League, and a solid Muslim front was created. N.R. Sarkar, B.P. Singh Roy and Maharaja of Cossimbazar were the Hindu caste ministers. They could hardly exercise any restraining influence. The tiger had tasted blood, and fanatic zeal was let loose on the province.

The Krishak Praja Party and the Muslim League formed a Coalition Ministry in Bengal in 1937, Fazlul Haq being the Prime Minister but real power remaining in the hands of the Muslim League. Fazlul Haq was made for dancing as the clever Leaguers like Suhrawardy, Shahabuddin and Nazimuddin wanted him to. At one place Fazlul Haq said to Congressmen, 'you have pushed me in front of the wolves'.[3]

Nazimuddin was the Home Minister, Ministry of Education was also given to Fazlul Haq. After some time, the Education Ministry was transferred to Azizul Haq, who was also serving as the Vice Chancellor of the Calcutta University. It was miserable that both of them had nothing to do with the academics. Azizul Haq was nominated as the Vice Chancellor and the Education Minister only on the basis of being Muslim. Very soon, his actual colour was exposed to the University. He had no strong will to do any work in the field of education. Dr. Mookerjee wrote in his diary on 23 January, 1939, "It is amazing how utterly indifferent he is to the work and needs of the University—except in so far as Muslims are concerned."

Thus, there was no one in the Bengal Government to look after the legitimate interests of the Hindus of Bengal. If the Congress High Command and the Bengal Congress had joined with Fazlul Haq in 1937, Bengal would have been a different province altogether.

However, it was the policy of the ruler to divide the communities with hatred and rule them. Lionel George Curtis (1872-1955), the British author, said, "If this principle of Communal Electorate is perpetuated we shall have saddled India with a new system of caste which eats every year more deeply into her life."[4]

Role of Dr. Syama Prasad Mookerjee in Bengal Legislative Assembly[5]

Dr. Mookerjee was deeply concerned about the improvement in the education system as he was of the opinion that India's political freedom could be achieved through the spreading of education. It is quite possible that the cause of systematic improvement in the field of education was first taken up by Sir Asutosh and his son was following the footsteps of his father. He expressed his like thoughts in the convocation addresses and in the assembly speeches and debates.

Dr. Mookerjee not only defended and extended the cause of education, which was his prime concern, but also showed a keen interest in other spheres of public life that were affected by the then political and administrative activities of the Government.

As he did not belong to any political party, he was not guided by any political ideology or party line at that time. Therefore, his responses to different issues were spontaneous and revealed his personal traits and reactions to those issues.

Syama Prasad was not elected as a Congress candidate, but

throughout his tenure as an M.L.C., he supported the cause of the Congress actively. He always fought in the Council for the cause of detenus who had been imprisoned during the boycott of Simon Commission and were detained in jails at that time. The Government kept the names and whereabouts of those prisoners secretively in the pretext that revealing this information would affect the public interest. He vehemently criticised the Government's policy of keeping that information secret. He stated that the reported acts of violence, torture and cruelty perpetrated by the authorities concerned upon political prisoners in jails, taken along with other manifestations of brute force outside the prison walls, had rudely shaken peoples' confidence in the British administration in India.

Though he himself did not take part in the salt *satyagraha* movement, yet he had a deep reverence for the *satyagrahis* and defended their case in the Council as a true patriot. His description of prisoners' sufferings proved that he was very much sympathetic towards the political prisoners.

Educational Freedom

A staunch believer of political and educational freedom, Dr. Mookerjee always sided the just and rational thoughts and talks in the Legislature and elsewhere. He even tried to save education from the narrow thought line of communalism. He exhibited his sorrow over communalism during the convocation address of Bombay University. He asked the students, "Do not hesitate to proclaim yourselves as Indians first and anything else next. One feels distressed to find the recent growth of communal and provincial feelings, which, unless checked, are bound to retard the progress of true Indian nationalism. I need not inquire into the origin of these differences, but it is true that if the idea of Indian unity is to grow permanently, it can do so mainly by the determined efforts of the youth of the nation. And who else can sound this call to unity than you who are entering into the fields of public activity after a full intellectual preparation, ready to face the struggles of life?...Let us unreservedly stand by our conviction that whatever our detractors may say, Indian universities are bound to play a large and noble part in the emergence of a new India which will be the mistress of her own destinies, the proud inheritor of an ancient civilisation, rebuilt and reshaped with the changing requirements of the age...At this crisis in the history of human civilisation when cherished doctrines of liberty and democracy are often discarded, and freedom of thought and opinion suppressed, let Indian universities and their sons and daughters proclaim the noblest ideals of Indian teaching and thought, which is truly her birthright. And let the Indian universities prove to the world that India can achieve this simultaneously with a progressive and systematic pursuit of western knowledge itself. Let the Indian Universities by the worthy participators in a constant movement towards a higher and nobler civilisation, a civilisation that will make its conquests without resort to war or oppression and achieve its greatest victories pursuing the paths of peace and justic...let a fervent prayer go forth from every member of this assembly in the soul-stirring words of Rabindranath Tagore that we may face our duties and responsibilities with courage and fortitude and make our contributions, however humble to the cause of national welfare.

Let honour come to me from thee
Through a call to some desperate task
In the pride of poignant suffering
Lull me not into languid dreams
Shake me out of this cringing in the dust
Out of the fetters that shackle our mind,
Make futile our destiny,
Out of the unreason that bends our dignity down
Under the indiscriminate feet of dictators,
Shatter this age-long shame of ours
and raise our head
Into the boundless sky,
Into the generous light,
Into the air of freedom.

Opponent of Communalism In Education

When the Bengal Government wished to add poison of communalism in education, Dr. Mookerjee criticised it sharply and said, "The universities must be given the amplest freedom to work out their salvation. We must free education from the undercurrents of political and communal strife. Let each University have a Constitution judiciously planned on academic considerations and truly representative in character. Let the men chosen for their administration be of the right type inspired solely by the idea of training youths who will be an asset to the cause of Indian progress."

Dr. Mookerjee was of the opinion that the university-trained youth should be saturated with the highest ideals of Indian life and culture and imbibe the best elements of western science and knowledge; however, he never wanted him to grow up as an aggressive nationalist utterly forgetful of his ultimate loyalty to the spirit of humanity at large. In the convocation address at Nagpur University, Dr. Mookerjee appealed the youth, "Let us...constantly bear in mind that the introduction of communal and sectarian factors in the field of Indian politics is sharply dividing her peoples into warring sections, each distrustful of the other. For the sake of our very existence, let us forget the supreme need of discovering a proper synthesis between apparently conflicting interests." He forcefully said that he didn't want any communalism in the field of education. He didn't want his students to be influenced by any communal hatred. In March 1938, League members, especially Mr. Ispahani accused Dr. Mookerjee of nepotism in the Calcutta University affairs ranging from appointment in different posts to reluctance in increasing the number of Muslim representatives in the Senate and the Syndicate of the University. In reply to this accusation and taking part in a general discussion on this matter, Dr. Mookerjee spoke on 17 March, 1938 in the Assembly. He stated that the existing Act provided that His Excellency the Chancellor (the Governor of Bengal) should make nominations to the Senate and that the Vice Chancellor had nothing to do with regard to the Constitution of the Syndicate. He also asserted that in the deliberations of the Senate, where there were 58 Hindus, 2 Indian Christians, 1 Anglo-Indian, 24 Europeans and 23 Mussalmans, there was no attempt to do anything, which would jeopardise the interests of the Mussalmans. He said the University either intentionally or even accidentally never carried out any educational policy, which would go against the interests of any particular community. The University could not appoint, as may Muhammadans as it would like to do but the fault did not lie with the University. It was very difficult to get qualified Mussalmans with regard to many of the teaching posts, which fell vacant in the University, and applications were very few. The standard policy of the University was to help in the progress of education of all communities.

He stated that the Hindus had taken a larger interest in the administration of the University than any other community had, due to the advances and contributions Hindus has made to education.

He presented the following data:

Institution/ Course	Hindu Students	Muslim Students	Others
Arts College	81%	13%	6%
Professional College	85%	13%	2%
High School	76%	22%	2%
Matriculation	21,700 students	5,000 students	-
Intermediate (Arts)	5,000 students	1000 students	-
Intermediate (Science)	3,199 students	190 students	-
B.Sc.	867 students	42 students	-
B.Com.	330 students	10 students	-
M.Sc.	191 students	06 students	-

Merit is Important, not the Caste

Dr. Mookerjee said that the dearth of qualified Muslims was a defect, which had to be remedied if the Muslims of Bengal wanted to stand up not only for the Muslims, but also for the people of Bengal as a whole. Regarding University's endowments, he said that out of 81 lakh rupees, the Hindus had contributed about rupees 80 lakhs during the previous 80 years, and only a sum of twelve thousand had come from the Muslim Community. He entreated the Muslim Community thus, "By all means, come forward and capture the University by dint of merit, service and sacrifice".

However, Fazlul Haq (in fact, most of the Muslim members of the Assembly) was not the person to be easily motivated to capture the University by dint of merit, service and sacrifice, as was earnestly requested by Dr. Mookerjee. Their intention was to capture the Calcutta University by undue reservation policy, turning non-Muslim seats into Muslim seats and through undue Government interference, financial and legal, even if their qualification, eligibility was not up to the mark for the posts they wanted to occupy. Therefore, the quality was degrading.

Discrepancies in the Budget: A Major Problem for Education Reconstruction

Dr. Mookerjee said that the Government had been wasting public money more to satisfy the communal ego of the Muslim community than to help the cause of general education. He stated that in the budget the problems were not tackled in the way in which they should be, and which would go not only to remove the wants of one community or another, but which would go to secure gradually educational reconstruction and usher in a new era of progress. He stated that Fazlul Haq had provided for two hostels for the Muslim student, but though he was the custodian not only of the interests of the Muslim community, but also of the interests of all communities in the province, he did not take into consideration of the state of things with regard to the Hindu students. Thus, the problems were to being looked upon as a whole but from a communal standpoint. The government had no policy for funding hostel accommodation for about 8,000 boy students in Calcutta. The government also did not maintain a single special hostel for hundreds of girls who were reading in the great city Calcutta. Nevertheless, provision had been making for the purdah college, but the Government did not feel it necessary that it should have some specific policy regarding the entire question of girl's education, including the problem of their residence.

Dr. Mookerjee reminded the Government that an appeal from the Calcutta University requesting the Government to assist the University in establishing a hostel, for girls reading in the affiliated colleges in the city was lying with the Government from January 1937. He stated that as the number of girl students was increasing, so he was thinking of constructing a hostel for them. He said that the University was prepared to spend at least ₹1 lakh or even half of the total cost, which would be incurred to construct such a hostel in which there would be a separate block for the Muslim girls reading in the colleges, if the remaining cost were borne by the Government. Nevertheless, the Government wanted to know first how many girls would come to take admission in the hostel before the Government could commit to any grant for the hostel. He replied that there were provisions for accommodation for only 230 out of 1,100 girl student's. However, the Muslim MLCs were not satisfied. Mrs Hasina Murshed demanded that they wanted a separate hostel exclusively for the Muslim girls. Dr. Mookerjee explained that the Government had withdrawn the modest grant of ₹3 and 8 annas per head for the Bethune College Hostel and reduced the library grant. Thus, the Government contribution was becoming less and less with the increase in the number of students of the college. The number of students had gone up to 300, and the contribution from Government decreased from ₹82,000 to ₹76,000. The situation of the Bethune College had come to such a point that it was much better than the college should be abolished altogether than maintaining the College in that inefficient manner. Time and again he exposed the prejudiced policy of the League.

As regards adult education, he stated that there were 16 million adults above the age of 18 years, who were illiterate. He said that for them the magnificent provision which the Government had made in that year's budget, was a sum of ₹13,000, which was less than half the sum, which had been given to Azad for the purpose of spreading communalism and creating division among different communities. He explained, "All this is due to wanting of policy and a lack of statesmanship. You are thinking with a great problem, you are giving something here and something there, but we remain where we are, you are spending 35 lakh rupees more on Education, but is it going to improve the system of education as a whole? What is educational statesmanship that prompts the department to impose a condition that no school will be allowed to be opened anywhere in Bengal without the approval of Board, is that educational reform? And is that going to be followed in this province where education has been based mainly on private support and enterprise? There is the University College of Science. It is not the monopoly of any community. It is a pride of Bengal and India. But what is happening there? The Government has refused to sanction grants for its development. The message of the government was clear—'restrict the education'.

Dr. Mookerjee deplored how the Government was trying to coerce the schools to accept its conditions by withholding the grants and other means. The Government rule was that if a school was to receive a grant-in-aid, the managing committee must have the approval of the District Magistrate. He stated that there had been case where District Magistrate on grounds, which could never be justified, had set election of members aside. If a number were a Hindu and was not in the good books of somebody who was a high official in a particular district or sub-division, then the Magistrate would give the order to set aside his election. It was an apparent attempt on the part of Government to officialise the educational institutions. The Government, with regard to the selection of teachers, was also doing such discrimination. If there was a private school, which was managing its own affairs out of its own fees, the school was considered educationally fit and proper to receive State aid, but from time to time as the school was inspected by the Inspector or in connection with private discussion, suggestions were thrown out that if teacher 'A' was not removed or if a teacher belonging to a particular community was not appointed, the grant will be stopped. Some schools were getting a large amount, and on the other side, some were not receiving any money, though it was supposed that the schools should receive a grant as per the number of students.

Dr. Mookerjee presented the data of the Government's prejudiced policy:

Schools	Students	Grant
45	13,500	Above 15 lakhs
557	1,50000	Approximate 15 lakhs
1000	Data not available	No Grant

Mr. W.C. Wordsworth (a representative of Bengal Chambers of Commerce) who was associated with the Education Department for 20 years also supported this view of Dr. Mookerjee. He said, "I agree with him entirely that if we could do something to give larger grants to our secondary schools, we should be making an enormous contribution to the social health of this province." Dr. Mookerjee was persistent in his request to the British Government using every conceivable platform, including the Legislature Council to increase the grant in aid for education. Unlike the popular belief, he was not pleading for aid to the schools of any one community for he wanted the grant in aid to be extended for the betterment of all the schools and for the benefit of the teaching fraternity irrespective of the communities managing the schools. The World War II, which had become a kind of sinkhole in which all the money, men and material of the British government kept on disappearing and expecting financial support was too much of asking but to Syama Prasad Mookerjee financial needs of the education sector wouldn't have been overlooked. Education was the foundation and sine qua non for the human being. Bengal had another problem to face in the same time span. A famine which consumed about four million people too tested all to the hilt, and the donations from private donors also dried up. In other words, the existence of the education department itself was on the brinks of extinction. Despite all odds came forward Dr. Mookerjee to emphatically exhort the legislators and all the stakeholders to pull education out of the huge husk of militarist mentality of the Raj.

Dr. Mookerjee Unveiled the Communal Outlook of the British Government

On 15 December 1939, in the Assembly, Dr. Mookerjee held the view that the best educational ideal should be to have such institutions where Students of all nationalities could read together. He said, "It will do a lot of good to every one of us if our education could cease to be a godless one as it has been during the last eighty years." However, the problem was that the Government began to impart primary education for all communities through maktabs, which were not following the common syllabus and curriculum.

Maktabs were meant to spread Islamic thoughts. However, children of other communities were supposed to read in such schools, Hindu community did not want that their boys and girls should receive instructions in those institutions under those conditions. They are definitely injurious to the interests of Hindu boys and girls. "I found a textbook, which says *'Murti Puja Pap Kaj'* idolatry is an act of sin. It may be that sort of instruction to the Muslim boys and girls is beneficial, although I doubt if that is so, in any case, we do not want that Hindu boys and girls should receive instruction under these conditions. In one of the textbooks, I was horrified to find the following words, "Beef is very tasteful". Perhaps it is so with regard to the Muslim community, but what right have you to say that such textbooks should be read by Hindu boys and girls, who will be compelled to receive that instructions in those institutions? If this programme of education continues in the way in which it is going on now, then it will really mean a goodbye to the educational progress of the Hindus of this province. If you say that there is no distinction between primary schools and maktabs, then I shall say abolish the maktabs and have only one kind of curriculum, one list of textbooks, and one method of recruitment of teachers which will be able to follow in all schools. If, on the other hand, you say that the Muslim interests demand that there should be separate treatment for the Muslims, then I say give us liberty to have our own textbooks and our own method of education for the Hindu boys and girls as you are claiming for Muslims."

Some MLAs tried to blame the curriculum of the Calcutta University for being the communal one, Dr. Mookerjee countered them with reasonable arguments. Dr. Mookerjee submitted, "I can assure...that the members of the University have much more to do than to be participators in a conspiracy to select pieces in their textbooks which will be especially offensive to a particular community...It exists not only for Hindus and Muhammadans, but also for other communities which may be residing in this province." Dr. Mookerjee said, "The University prescribes the Bible as a compulsory textbook from intermediate to B.A. standard... they were introducing this book as part of literature because they felt that if English literature was to be properly taught, some parts of the Bible, adapted to Indian students, must be in the hands of Indian boys. With regard to the Bible, there has not been any suggestion by the Muslims that the University has been responding for introducing feelings and sentiment which are offensive to their community as being anti-Muslims."

He also stated, "These writings contain some good and noble sentiments and feelings, which are placed in the hands of the boys. We never ask the students that they must go and actually practise what is preached there. Take, for instance, the story in the Intermediate Bengali textbook taken from the famous novelist Sarat Chandra. There a picture has been given depicting the life of a Bengali Muhammadan peasant—how he would stand against oppression, how he would admire courage and devotion to truth, how he defies the powers that be for the sake of the ideal which he thought was his own. And therein one place he praises and cries in the name of Allah—does that mean that all Hindus are being asked to pray in the name of Allah and not in the name of Hari? Or, if the word *'Horibol'* is uttered, does that mean all must pray in that name? It would be absurd if you go on arguing in that fashion...There is no question of imposing the faith of anybody upon anybody else."[6]

He also stated that as far as the Hindu ideas and ideals, which are narrated in the extracts made by Maulvi Abul Quasem (He made an objection on the curriculum with reference of many pieces of the Bengali selection for Matriculation Examination, i.e., extracts from Rabindranath Tagore's poems 'Bichaar' and 'Pujarini') are concerned, "They have been handled in the same way by Muslim authors as well. I have here in my hand a number of copies taken at random of an influential Muslim monthly magazine, the *Masik* by Muhammadan poets dealing with some portions with Hindu idea and ideals."[7]

When Maulvi Abul Quasem made an allegation of de-Islamising the Muslim students by making them read history books written by authors like K.P. Mitra as Mitra gave a contrasting picture of Hindu rulers and Muslim invaders, Dr. Mookerjee said that the textbook in history, referred to by Maulvi Abul Quasem, had been prescribed by Patna University. No objection had been taken either by the Patna University or by the Bihar Legislative Council to its introduction. The author in some places referred to Hindu rulers as buffoons, cowardly and weak. However, no Hindu objected to that. Every book can be condemned in that way, even written by Europeans. He also reminded that there was not a single Muhammadan writer, who during the previous six years submitted a book on Indian History; and that was not the fault of the University or of the Hindus. He urged that competent Muhammadan writes should come out, write books, and indicate the standard they desired to see followed. He said, "Authors, be they Hindu or Muslim, must remember they are to write history and not story...If it is said that in some periods, Hindus and Muslims fought with each other, I am not afraid of that. What is the lesson we have learnt from such fights between the Hindus and the Muslims?...We want them (students) to remember if they want to be the masters of their country, they must unite, and must not fight with each other in the way in which they have done in the past". He commented, "The present atmosphere of mutual distrust and suspicion is ruinous and may we not unite to distrust the correct path of permanent reconciliation?" There should be brotherhood and unity in both communities.

Catholicity in Dr. Mookerjee's Thoughts

In Patna University convocation, Dr. Mookerjee pointed out the mixed culture of India and said that India is a liberal country and it is catholic and sympathetic towards the world. "How can we say that India ignored the teachings of different religions and cultures when we find saints like Nanak and Chaitanya, Namdev and Tukaram, preaching the brotherhood of man and the futility of caste in matters spiritual? Although attempts on Hindu culture and institutions fill the pages of Indian history, how can we assert that Muslims ignored the appeal of Hindu culture when we find Muhammad Jayasi weaving a beautiful romance to illustrate the teachings of Hindu philosophy, when we read the simple devotional hymns of Kabir and Sheikh Farid, who refused to recognise the barriers of caste and creed on the high road to God's kingdom? "Utter not one disagreeable word," said Farid, "since the true lord is in all men. Distress no one's heart for every heart is a precious jewel." In the same strain did Kabir proclaim, "There is the same God for the Hindu as for the Muslim."

Dr. Mookerjee did mention the great kings like Ashoka and Akbar in his address. He said that India found an Akbar to put an end to political chaos and social disharmony and a Shah Jahan to dream a dream in marble the like of which is not to be met with in the world. In his Vice Chancellorship, Dr. Mookerjee started a course in Islamic culture. During his headship of Asiatic Society, he arranged lectures on the teachings of Paigambar Mohammad. He was having an in-depth knowledge of Buddha philosophy.

Here we can add an instance of a great and famous Bengali Muslim poet Kazi Nazrul Islam who was recognised later on as the national poet of Bangladesh. This will present Dr. Mookerjee as an absolutely non-communal and the most generous one. Kazi Nazrul Islam, born into a poor Muslim family, pioneered poetic works espousing intense spiritual rebellion against fascism, oppression and religious fundamentalism. Once he had run up a huge amount of debt because of the illness of his wife and the cost of her treatment, for which he had to borrow money, he was facing a financial crunch. At this stage, Fazlul Haq, to whom he was close, asked him to take over the editorship of his party paper, '*Nobojug*' and said he would take care of his debts. However, to join Nobojug, he let go of music directorship of a Bengali film. To his dismay, Fazlul Haq didn't pay any money to Nazrul Islam for several months. It was unfortunate that the great literateur was in a terrible state and finally approached Dr. Mookerjee. Dr. Mookerjee not only arranged for repayment of his debt but sent him to Ganga Prasad House, Madhupur for change and recuperation. Nazrul stayed there with his wife for nearly two months. This made a difference to Nazrul. Kazi Nazrul Islam wrote a letter full of gratitude to Dr. Mookerjee. (see appendix I) He said, "...Your greatness, your love for me, your fearlessness will remain forever embedded in every atom of mine." Around that time, Nazrul had begun to suffer from a neurological disorder. In 1952 Dr. Mookerjee and other admirers of Nazrul formed an organisation called 'Nazrul Treatment Society'. This society arranged for him to travel to London and Vienna for further treatment. It is to be known that Nazrul and his family shifted to Bangladesh on its invitation in 1972, where he died four years later.

Another eminent poet who received help from Syama Prasad was Jasimuddin, a rural Muslim from a poor agricultural family and a student of Calcutta University. He told in an interview (to Professor Vishnu Kant Shastri, Calcutta University) that once there was a tie for a scholarship—one scholarship, and two aspirants with equal marks, one Hindu and one he himself. However, Dr. Mookerjee analysed the situation with honesty and, on the basis of economic background and financial need of the aspirants, decided to give scholarship to Jasimuddin.[8]

One more example should be quoted here. Maulavi Abdul Qadas, the Vice President of Islamia College Union, wrote a letter to Dr. Mookerjee in April 1938, "Like your father, you (Dr. Mookerjee) are the personification of generosity. You always help the destitute just like your father. You want to throw communalism outside the nation."

Dr. Reena Bhaduri told us that the thought of Hindu-Muslim disparity never entered in 77, Asutosh Road, Bhawanipur. She told that there were a lot of friends of Dr. Mookerjee belonging to Muslim and other communities who were frequent visitors there. Dr. Mookerjee always tried to resolve the problems of the complainants whatever religion they belonged to. Dr. Bhaduri told us that Humanyun Kabir, a politician and writer, was a frequent visitor there and he used to call Dr. Mookerjee, 'Dada'. Dr. Mookerjee was never in disfavour of Muslims or other religious communities. Whenever he showed his confrontation, it was for the biased policy of the Muslim League. His differences were with the political party and not with the religious community.

Syama Prasad in a meeting at Calcutta University Institute in 1940. Sarat Chandra Bose and Smt. Sarojini Naidu are in the Photograph

It is important to know that while giving his resignation from the post of the Finance Minister of Progressive Coalition Cabinet, Dr. Mookerjee said, "Let me make this appeal to all sections of this House so that we may unite in our own struggle to uproot tyranny and oppression... A Hindu and a Muslim may differ on many things, but do they not equally detest slavery—and it is for ending the state of intolerable slavery that I am asking for your support and cooperation."

In the foreword to 'Educational Speeches of Dr. Syama Prasad Mookerjee', Radhakrishnan wrote: "His religion was not of the narrow kind. He was catholic in his sympathies and broad-minded in his outlook. Patriotism is not merely loving of the land in which we are born; it is respect for the ideals by which we are sustained. That man has a spiritual dimension that its development can take place in various ways, that we should have respect for all these ways are some of the cardinal features of Indian tradition. It is Indian and not merely Hindu. Syama Prasad Mookerjee was an ardent advocate of these great ideals."

The Strong Voice against the Secondary Education Bill, 1940

Dr. Mookerjee was an open-minded educationist whose aspiration was to see the holistic development of education. However, the Bengal government was severely attacking the whole fabric of education by introducing the Secondary Education Bill, 1940. Fazlul Haq presented the bill in the legislature on 21 August 1940. The nature of the bill was communal. Fazul Haq's real intentions in bringing the 'Secondary Education Bill, 1940' were three-fold. One was to capture the decision making body by his community. The second was to Islamise the education system of the province through the Matriculation Syllabus committee and publication committee which he envisaged in the Bill as two of the many committees under the Board. His third intention was to increase the number of Muslims by providing reservation in different appointments in the Board and the schools, functioning under the Board, by virtue of their majority in the Board and the Government.

In respect of the relationship between the new Board and the University, the Bill provided that the Matriculation Examination would remain under the control of the Calcutta University. The Sadler Commission desired to provide for united control in the sphere of secondary education, and one of their chief recommendations was that the examination must be left in the hands of the Board. But, according to the bill, Dr. Mookerjee explained, the University would be called upon to hold the matriculation examination with whose syllabus and courses of study, it would have little concern. He stated that it was against all canons of sound educational efficiency and administration to empower one body to frame the curriculum and ask another body to hold the examination.[9]

Syama Prasad with Sir Prafulla Chandra Ray in Anti Communal Award Conference on Secondry Education Bill of Bengal Assembly at Calcutta on 25-08-1941

Dr. Mookerjee called this Bill a 'Black Bill' as it was reactionary in character. He asserted that even if the Bill became law, they would not obey it, and would oppose it. He goes on the detail methods by which they would oppose it. He wrote in his Diary, "We had a stirring agitation on the Calcutta Municipal Bill and the Secondary Education Bill. I was more intimately connected with the second and indeed did my best to make the agitation fruitful. The Bill was held up on the floor of the House when all attempts at an honourable settlement failed. Here also, my attitude was dictated by the actualities of the situation. I was not for any form of communalism in education. I felt, however, that if the Muslims were determined to give educational administration an aggressively communal turn, it was not for us, Hindus, to try to save them. They would not listen to us in any case. We should demand, therefore, that we must have our own Board to look after our education. Although we were a minority in the province, eighty per cent of the school-going population, secondary education, was borne by Hindus, and ninety-nine per cent of the schools owed their birth or continuance due to Hindu generosity. We were therefore entitled to say, 'You do whatever you like with the education of our boys, but we do not believe that education should be made the plaything of communalism' or 'Politics must have the freedom to shape the education of our children according to our own light and judgement, and the State must give grants according to number of pupils attending our schools.' This idea was not at first acceptable to a section of Congressmen who thought they were slowly dragged into the net of Mahasabha politics. But, fortunately, the majority agreed, including Sarat Bose and Haren Chaudhary, and our demand was voiced accordingly."

Dr. Mookerjee was opposed to the main principles underlying the Bill. He regarded this Bill as a reactionary step, which required the strongest possible resistance both inside and outside the Legislative Chamber. He said that Fazlul Haq's community was not as sincere and genuine in making their 'effective voice' felt in the educational system of Calcutta University as Fazlul Haq demanded it to be. Chief Minister Fazlul Haq earlier had regretted that the registered graduates never elected a Muslim Fellow. Dr. Mookerjee explaining the reasons said that the University had 2 Muslim registered graduates in 1914, 4 in 1924, nil in 1934 and 4 in 1940. "Does this much advance the insistent claims of my friends to the left for an effective voice in all public bodies merely because they are numerically larger in population?"

Regarding endowments he stated that the University had received nearly one crore of rupees mostly during the last 34 years, a period when according to the Government it started on its course of deterioration and out of that one crore rupees a sum of rupee twenty-four thousand came from our Muslim countrymen. He stated that if the Muslims wanted to control the University because they were the majority community in Bengal, then they should treat the University as liberally as the Hindus had treated their alma mater.

Dr. Mookerjee proceeded to explain that the Secondary Education Bill was not in accordance with the Sadler Commission report, but was much against the spirit of the Commission. He stated the fundamental defect of the Bill was that it tightened the grip of official control over secondary education and placed it entirely at the mercy of the Government. The Sadler Commission made it abundantly clear that 'the Board must be autonomous in so far as its administration was concerned, and it must be free from official influence and interference'.

In the financial matters also, the Board would have no say of its own. Dr. Mookerjee continued that the Commission had said that with regard to financial matters, the Board would submit its estimates to Government and the latter would have the opportunity of withholding its assent from any proposals, which did not meet with the approval of Government. Notwithstanding, the extent of control, envisaged by Government under this Bill not only the Budget was to be passed by Government, but also the Board could not spend even a single penny even though it might have money of its own which had not been sanctioned previously by the Government. Even the inclusion of an item of expenditure in the Budget might not get Government sanction in some circumstances. The Board would virtually be part and parcel of the Secretariat.

The Sadler Commission suggested that 'the regulations of the Board will be published and would, therefore, come within the cognizance of the Government and the Legislative Council and be open to criticism from either body'. Dr. Mookerjee argued that there was no provision that every regulation has to be submitted to the Government for previous approval as was mentioned in the draft. Such criticisms, the Commission proceeded to say, would naturally carry great weight with the Board, but it was left there. But, according to the draft bill, the regulations would be subjected in each case to the previous approval of the

Provincial Government, and all matters falling within the purview of the Board were to be conducted under the direction of the Government. Conditions of grants-in-aid, recognition of schools, the appointment of staff, fixation of fees, examination results, and admission of students, supervision and administration of schools were some of the vital matters, which would fall within the scope of the regulations. Those were not only to be determined by the Board which would itself be subservient to the Government, but also such determination would again be subject to the previous approval of the Government. He said, "And yet, Sir, the Hon'ble Chief Minister, expects us to believe that he piously intends to follow the report of the Sadler Commission." He categorically stated, "The one object of the Bill is to officialise education, and that has been done with a full vengeance in utter disregard of the educational traditions of this province and forgetful of the warnings of the Sadler Commission itself."

Sir Manmatha Nath Mukherjee, Sir P.C. Ray, N.C. Chatterjee, Prof. Charu Chandra Bhattacharya, Principal Panchanan Sinha, Syama Prasad Mookerjee at Hazra Park, Anti-Secondary Education Bill Conference, 1940

Left to right: Syama Prasad, Sir P.C. Ray, Sir Manmatha Nath Mukherjee, Nirmal Chandra Chatterjee – in a protest meeting on Secondary Education Bill of Muslim League Government of Bengal on 22-12-1940

For the prizes and scholarships awarded on the result of the Matriculation Examination ₹1,75,000 had been endowed to the University which was used to maintain 86 scholarships, medals and prizes and out of this sum only rupees one thousand three hundred had come from the Muslims. He asserted that all these 86 scholarships barring only 4 were open to all the communities. He explained that Hindu donors were sufficiently liberal and were inspired by only one ideal and one alone, the encouragement of education irrespective of caste, creed or community.

Dr. Mookerjee stated that in matters of the grant, favouritism had been openly shown. Old institutions which deserved assistance had been kept out of the list or in the alternative conditions were attached to grants, which it was impossible for them to accept consistent with educational needs and traditions.

He presented various examples of the government's biased policy:

School for girls of all communities	200 girl students	4 rupees/month grant
Madrasa for only Muslim girls	Approximately 150 girl students	150 rupees/ month grant

According to a Government decision, the post of Secretary to the Text Book Committee in Bengal was reserved for a Muslim. Dr. Mookerjee accused the Government of showing communalism even in this particular sphere. He stated that with regard to the inspection staff, nearly 75 per cent of the appointments had gone to Muslims during the previous three years. He presented a list of some qualified Muslims in the Education Department, who were superseded and whose cases were not taken into account for obvious reasons, not because of communalism, but because they failed to pander to the needs of party politics.

All the nominated members were gone to the Muslim community. With regard to districts where the Muslims were in the majority, the excuse was that as Muslims were in a preponderating majority in those districts, obviously the nominations should go to the Muslim community. But in Howrah, where no Muslim had been elected, all the nominated seats went to Muslims because that was a district where the Hindus were in the majority, and the Muslims were in the minority, and the protection of minority interests was one of the privileges of the existing ministry of Bengal. That was how the administration of District School Boards had been going on under the control of the Minister of Education. Teachers had been appointed not on the ground of merit, but communal percentage had been raised in reference to the population in a particular district. In a particular district, where 70 per cent of the teachers in primary schools must be Muslims, irrespective of qualifications, but in West Bengal, where the Muslims were in the minority, the doctrine of fifty-fifty had been followed.

The Bengal government was unable to face the severe opposition against the bill. So, it requested Dr. Mookerjee to be part of the select committee which was intended to set up for a rethinking of the 'Secondary Education Bill, 1940'. However, Dr. Mookerjee did not agree to serve on the Select Committee, as he knew that 'the principles, the fundamental principles, of the bill were such that they must be altered, if it is going to be an educational measure at all, and when there was no chance of that being done, it was useless to serve on the Select Committee'. He said, "Fortunately, for the sake of the justice of the cause, in spite of political and other differences, all sections of Hindus have combined to oppose the operation of this Bill."

Dr. Mookerjee asserted, "We shall never accept this Bill and shall paralyse its operation if it is forced upon us...We cannot allow the 'death-knell' of our culture and progress to be sounded by a band of reactionaries...It may be-that resistance to this Bill may bring us into conflict with the authorities, and it might lead to situations which will involve menace."

That the Calcutta University though dominated by the Hindus imparted secular education, and there was nothing to call Hindu culture, was supported by a Muslim member of the Assembly named Mr. M. Shamsuddin Ahmed. He commented, "I do not find anything of Hindu culture in the University education that is being given to us today." Where Dr. Mookerjee called this Secondary Education Bill, 1940 a 'Black Bill'. Mr. Pramatha Nath Banerjee called it a 'Cobra Bill'. Therefore, he gave whole-hearted support to the motion for circulation of the Bengal Secondary Education Bill for eliciting public opinion thereon. Sarat Chandra Bose, the opposition leader, said, "Mr. honourable and learned friend Dr. Syama Prasad Mookerjee has demonstrated to the House quite clearly that none or practically none of the recommendations of the Sadler Commission have been incorporated in the report." He asked, "Then why call the Bill the Bengal Secondary Education Bill? Why not call it rather the Calcutta University Deprivation of Powers Bill or possibly in slightly better language, the Calcutta University Spoliation Bill? He asserted, 'We shall consider it our duty both inside and outside the House to take such steps as will make the Bengal Secondary Education Bill a dead letter in this Province...We should be untrue to ourselves and to the system of education, which gave us birth if we were to adopt a more compromising attitude." This debate raised furor in the Assembly.

The Secondary Education Bill, 1940 was again brought to the House for discussion in September 1941 after the report of the Select Committee was placed in the House. On this issue, Dr. Mookerjee observed in the Assembly on 4 September 1941. "So long as Communal Award and separate electorates continue, we see no prospect of the establishment of a really representative Government which will command the confidence of the different sections of the people. In particular, the administration of the province for the last four years under the control of the present Ministry has left us with bitter experience...In Bengal, political and official domination is closely linked up with communal squabbles, which, if unchecked, will sound the death-knell of true education to develop purely on secular lines."

Supporting Dr. Mookerjee, Sarat Chandra Bose stated, "We carried with us the sympathies, the support, and may I add, the convictions of the entire Hindu community and an overwhelmingly large body of educated opinion in this province. Sir, we offered uncompromising opposition to the Bill because we felt that the Bill was communal both in inspiration and intention... I asked to myself twelve months ago, and I asked today if this bill was and is a purely educational measure, where and how this question of loyalty to Islam came in." Mr. Fazlul Haq retorting the accusation of communalism said, "So long as the Opposition is un-Islamic, so long as the Opposition is communal, so long as the Opposition is unjust and unfair, our reply will be Islamic, communal and from our point of view, just and fair. If the Opposition is un-Islamic, the retort from this side is Islamic." To this assertion of Fazlul Haq, Dr. Mookerjee asked, "Will you define what Islamic Opposition is?" Fazlul Haq stated that as far as Muslim interests were concerned, there was a strong feeling among the Muslims that there must be included within the system of general education such elements of Islamic religion and tradition that considered vital for the completion of the education of their children." Amrit Bazar Patrika fully covered the protests and the conferences held against the communalisation of education.[10]

To this assertion of Fazlul Haq, Dr. Mookerjee reacted that the Hindus wanted a general secular and national education. However, if the Muslims were bent upon having such education that would enable them to educate their children on Islamic line, then the education system must be divided in such a way so that it would leave the door open for secular education where Hindus, Muslims and Christians might flock together without any reserve. At the same time, it would leave the door open to those Muslims, who desire to receive their education based on their faith and on their culture. It would also give a similar right and privilege to the Hindus of Bengal, and lastly, it would leave the door open even for the Hindus and Muslims to receive their training according to strict orthodox lines as has been the case during the previous one century or more in Bengal. It was only then that it would be possible for the Board or any other constituted authority to frame a national system of education suited to the best ideals of their beloved motherland."

Impartial Approach Towards All the Educational Institutions

Dr. Mookerjee strongly felt the need to have an unbiased approach towards all the educational institutions big and small and irrespective of their religious roots and affiliations.

Therefore, he openly expressed that he absolutely had no problem with more grant in aid given to the educational institutes like madrasas run by Muslims. In fact, he always exhorted to undo the communal overtones in the policy matters concerning the sphere of education. He felt that every single school or any other such institution engaged in the dissemination of education and, thus, serving the cultural and social mosaic of the country.

He advocated an honest effort on the part of all the communities to understand the ideas and opinions of one another and only by doing this; the people would be able to give their best to the country. The dirty politics in the field of education was not at all tolerated by Dr. Mookerjee. This also heralded a new stage in his career. He came out of 'academic seclusion' and became a full-time active political leader by joining Hindu Mahasabha. One historian has remarked, "For the first and last times the Hindus of Bengal found a spokesman who did not care at all for political expediency or personal interest." Dr. Mookerjee successfully foiled the League's plans to dominate the education. His resistance to the Secondary Education Bill purely through constitutional means showed the quality of the man as a constitutional and parliamentary politician.

It is noticeable that the next government was the coalition government[11] of Fazlul Haq and Syama Prasad, where Fazlul Haq accepted the policy of communal brotherhood. Fazlul Haq initially faced a lot of opposition from his party colleagues regarding the inclusion of Dr. Mookerjee in the cabinet, because of his pro-Hindu credentials and his trenchant criticism of Haq when Haq was blindly pursuing the anti-Hindu policies of the Muslim League. In reply to this opposition, Haq told Abul Mansur Ahmad, one of his closest associates, "Listen, Abul Mansur, you do not know Dr. Mookerjee, I do. He is the son of Sir Asutosh. It doesn't matter that he belongs to the Hindu Mahasabha. You will not find a more liberal person or a better well-wisher of Muslims among Hindus. If you trust me, you must trust him too".

Mahatma Gandhi's Faith in Dr. Mookerjee

Gandhi welcomed Dr. Mookerjee's entry into politics. Gandhi was impressed by the nationalistic approach of Dr. Mookerjee. He was always kindly disposed towards Dr. Mookerjee, and had once remarked that he wished him to be a 'Hindu leader with a congress bent of mind' after late Pandit Madan Mohan Malaviya, just as 'Patel was a Congress leader with a Hindu Mind'. Dr. Mookerjee remarked sarcastically, 'but you will call me communal.' Gandhi replied, "Like Shiva who drank the poison after churning the sea, somebody must be there to drink the poison of Indian politics. It can be you." Gandhi was in full praise of the capabilities and qualities of Dr. Mookerjee. It was Gandhi's insistence that Dr. Mookerjee was included in the first cabinet of free India. He was given the important portfolio of Industry and Supply. This showed the faith the Congress leaders had in his integrity and in his understanding of vital industrial and economic problems of India. This assignment gave Dr. Mookerjee an opportunity to lay the foundation of India's industrial policy and prepare the ground for the nation's industrial development in the years to come. His biographer Balraj Madhok says, "The loss of education and cultural life was, thus, a gain to the economy and industry."

The leaders of independent India decided to designate the work of preparing the constitution of the country to a 'constituent assembly'. Dr. Mookerjee was also made part of the constituent assembly as a member. His non-partisan and egalitarian principles got a fair amount to expression in 'constituent assembly' debates as he professed that 'all the citizens of Bharat should be given equal opportunities, equal status and equal freedom, so as to enable them to march ahead fearlessly to attain success according to their capabilities and in the service of the motherland.'

His political engagements, however, could never be able to hold him completely away from his responsibilities arising out of his engagements in the academic world. He kept on contributing tirelessly to shape the educational landscape of the country in the capacity of the president of Post Graduate Council of Arts and Science of the Calcutta University.

"Why should we not both (Hindus and Muslims) agree to be loyal to our respective culture and religion and build up a common nationalism which will protect both of us and also merge us together in the highest ideal of service to our common motherland?"

—Dr. Syama Prasad Mookerjee

After Signing the Constitution of India

Syama Prasad with Dr. B.R. Ambedkar in front of Parliament at New Delhi-1949

First Cabinet of Independent India

Dr. Mookerjee working at his residence in New Delhi

Endnotes

1. On August 16, 1932, the British Prime Minister McDonald announced the Communal Award. Thus, it is also known as McDonald Award. The Communal Award was basically a proposal on minority representation. It was declared by Gandhi for more than once that the separate electorates for the depressed class was an attempt to divide and detach the depressed classes from the main body of Hindus. It seemed to him the Britishers are going to break the country on the basis of the communities and so, he wrote a letter to the Prime Minister that if the award, so far it was related to the Depressed class, is not changed, he would sit on a fast unto death. On 20 September 1932, Gandhiji sat on the fast unto death in the Yarawada Jail, in which he was lodged at that time. The Hindu leaders woke up and went directly to Dr. Ambedkar, to negotiate on this matter. The outcome of these negotiations was Poona Pact of 1932.
2. Banerjee A.C., A Phase in the life of Dr. Syama Prasad Mookerjee 1937-1946, AMMI, 2000.
3. Mookerjee, Syama Prasad, Leaves from a Diary, Oxford University, 1993.
4. Curtis, L.G. Letters to the People of India on Responsible Government. London: Macmillan & Co. Ltd. 1918.
5. We are indebted to Dr. Naba Kumar Adak for we thoroughly studied his book 'Syama Prasad Mookerjee : A Study of His Role In Bengal Politics (1929-1953)' (available on Amazon.in) to understand Dr. Mookerjee's role in Bengal politics. It helped us in writing this chapter.
6. Adak, Naba Kumar, Syama Prasad Mookerjee, New Delhi, Kunal Books, p. 98.
7. Ibid.
8. Tathagat Roy, The Life and Time of Dr. Syama Prasad Mookerjee, Prabhat Prakashan, New Delhi.
9. BLAP, VOL. 57, NO. 4-7, 28.8.40, P. 263-264
10. Poromesh Acharya. 'Education and Communal Politics in Bengal: A Case Study'. *Economic and Political Weekly*, vol. 24, no. 30, 1989, pp. PE81–PE90. *JSTOR*.
11. It was known as 'Syama-Haq Cabinet'.

□

7

The Great Educationist: Dr. Syama Prasad Mookerjee

Our ideal is to provide extensive facilities for education from the lowest grade to the highest, to mould our system in such a way as to unify our educational purpose and to draw out the best qualities that lie hidden in our youths and to train them, intellectually, physically and morally, for devoted service in all spheres of national activity—in villages, in towns and in cities. Our ideal is to make the widest provision for a sound liberal education, and vocational and technical training, remembering always that no nation can achieve greatness by turning its youth into a mere machine-made product, with nothing but a material end in view. Our ideal is to afford the amplest facilities and privilege to our teachers so that they may be endowed with learning, character, and freedom and may regard themselves as not only the torch-bearer and interpreters of knowledge and conquerors of new realms of thought but also as makers of men and women, of leaders and workers, true and brave, upright and patriotic. Our idea is to make our universities and educational institutions the home of liberty and sane and progressive thought, generously assisted by the state and the public, where teachers and students will meet and work in an atmosphere of harmony and mutual understanding, where none will suffer on grounds of caste, sex, creed, and religious or political belief.

—Dr. Syama Prasad Mookerjee

(Excerpt from the speech delivered at the Calcutta University Convocation—22nd February 1936)

As we have mentioned earlier, the milieu in which Syama Prasad was destined to spend his formative time was extraordinary on many accounts. As a matter of fact, he did not become a leader and a scholar par excellence merely by an accident of birth. He indeed inherited rich literary and scholarly family antecedents which had an immense impact on his growth as an educationist. However, we cannot deny the fact that there were conscious efforts on the part of Syama Prasad himself to acquire and grow and eventually reach out to the goals he had set for himself. If we deconstruct his life, especially the time he spent as a student of the university, we find that the time itself was a great catalyst in acquiring the persona and greatness. Many points we have already discussed in earlier chapters, now let us tread the portals which led him to become the benefactor of the Indian education system. He delivered approximately two dozen convocation addresses at Calcutta University, Nagpur University, Mumbai University, Patna University, Agra University, Banaras Hindu University, Gurukul Vishwavidyala, Vishva Bharati University, Delhi University, etc. His educational speeches delivered at All India University Conference, All Bengal University and College Teachers' Conference, Indian Science Conference, All India Academic Conference, British Association for the Advancement of Science, Indian Statistical Conference, Indian Institute of Cultivation for Science and meetings of Inter-University Board, etc., are the testimony of his vigilance in the field of education. The best way to understand his educational ideas, philosophy and policies, etc., by peeping into his mind through his various lectures, convocational address, letters he exchanged with the greats of the times he lived in.

Dr. Mookerjee considered the role of education the most

important one in the nation-building. The process of revival in the field of education was an integral part of the reconstruction of a Nation faced with colonial oppression and destruction of its time tested institutions hampering, thereby the very process of getting independence. He said, "It is through education that the ultimate battle of Indian freedom will be won. The gigantic task of reconstruction, culture, social, economic and political can be rendered possible through the coordinated efforts of bands of trained and disciplined Indians."[1]

The education policy, determined in the days of Bentinck and Macaulay, was influenced not by considerations of the welfare of the Indian people but of the advancement of the interests of the ruling class. In no country has education properly developed unless it has drawn its inspiration from the foundation of its own national life. Education, with its roots cut off and superimposed by the edicts of an alien power, is doomed to ultimate failure. Applied to a subject-race which has not entirely lost its intellectual curiosity and virility, such a system may for some generations foster an artificial growth; it may even produce a race of able imitators, but it can never inspire or elevate the people as a whole, far less advance their permanent welfare.[2]

In the introductory chapter, we discussed how Lord Bentinck and Lord Macaulay were afraid of the possible dangerous results of the spread of knowledge among the masses of the people. They chose to favour a select class of Indians and train them on Western ideas not to help them develop into self-reliant and patriotic Indians, but to form a class of clerks and bureaucrats. They indeed portray a remarkable over-emphasis on the so-called virtues of Western culture and unconcealed contempt for everything Indian. It was an intentional assault to make the roots of Indian culture weaker. However, Dr. Mookerjee was very well aware of the selfish motive of the English educational policy. The gate of western knowledge was thrown open to Indians, but at the sacrifice of India's cultural heritage. Dr. Mookerjee said that the proper synthesis between the two systems was needed and security must be given to the 'Indian base'. It might be the envy of any civilised nation that there was a time when many of the European countries remained steeped in ignorance and barbarity, India's great seers and sages like Panini had attained an intellectual eminence.

One major characteristic of Indian education lies in its continuity. We have archaeologist evidence of the Indus Valley script. Though we are still unable to decipher that script and that is the reason we cannot say more about it. However, since the Vedic age, the inherited perceptible practise of Indian education system has been alive in its intact form. There was never existed the dark age of Indian education and culture. In this country was developed a state of society which encouraged not merely scholastic learning, philosophy and religion, but also art, architecture, medicine, science, astronomy and engineering. Dr. Mookerjee thought that it should be mandatory to assimilate the tradition, ideas and thoughts of the nation in its education policy.

The prophecy of Macaulay and his colleagues was partially falsified in their schematic policy as the national consciousness of educated Indians could not be suppressed. The educational system failed to serve the real needs of India, and its defects were soon manifest to patriotic Indians. Attempts have, no doubt, been made from time to time to introduce far-reaching changes in the educational system by the needs and aspirations of the people. The problem of education could never be fully solved until and unless it was freed from foreign domination. To its contrast, without education, properly outlined and directed freedom could not be attained. Without freedom and full control over our destinies, we could not reshape an education policy entirely according to our will and requirement. The solution was depended on the political freedom of India. However, with continuous efforts and movements in colonised India, some changes and reforms were possible on which laid the backbone of India's freedom.

The Need of Financial Support to Academic Institutions and the Reconstruction of Education

Education may not be static. Its course must change with time and with the altered conditions of the community, it seeks to serve and elevate. It must always be closely related to the life of the people. Otherwise, it becomes stagnant and soulless, and instead of uplifting society tends to retard progress.

Only education can give concrete shape to national aspirations. Education is the basic mantra that can write the story of socio-economic and political renaissance on the Indian surface. For this sacred purpose, every section of society requires an atmosphere of unity and harmony so that all of us can work for the betterment and upliftment of our country by forgetting our small differences. Dr. Mookerjee has strongly reiterated that we will be able to restructure our country's education by our national needs only if our nation is independent. Our Constitution will give us the real strength, and Swaraj will be established in its original form. He said that India is the creator of its destiny. A healthy India will be created by eradicating poverty and preventing diseases. The Government of India must spend on education with a more generous heart. The plan of rebuilding education is impossible unless it is given financial support. He thought that university education provides a strong foundation for primary and secondary education, so it should be expanded.

Education should be kept as cheap as possible, and quality should be high. Dr. Mookerjee, in his statement, gave examples of countries where education is kept free. The British government wanted to curtail Indian education in place of further spending and even wished to close down many institutions of the highest education. In a number of statements, in the Assembly and Legislative Councils debates, he condemned the designs of fog plans of the foreign government on education and exposed the hollow policies of foreign rule in front of the people. He encouraged individual donors to spend a portion of their wealth in raising their countrymen, spending money in redressing the grievances of the distress and providing financial services in the upliftment of Indian culture. As much as possible, education should be affordable, and its quality should also be maintained at the highest level. He said we must emphasise that the private charities by our universities should also be driven to a more comprehensive level than they have done so far. In view of the situation then, Dr. Mookerjee said that our poor country should spend money in the propagation and dissemination of education by cutting down the cost of building buildings, fearing that there should not be a group of so-called Indians who have their living and attitude, rather who should devote their lives to the service of their less fortunate Indian brothers.

Education cannot be separated from the social and economic environment of the masses. Dr. Mookerjee related the solution of the growing problem of unemployment with the reconstruction of the education. The institutions which bear the responsibility for imparting education cannot ensure that all the youth are provided employment. So, the education system should be regulated in such a way that the training imparted to them is helpful for them and not a hindrance in earning a living. Education should be multi-dimensional, and various institutions should be promoted to train people in different sectors in line with the economic and industrial progress of the country. Business, Commerce, Agriculture and Industry should have coordination with the activities of educational institutions. It should be the aim of all to serve the nation, and therefore, there should not be conflict in the interests of various agencies. Trade, Agriculture, Industry and Commerce should have a close relationship with education so that the trained persons in different branches of professional skills are provided with the work area according to their skills. If the universities are not concerned with such institutions, only technical education will not solve the unemployment problem.

Autonomous Education

Dr. Mookerjee was in favour of autonomy for education. He asserted that it should be freed from politics and communalism. He wanted the universities, and school boards should have the charge of their system. In the Bengal Legislative Assembly, he said that he wanted an autonomous Secondary Board of School Education. That Board would be a representative body. He wanted it to be constituted in such a manner that the academic interests would be paramount and it would have ample funds so that education of all the communities might progress.

The Goal of Education

The aim of education has to be defined with charity and precision. Briefly put, the object should be to develop every Indian child as ultimately as poșsible so that he may feel himself consciously at one with his community, share in its traditions of past, its life and action in the present and its aspirations and responsibility for the future. The aim should be to inculcate in the mind of every child a passionate loyalty to the spirit of Indian unity and so to regulate the daily work that he may become aware that what he is doing is for the advancement of his nation and through his nation of humanity at large. The aim of Indian culture and education has been the complete realisation of life.

Reorganisation of the Curriculum

Dr. Mookerjee wanted that various subjects should also be restructured to suit the needs of the country. We have already discussed in the book that while at the post of the Vice Chancellor at the Calcutta University, he had started the process of restructuring the curriculum. History, Economics and Social Sciences should be composed in the context of the Indian environment. On the subject of science, he said that because it is beyond the geographical boundaries, it should be at the same level as is being taught in other parts of the world. It is necessary to enrich the libraries, laboratories, seminars and museums in any system of national education. It was necessary to inaugurate the new policy of education to consolidate the foundations of nation-building. He said that the time has come when we work to bridge the gap between us, that is best for our larger population. He said that education presents a field of activities where all sections can work with full brotherhood and cooperation and if we really want to achieve some of the important things from these reforms, we have to come forward with enthusiasm, where there is no conflict in our objectives and ideals, where there is no place for selfish interests where there is no unethical interference of the government administration. The atmosphere of distrust and doubt has to be eliminated forever if we are to take part in rebuilding the nation.

The syllabuses, courses, systems of training and examination should be remodelled and reorganised so that the students may grow up not as a mechanised recorder of information and theories, not as a dry specialist, but as one whose latent power is well roused, whose critical judgement is strengthened and whose capacity for broad thinking and application of knowledge to problems of life is developed to the fullest extent. The students should not be locked up in beautiful buildings of the school. They should not be burdened with the books; otherwise, their natural talents would be strangulated. The curriculum should lead the students to all-round development. Dr. Mookerjee's thoughts remind us of Rabindranath Tagore's 'Parrot's Tale' *(See appendix III)*. Rabindranath Tagore had taken steps to bring about a revolution in the education world. Tagore has very elegantly expounded the nature and status of education through the story.

Dr. Mookerjee strongly criticised the students for their habit of answering without understanding the concepts. He condemned the "cram-book spirit" which dominated the then academic system. He was of the view that any short cut can never capture success. In terms of rebuilding the curriculum, he was of the view that scientific and rational education should be imparted in mother-tongue without neglecting English to benefit more and more people. More than 90% of the Indian population was illiterate in the then system. This could not be tolerated, and an immediate solution to this problem was needed. In his every convocation address he forcefully said that the medium of instruction should be the mother-tongue of the students while giving a working knowledge of Hindi and English. He advised that a bureau should be set up in each of the provinces which would prepare curriculum books in various Indian languages under the supervision of scholars and in collaboration with universities.

Dr. Mookerjee himself had a particular interest in the affairs of the Bengali language Department for the development of his mother-tongue even after his retirement from the post of Vice Chancellor of the university. Dr. Mookerjee always gave respect to the top-ranked litterateurs of Bangla, like Sharad Chandra Chatterjee and Bharat Chandra Rai. Sharad Chandra, the creator of novels like *Srikanth* and *Devdas*, had made outstanding contributions to prose literature. He remains the most popular, translated, adapted, and plagiarised Indian author of all time. Bharat Chandra Rai was the last best poet of Bengali literature. He is mostly known for his poetic work, *Annadamangal*. Dr. Mookerjee attended the homage celebration in the memory of Sharad Chandra Chatterjee in 1939, the next year of death of Sharad Chandra Chatterjee, at his village Debanandpur. He expressed his sorrow by saying that no encouragement was given to the excellent works of these great works of literature by the then Bengal Government.

Syama Prasad at Debanandapur on occasion of Sarat Chandra Chatterjee's first death anniversary

The Development of Hindi and other Indigenous Languages

In the convocation address of the University of Delhi, in 1952, Dr. Mookerjee said that he was in favour of making Hindi as a powerful instrument of expression in all the states of India. All should learn Hindi without any hesitation. He considered it as a powerful unifying force. Different phrases and idioms of different regional language should be absorbed in Hindi. He was of the view that the authentic Hindi dictionary should be composed in which specific words and phrases of all Indian regional languages should be inserted to create a coordinating dictionary and draw all the languages of India closer to the Hindi language. Dr. Mookerjee was the proficient speaker of Bangla and English languages. After becoming president of *Bharatiya Jana Sangh*, he had to deliver speeches in Hindi from one place to another. So, within a year, he learnt many words of Hindi through English-Hindi dictionary and became a strong orator of Hindi in the same year. According to Dr. Mookerjee, While Indian languages must be fostered and developed in the broadest possible manner, we need not, and we must not take a hostile attitude towards English. There should not be any prejudice against the English language as such. It is one of the most significant languages of the world through which we can make ourselves familiar with essential knowledge and information, to exclude which would render our education imperfect. A comparative study of Indian languages will be significantly facilitated if, under state patronage, a scheme is formulated for bringing out a well-known publication from different Indian languages in their original texts, but printed in *Devanagri* script. He also urged for the revival of the study of Sanskrit and granting of special facilities for this purpose. It is necessary for the proper appreciation of our cultural unity and heritage. Sanskrit is a secure repository of our cultural heritage and knowledge.

Syama Prasad inaugurating Nikhil Bharat Banga Bhasha Prasar Samiti Meeting at Calcutta. Also in the picture: Dr. Harendra Coomer Mukherjee, Governor of West Bengal (Also Syama Prasad's Teacher), Smt. Banga Bala Mukherjee (wife of the Governor), Maharani of Burdwan.

Dr. Mookerjee wanted the university's teacher and student groups to participate in various activities under the planned exchange programme in various universities and understand the uniqueness and problems of different languages in different regions.

Dr. Mookerjee was always fond of regional languages. All regional languages of the country should be given full consideration. He opposed any kind of imposed unity and considered it contrary to Indian tradition. To achieve unity in diversity has always been the target of India. Given this fundamental element, the opportunity should be given to enrich all regional languages. The advancement of one language cannot be condemned or degraded by another language.

The Functions and Duties of a University

Indian University must regard itself as one of the living organs of national reconstruction. It must discover the best means of blending both the spiritual and the material aspects of life. It must equip its alumni irrespective of caste, creed or sex, with individual fitness, not for its own sake, not merely for adorning various occupations and professions, but in order to teach them how to merge their individuality in the common cause of advancing the progress and prosperity of their motherland and upholding the highest traditions of human civilisations. That constitutes the perennial ideal of a university, rooted in Indian soil and expresses one of the greatest needs of the hour.

Syama Prasad addressing Calcutta University Senate meeting – 1949

Agriculture must form a distinctive part of the work of the university and the possibility of increasing the productive power of land with the aid of science explored and explained.

Dr. Mookerjee in his presidential lecture in the first All India University Teachers Convention at Allahabad on 24 December, 1947 said, "If we are to increase the standard of education and research, the universities must have more freedom and more finances on a secure basis. Let there be periodic surveys made of university activities by a body of impartial and well-reputed educationists, but each university must be provided with adequate statutory so that they may live and grow in an atmosphere of peace and freedom."

Sir Fredrick Burrows, Chancellor of Calcutta University and Governor of Bengal addressing the Convocation meeting Syama Prasad and J.L. Nehru sitting behind – 1946

University must always help in spreading the bounds of knowledge and also in other ways strengthen the intellectual life of the country, one of its primary duties must be to devote itself directly and indirectly to the progressive welfare of the student community in general, acting in close cooperation with schools and colleges under its jurisdiction.

The universities must not regard themselves as private institutions which exist apart from the currents of the country's life. They should train their alumni in a worthy manner. University must always help in spreading the bounds of knowledge and also in other ways strengthen the intellectual life of the country, one of its primary duties must be to devote itself directly and indirectly to the progressive welfare of the student community in general, acting in close cooperation with schools and colleges under its jurisdiction. Saturate the students with the lessons of Indian history and civilisation, instill into them unity and reason, strength and dauntlessness, inspire them with skill and knowledge and teach them to apply themselves devotedly and unselfishly to the service of their fellow men.

The promotion of military studies among its students, which though limited in extent, will lay the foundation for training in a sphere of activity capable of vast possibilities in building up national life and character.

Syama Prasad at a meeting with Smt. Vijay Laxmi Pandit at Calcutta University Institute –1946

It must foster the establishment of student's organisations within each college, pledged to their corporate welfare and controlled and managed by themselves, for which they must be genuinely encouraged to undertake responsibility.

Providing practical training in the technicalities of trades and for helping our youths in other directions.

Programmes of corporate activities for the benefit of its students and strive to equip them for active service in different spheres of useful and constructive work.

If with the cooperation of the principals and professors and the students themselves, a scheme of work, aiming at simultaneous growth of intellect and building of health and character, steadily continues and develops, if this can gradually sow the seeds

Syama Prasad addressing a meeting at the Calcutta Medical College

of unity, organisation and discipline even among fifty per cent. Of thirty thousand of Bengal that will produce at a moment's notice thousands of able-bodied intellectual youths Hindus, Muslims and Christians, trained and brought up according to the highest ideals of service, capable of responding to the call of the nation and ready to unfurl the flag of truth and sincerity of progress, unity and freedom.

She must produce through her educational institutions a race of men and women, strong in body and mind, pure, resolute and self-reliant, burning with lofty patriotism and idealism, not carried and reasonable judgement, trained both to be leaders and soldiers, amenable to discipline—discipline imposed by the combined will of themselves—devoted to duty, determined to work not as a class or community, but in a spirit of corporate service, and ever willing to place their services in all capacities, humble and high, for the good of society.

University may now and forever be the national home of progressive culture and enlightenment, the torch-bearer of knowledge and freedom and bring to its doors all classes and communities, which may be willing to join us in serving the cause of education and so far and wide permanent seeds of national development.

Dr. Mookerjee pointed out the necessity of a reorientation of university education in India to suit the changing conditions of then India. He said that the universities should not continue to be merely training grounds for the professions and the services. They must offer a kind of education which will enable Indians to regain their supremacy in the domain of culture as well as in the social, economic and political spheres of activity.

Dr. Mookerjee asked the universities to play their part in the task of supplying trained statisticians as they were required in the domain of commercial enquiries. He said that programmes and policies for new India must be broad-based on accurate data, such as figures relating to income and wages, cost of living and indebtedness. He urged the economists to take up such problems and evolve the technique necessary for measuring the relative well being of different classes and communities. He pointed out the problem of comparative tax burdens of various groups. The question of compiling the statistics of production about agriculture and fisheries, forests and minerals, organised and cottage industries were equally important. He said that the calculations should be accurate based on a scientific basis. He asked the universities to expand the courses related to economics, Banking, Statistics and foreign trade, etc. He wanted to see economically secure and free India.[3]

University occupies an integral place in our society and public life. It must address itself whole-heartedly and unreservedly to the advancement of knowledge, the study of problems, from whatever source they come and the training of men all at the highest level of possible effort. Teaching and research constitute its twin functions—teaching to train up the personnel of our society and research to seek out new forms and relationships both of man and matter.

For Teachers

Teachers should consider it their sacred duty to be interpreters of India's heritage, the seekers of truth and knowledge, and prove to the world that Indian scholars are second to none in their efforts to serve the cause of the humanities and the sciences in relation to the unfettered progress of India and of human civilisation itself. Teachers are the moral guardians of our society.

Teachers must claim for themselves their rightful place not only in the sphere of academic administration, but in shaping the policy of education as a whole. Theirs must be the primary responsibility to serve as the connecting link between the people at the bottom and the legislators and administrators at the top.

The test of a good teacher undoubtedly is that he should be able to inspire the confidence of his pupils. "The true object of education," said one great German philosopher, "is to form tastes and not to impart knowledge." A good teacher should be able to form good tastes in his pupils. He must try to build up their character by the example of his own personality, character and erudition. Dr. Mookerjee asked the university teachers to pursue research in educational problems as it lays firm foundations for a progressive practical life.

For the Scientists

Dr. Mookerjee observed that the responsibilities of the scientists towards the revival of nationalistic feelings are indeed immense. He said that the first and foremost liability of them was to raise the standard of education; to enrich its quality by interpreting the manifold discoveries of science to the lay public in non-technical language, preferably through the vernaculars; to unfold how the secrets of Nature have been brought to light, how resolutely darkness has been chased away, how science, like sunshine before mist, has cleared away doubt and superstition and opened up a never-ending vista before despairing humanity. The scientists have taken upon themselves the sacred task of widening the boundaries of knowledge. India's prestige and reputation as a home for scientific and technological study and research rest upon the scientists. Dr. Mookerjee asked them not to remain satisfied with academic achievements only. Dr. Mookerjee adjured the scientists, "It is for you to undertake a systematic and scientific investigation of India's industrial problems, the solution of which would result in the improvement of our economic condition. Who is better fitted for this great work than you, who are expected to act inspired solely by the lofty motive of serving your country and humanity and not for personal gain or profit? What nobler return can you give for all the facilities which you have been privileged to enjoy and for the confidence which your countrymen have reposed in you?...Have you considered how science should be applied towards the alleviation of poverty and sufferings of millions of your countrymen?" He asked them to utilise their attainments in such a way as to benefit the humanity—to regard science not as a powerful instrument of destruction but as a vital factor for the promotion of the good of mankind. If truth and sanity are to rule the world, the impartial problem-solving attitude of mind must be obtained. The scientists must indicate how to develop this scientific habit of mind. They should open the Temple of Truth and Service for all seekers of knowledge, irrespective of caste, creed or colour. "The view of science should be supplemented by the vision of beauty and truth," pronounced Dr. Mookerjee.[4]

Dr. Mookerjee along with Sardar Vallabh Bhai Patel and Dr. S.S. Bhatnagar at National Physical Laboratory, Delhi

Sardar Patel addressing the gathering on the occasion of the opening of the National Physical Laboratory at Delhi on 21st January 1950. Among others present are Dr. Mookerjee, Pt. Nehru, Sh Rajagopalachari and Dr. S.S. Bhatnagar

Dr. Mookerjee and Dr Bhatnagar at NPL, Delhi

For the Youth

Remember that any 'short-cut' process can never achieve success. You have to toil and work hard during this formative period of your career, and you will find that it will turn into a profitable investment. Whatever work you undertake, do it seriously, thoroughly and well never leave it half-done or undone, never feel satisfied unless and until you have given it your very best. Cultivate the habits of discipline and toleration. Surrender not the points of view of your opponents. Remember that respect for and obedience to your superiors constitutes no sign of weakness in human character. Abandon everything false, sham and hypocritical. Forget not that labour and social service form the two fundamental principles of life in society. Contempt for labour and indulgence in luxury make a person a parasite and perpetuate national subjugation. Use all in your power to assist others by doing at least one good deed everyday, thus paving the way for the more important work of national reconstruction. Remember that the blessed work of helping the world forward does not wait to be done perfect men and you are fully equipped for this task.

Form the spirit of love and charitable sympathy for your friends, neighbours and different communities, endeavouring to work together in righteousness and to co-operate to the best of your ability.

Toleration and Catholicity

Dr. Mookerjee always gave importance to two cardinal values, toleration and catholicity, which were adhered by his beloved nation India. Be it his Convocation addresses or any conference lecture or his debates in Bengal legislative assembly or the parliament of India, he always gave priority to these values in his speeches. Here are some of his thoughts on these values:

India has been styled an epitome of the world. She has had a splendid past. From time immemorial, she has been known for her toleration and catholicity. She always extended welcome to her visitors. Toleration and concord were the watchwords of the rulers; benevolence and righteousness inspired their subjects at large. She never followed the path of violence. Indian culture has retained its vigour and vitality and has found a worthy place among the citizens of all ages.

यूनान मिश्र रोमन, सब मिट गए जहाँ से,
बाकी मगर है अब तक, नामो निशाँ हमारा,
कुछ बात है कि हस्ती, मिटती नहीं हमारी,
सदियों रहा है दुश्मन, दौर-ए-जहाँ हमारा।।

—मोहम्मद इक़बाल

(Greeks, Egyptians and Romans have all vanished, but we are still here. There must be something special that we still exist despite the whole world against us.)

Dr. Mookerjee said that although Indian culture was not getting support from an independent national state, the Indian philosophy and teachings were very ably giving inspiration to millions of human beings. For this thing, the credit should be given to India's catholicity and universal sympathy. The ancient Indians believed in assimilation and improvement. The Macedonian and the Greek, the Saka and the Kushan came to conquer and slay but remained to wonder and pray. Swami Vivekananda quotes, "Civilisations have arisen in other parts of the world. In ancient and modern times, wonderful ideas have been carried forward from one race to another...But mark you, my friends, it has always been with the blast of war trumpets and the march of embattled cohorts. Each idea had to be soaked in a deluge of blood..... Each word of power had to be followed by the groans of millions, by the wails of orphans, by the tears of widows. This, many other nations have taught, but India, for thousands of years peacefully existed. Here activity prevailed when even Greece did not exist... Even earlier, when history has no record, and tradition dares not peer into the gloom of that intense past, even from until now, ideas after ideas have marched out from her, but every word has been spoken with a blessing behind it and peace before it. We, of all nations of the world, have never been a conquering race, and that blessing is on our head, and, therefore, we live...!"

India values toleration, but it knows how to protect herself. Despite the Pacific Hindu teachings, she produced the valiant rulers like Chandragupta, Maharana Pratap, Shivaji and Ranjit Singh, etc. Indian sages and philosophers never suggested that cowards and weaklings would ever be the torchbearers of India's great heritage. None but the valiant can achieve salvation. Dr. Mookerjee asked youth to follow the teachings of the Gita. Do not allow narrow selfishness, jealousy and distrust to overpower your soul. He asked the youth to remember the great personalities of India. India has been the motherland of great souls like Buddha, Mahavir and Vivekanand, etc. He gave reference of Gandhi, an apostle of peace. He said, "...every civilised country in the world finds in Mahatma Gandhi a new messenger of peace, an embodiment of truth and non-violence who can brave the wrath of the mightiest and suffer nobly and patiently for the sake of his ideal." He asked Gandhi to redefine the non-violence.[5]

India ungrudgingly gave her best to the strangers needed spiritual solace. Dr. Mookerjee always asked the youth to have pride in their nation's age-old values. He asked them to respect India's ethical values—tolerance and catholicity, imbibe human values and assimilate the ethical principles of the western world. Max Muller, the German philosopher, praises India, "If there is a country which is complete and ideal for humanity, then I will lift fingers towards Asia where India is." Dr. Mookerjee asked the youth to read the scholars from all over the world and get to know how they were in praise of their nation.

On Liberty

Dr. Mookerjee said that no reforms of a radical character in any field of activity would ever be possible until or unless the nation is free. No material gain, no earthly possession can ever compensate for the loss of man's liberty. Nations should be free from alien domination. Liberty is not a single and straightforward conception. It has four elements—national, political, personal and economic. The man who is fully free is one who lives in a country which is independent; in a state which is democratic; in a society where the laws are equal, and restrictions at a minimum; in an economic system in which national interests are protected and the citizen has the scope of a secure livelihood, an assured comfort and full opportunity to rise by merit. *(from Patna Convocation address)*

Within the nation, the individual should be free, free to think, worship, speak and act as he would, subject to the similar rights of others, free under the protection of equal justice to pursue his lawful business as he chooses. Men should no longer be bound down from birth to death by the hampering restrictions that come from bondage, poverty, overwork and environment. Freedom consists not only in the absence of restraint but also in the presence of opportunity.

Physical Education

At the Calcutta University, Dr. Syama Prasad Mookerjee, in his first convocation address, clearly expressed that the focal point of education is to produce healthy students both mentally and physically. He said, "*What is education worth if our youth, in general, are physically weak or unfit, unable to stand the stress and strain of modern life? What is education worth if we cannot turn them into men physically strong and well-equipped sane and robust?".*[6] He thought that physical education programmes increase attention to human wellness and healthful living. Teaching for wellness involves exploring concepts that help students develop an active lifestyle. He emphasised the imperative need for improving the health, vigour and vitality of the students. He urged them to participate in games and physical exercises actively. The objective of education is to make the youth prepare for life, and this cannot be achieved by fostering intellectual activities alone. He said, "We have to raise the physical standard and efficiency of the rising generation and must aim at creating a sound mind in a sound body. Physical education must be made compulsory in schools and colleges."[7] He advocated for the abundant provision of playing fields and gymnasia and above all, a regular supply of skilled physical trainers.

The Thrust on Moral and Social Education

Dr. Mookerjee had abundant faith in the glory of youth, and he wanted them to be given a chance to live, an opportunity to enjoy life and the amplest facilities for the development of their health and character. The youth is the real asset of the highest interest for the motherland. He was curious to devise ways and means for the progressive welfare of the student community. He wanted to promote not only the physical wellbeing of the students, but also a sound moral character in them. He wanted universities to create men and women who, in the home, in the village and the city, in their influence on government and local administration and national policies, would act righteously, fearlessly and for the attainment of the general welfare. He observed that the moral and social aspects of education were necessary if students want to live full and active lives as part of their local and the global community. Students must understand how to participate productively in a diverse and plural society and learn how to engage with societal institutions and processes effectively. Students must consider the consequences of personal and societal decisions in the broader community—local and global—and the environment and future generations.

Students and Politics

Dr. Mookerjee urged the students forcefully not to make the educational institutions the forum for expressing their disapproval of questions of public policy which might deeply stir their minds. He stood for the fact that education should be free from the undercurrents of political strife. Though, he was not one of those who favoured university students remaining aloof from the burning question of the day. Students can have their opinion, or they can even sympathise with a particular school of political thought. However, he did not like them to be engrossed in party politics. According to Dr. Mookerjee, the students should maintain their independence of outlook and zealously cultivate the spirit of clear and critical thinking. They should also imbibe the power of analytical reasoning, and it would serve their essential aid as they face the outer world after graduation. Nothing should prevent them from an ongoing study and discussion of all important political questions of the day. Dr. Mookerjee was frank enough in saying that occasional outbursts of youthful feelings should not make educational administrators anxious. University and college unions should provide an excellent training ground for future citizenship. However, Dr. Mookerjee was against any disturbances in the routine of academic work. There should not be any deadlocks on issues as they tend to destroy the very foundation of the robust and disciplined character which must be an essential possession of the youth anxious to dedicate their lives to the cause of their country's liberty. Nations live or die according to the character of the people.

Students and Discipline

Discipline should come from within. Modern psychology tells us that the mind of man cannot be built up by superimposed ideas and instructions without regard to its living impulses. Dr. Mookerjee observed that "teachers should be untrue to their work if they fail to make the right appeal to the student community and make them realise that the maintenance of sound discipline in educational institutions is a duty not cast on administrators and teachers alone, but must readily be shared by the students themselves. The mass student mind is sound and pure. In every country, the youth adores the spirit of patriotism. The time for youth is the time for initiative and enthusiasm...Mazzini says, 'Adore enthusiasm, worship the dreams of the virgin soul, and the visions of early youth, for they are the perfume of Paradise, which the soul preserves in issuing from the hands of the creator.'" Dr. Mookerjee further explained that 'in a subject country, the patriotic impulses of youths were apt to be all the more fervent and outspoken'. Their thoughts and ideas should be appreciated by their elders. It is the students' duty that they should retain the sanctity of the academic atmosphere in colleges. Students' strikes and demonstrations within the colleges cannot solve the national problems. It is always better that students should secure a better education for themselves. It will pave the way for better preparation for life. He asked the youth to take lessons from the proud history of India and remove the clouds of distrust and prejudice with all solidity and vigour. No man lives to himself. No task can be more patriotic than that of binding the whole community together by common association and aspirations. Dr. Mookerjee had an intimate association with the student community. He asserted on several occasions that the teachers should discuss with them all those problems that agitate their minds, even though they may have no direct connection with their academic work. It creates an atmosphere of mutual trust and confidence whose value cannot be overestimated.

His Thoughts on Religion and its Role in Education

Dr. Syama Prasad Mookerjee was a staunch believer of the ancient Rig Vedic dictum "*Ekam Sat Vipraah Bahudha Vadanti*" (Truth is one expressed by sages differently). He not only openly acknowledged the diversity in Indian religions landscape but also exhorted ceaselessly that the followers of all creeds should be given the opportunity for intellectual and cultural development. He also believed that the followers of every religion should be upright to their faiths and their conduct should instil a sense of cooperation and confidence amongst the followers of other faiths so that the very fabric of fabled Indian unity may remain active and everlasting.

Moreover, he also opined that religious education had played a very significant role in shaping the course of human development. However, it also had shown in the past some negative shades as well, which, in turn, showcased the vulnerability of the best of the religious creeds when it falls in the hands of formal elements of the society. In other words, religion, has always been a safe shelter for human beings when they encounter confounding and challenging times, however, when narrow-minded people with vested interests hold the reigns of the religion then they can often use it as an instrument of suppression of the same spirit which upholds the apotheosis of the virtues of any religion. Therefore, when interpreted narrowly, religion becomes a tool for atrocity and mistreatment of the human being. Dr. Mookerjee also believed that the practicality of religion being included in the education brings with it a potential confusion and chaos if the preachers lose sight of its ideal form and concentrate on its practise in a narrow ritualistic facet.

Moreover, if it happens, then there would be a fear of bigotry which, as a consequence, will hamper the growth of Indian nationalism. As a result of this fear, he advocated that people must imbibe religious spirit in its highest humanistic form from the influences coming from home and hearth. However, he also maintained that the truth and beauty of the religions should be inculcated in such a way that they help in the peaceful coexistence of all the diverse strands of religions leading the human soul to the bliss of truth and beauty that is inherent in the teachings of all the creeds. He suggested that there could be a text which would record the ultimate triumph of truth and righteousness and lay stress on the essential unity of all religions and aim at the foundation of common sympathy, a just and equitable understanding, and a sense of universal brotherhood.

The Teachings for the World

At that time, the world was struggling with a peculiar challenge that had no precedent in the human history. The western civilization had failed to provide the twin ideals of liberty and peace to the world. Despite material, scientific and industrial developments the ruling class of Europe was largely influenced by the evil tapestries power, supremacy and wealth. The prosperity of the whole world was dependent on the bigotry those who were promoting the nefarious and selfish interest of only a few powerful countries. Allthough these countries had put equality, democracy and liberty on the pedestal as the lofty ideals for human civilization, they didn't stop their own exploitation of the weak and developing countries for their selfish gains. Dr. Mookerjee said the the future of the world rested with the union of independent nations, where young nations could develop according to their own traditions and ideals.

According to Dr. Mookerjee the education system across the globe required complete overhauling and restructuring to nurture international relations and understanding of universal brotherhood. It is important that an individual should be compassionate towards his fellow beings. Every individual should be given an equal opportunity to take advantage of natural facilities to augment his mental, intellectual and physical upliftment.

A person's sense of social responsibility should be so strong that he should not hesitate in sacrificing his personal interests at the altar of common good and welfare. A person should be tolerant enough to the difference of opinion with grace and humility. He should acknowledge and respect that he should not only belong to his own country but also transcend the geographical boundries of his country to be a world class citizen.

Justice should be equal for everybody and government should be dependent on public welfare and mutual Co-operation.

Dr. Mookerjee's legendary speeches and his distinguished

contribution in the field of education in Calcutta University made him a household name as a highly influential educationist in india.

He was everready to accomplish educational and social works of national improtance; that is why he was always surrounded by people seeking his advice, guidance and mentorship on the matters of grave importance. He gave everybody his undivided attention and tried to extend his support to them in every possible way. Students, teachers, researchers, unemployed, destitute and the poor—all were beneficiaries of his friendly and benevolent nature. He was indeed a man of simple living and high thinking. He continued to be a guiding pillar of concern and support for the educational challenges of young india, despite being appointed as a Minister for Industry and supply in the first cabinet of the independent India. He was keenly contemplative of the unique problems of the academic field for strengthening the quality and quantam of education in India.

In the first budget session of the independent India, he laid utmost emphasis on increasing the financial aid to the field of education. His conceptualization of the ideal education for a new India transcended petty political considerations and appeasement practices.

We have already discussed his last convocation address in connection with the development of Hindi language. He lauded the report of Radhakrishnan that it did justice to the need of planned restructuring of university administration and teaching. However, unfortunately that commission also didn't pay much attention on the financial needs of education sector.

Dr. Mookerjee said that "The university's vital needs relate to improved methods of teaching and research and abundant facilities, both academic and extra-academic, to the staff and the students for performing their essential duties. This can hardly be fulfilled without adequate state aid. A university that has to depend for its existence principally on its fee income can never meet its obligations, however much it may compromise with sound academic principles for artificially raising such income."

In Delhi University convocation address, he applead for the autonomy of universities.

"No external authority set up by the government can ever hope to secure co-ordination of work or enforce a common standard among all universities in India. It will, thus, become a super-university by itself, developing a piece of extremely complex machinery, deadening the soul of all universities in India and making them rigid and stagnant. If such an authority is to enjoy executive powers, it will lead to the regimentation of university education which even totalitarian countries or autocratic regimes dared not experiment in."

He said that all necessary reforms of the universities should be taken up in this manner that first, regional requirements balance with national progress; secondly, by the Inter-University Board which, though having advisory powers, must be helped to develop healthy conventions and whose well-considered recommendations cannot be easily flouted by any university; thirdly, by well-informed deliberations in state legislatures and Parliament at the time of voting of demands on grants and lastly, by the Universities Grants Committee, which, functioning on the model of the British Grants Committee, can always exercise a healthy and decisive influence on both the administrative and the teaching activities of the universities concerned. Various educational and cultural organisations had included him in some form or the other in their various important bodies to avail his guidance. His contribution in providing a strong foundation to the various eminent educational and cultural institutions is noteworthy. Some of those institute's brief deliberation is as follows:

Royal Asiatic Society of Bengal

Dr. Syama Prasad Mookerjee proved to be very successful in the handling of the great tradition as the President of the Royal Asiatic Society (RAS), which was successfully established by his predecessors in the history of nearly 150 years. It is essential to know that the RAS was founded in 1784 under the chairmanship of Sir William Jones. His name is familiar to anyone who has studied history, archaeology and literature of India. He dreamt of developing a centre of research wherein would be co-ordinated the multitudinous currents of oriental culture, language and literature, law and social institutions, religion and philosophy, civic and natural science of Man in India against the background of the history of Man in Asia, and this dream was realised by him although his premature death prevented its full achievement.

Formerly RAS was known as the Asiatic Society of Bengal. It was named as Royal Asiatic Society of Bengal in 1936. However, before 1929, Indians were not allowed to become a member of RAS. Some worth noting former presidents of RAS were Rajendra Lal Mitra, Sir Fraser, Atkinson, Sir Asutosh Mookerjee and Hariprasad Shastri. It is worth noting that after Dr. Mookerjee in 1945, his best friend Dr. Meghnad Saha adorned the position of President. In 1949-1950, Mookerjee's elder brother Justice Rama Prasad graced the position of President of RAS.

In the office of Dr. Mookerjee, all the works of the Society like lectures, scholarships, publications, manuscript library, etc. were all proceeded very smoothly. Dr. Mookerjee kept alive the old tradition of maintaining the scholarships and objective inquiry amid the strains of civil administration and politics. Even the war period did not bother Dr. Mookerjee in running the whole thing with absolute fairness. As President of the Society, Dr. Mookerjee gave directions to solemnise many compact works. He inspired famous scholar Dr. Baini Prasad for editing the Arabic translation of Srimad Bhagavadgita. The following main tasks took place during his presidentship:

Maathir-ul-Umara (Vol. II), translated in English by Dr. Baini Prasad

The Doctrine of Nimbark (Vol. III) by Dr. Roma Chaudhary

Publication of *Kuttanimatam* ed. by Pt. Madhusudan Kaul of Kashmir

Publication of *Haft-Iqlim* (Vol. II) written by Prof M Mahful-ul-Haq

Dr. Mookerjee always took a personal interest in the research papers that were published in the Royal Asiatic Journal. He used to read them before printing and often gave suggestions. Prominent lectures conducted by the Society under the headship of Dr. Mookerjee are:

- American Medicine in the Second World War.
- The Life of Prophet Mohammed and the expansion of Islam.
- Sikkim.
- Old Theatres in India.
- Occupation of Sicily and Italy.
- The Epic Age of India.
- Dawn of Law in Ancient India.
- Tibet.
- The gods and goddesses of India.

Dr. Mookerjee formulated post-war reconstruction schemes related to culture. In 1944, he actively contributed as a member of the Society's Cultural Advisory Board. Dr. Mookerjee was also a member of 'Dr. Bimala Charan Law Gold Medal' Advisory Board. He showed interest in opening an institute for the study of Jainism in November 1949, which was aimed to spread the principles of Jainism and to develop intellectual, moral and literary interests in the public.

Jain Bhavan was established in Calcutta in the year 1945. Regarding the culture reconstruction in India, Dr. Mookerjee emphasised the following:

Establishment of a School of Indian Architecture, the further protection of the aboriginal tribes, establishment of National Parks, National Academy of Fine Arts and Culture, and a National Museum at New Delhi.

In 1945, the Royal Asiatic Society of Bengal under the chairmanship of Dr. Mookerjee appealed to the Government of India for the establishment of the National Cultural Trust. Three academies were set up in the National Cultural Trust—Dance, Music and Drama Academy, Sahitya Academy and Lalit Kala Academy. After independence, a conference on art was organised in Calcutta in 1949, and two conferences on literature were held in 1951. All these conferences resulted in the formation of Sangeet Natak Akademi, Sahitya Akademi, and Lalit Kala Akademi. Dr. Mookerjee took the great initiative to preserve literature, art and culture.

While holding the post of the President of the Royal Asiatic Society of Bengal, Dr. Mookerjee not only gave unprecedented direction and momentum to the cultural conservation, but also emphasised that the establishment of many more such institutions of Indian culture would help preserve and maintain our culture.

He played an essential role in the establishment of the National Museum of India. It is noteworthy that the committee headed by the then Vice Chancellor of Delhi University, Maurice Gwayer, was assigned with the responsibility of establishing the National Museum. An interesting fact about the establishment of the National Museum is that the British Government was insisting on developing this museum as a part of the World War Memorial, but Dr. Mookerjee was in favour of developing the National Museum as two different units—War Memorial[8] and National Museum. A letter written by Dr. Mookerjee to Sir Ramaswamy Mudaliar, who was the Diwan of Mysore and chairman of the Imperial war committee and the Gwayer committee, suggests that he insisted on developing the National Museum as the world's best museum and research centre for culture. He wanted to see this museum as a guiding institution. He remained as a member of the Royal Asiatic Society of Bengal[9] till his last breath.

Sahitya Akademi

The National Academy of Letters (Sahitya Akademi) Committee was formed in May 1951. Dr. Mookerjee played the role of a member of the Committee. It was the responsibility of the Committee to coordinate and encourage all Indian languages in literary activities. Dr. Mookerjee along with Shri Shankarrao Dev, Sh. Kakasaheb Kalelkar, and Sh. Nimani Fukan (Assam), played a significant role in the constitution of Sahitya Akademi. Dr. Mookerjee was always in favour to set up the Academy of Letters. He proposed it while he was the Chairman of the Education

Advisory Committee of the Government of India. Dr. Mookerjee, along with others, emphasised the new goals of Sahitya Akademi:

- Encouraging the establishment and development of representative literary association exclusively concerned with the development of language and literature and promoting cooperation between literary associations, universities and cultural organisations.
- Translation of Indian languages from one Indian language to other Indian languages and foreign languages and related literary books:
- To help in the publication of literary materials.
- Organising Literature Conferences at All India Level.
- Rewarding authors for distinguished work in literature.
- Promoting research in Indian languages and literature.
- Promoting regional languages and literature in different parts of the country to build national unity.
- Promoting Devanagari script.

Mahabodhi Society

In the year 1942, Dr. Mookerjee was elected the President of Mahabodhi Society.[10] This major organisation of Buddhists had its head office in Calcutta. Dr. Mookerjee continued to bring the 'Tripitik' message of Buddhism to various sections of the society through the Mahabodhi Society till his end. Dr. Mookerjee had introduced many teachings of Buddhism in his moderated lifestyle. Right thoughts, Right Speech, and Right Conduct were integral parts of his life. His conviction was firm that Buddhist thought and culture could bind together South-East Asian and East Asian countries with India. The Mahabodhi Society acted as a bridge in strengthening international cultural relations.

As President of the Mahabodhi Society, Dr. Mookerjee was performing many duties which were of international importance. His contemplation of India's relations with the nations of the Far East shows thinking ahead of his time. This thinking of his can be seen as a significant form of foreign policy like 'Look East' by the Indian State Department.

Meeting of Mahabodhi Society at Calcutta

At sanchi: Pandit Jawahar Lal Nehru addressing a function on handing over Buddhist relics. Others in the picture: Syama Prasad, Dr. S. Radhakrishan, Shankar Dayal Sharma

On 21 December 1945, Dr. Mookerjee delivered a speech on Buddhist education in the context of Indian culture at the Mahabodhi Conference held in Sri Lanka. The objectives that Dr. Mookerjee considered necessary for the upliftment of the society through the society were—Renaissance of Buddhism in India; Promotion and propagation of Buddhist Literature written in Pali and Sanskrit languages; To teach Household science, Technical Industries and Local crafts to illiterate people; Translation of Buddhist Literature into English and other regional languages; Opening of arts and crafts schools for boys and girls in villages;

Establishment of Institute and hospital for expansion of the Buddhist system of medicine; Open an orphanage; Opening of schools to train teachers.

Dr. Mookerjee wanted to make efforts towards realising the dream of establishing all-round universities, like Taxila and Nalanda for discharging the glorious tradition of Indian education through the Mahabodhi Society. Dr. Mookerjee contributed significantly to the development of Pali, the language of the Buddhist *Tripitaka*, even while staying at the University of Calcutta. He believed that Pali is not just a language, but a significant cultural movement. On the restructuring of the syllabus at Calcutta University in 1951, Dr. Mookerjee had said that the Pali subject had been taught for the last 50 years, the subject should be expanded. The proposal for a postgraduate degree in Pali language was approved and changes were also made in the curriculum at the undergraduate level. He emphasised the importance of Pali language after Sanskrit in ancient writings as it offered many possibilities for research.

At the time, the propagation of Buddhism under the aegis of Mahabodhi Society took the form of a religious movement. As a result, cultural and religious ties between many countries of Asia became very strong. Dr. Mookerjee was the most decisive contributor to the revival of Buddhism in India. He brought back the sacred relics and souvenirs of Lord Buddha's disciple Sariputta and Mahamouggallana from the Museum of England and installed them at Sanchi Stupa.[11] The Mahabodhi Society urged the British government to return the sacred relics and souvenirs to India. In the late 1940s, the British government completed the process of transferring the holy relics to India. The relics were taken to Sri Lanka before being brought to India, where they were welcomed with great pomp. The relics were kept in the Colombo Museum for two-and-a-half months, where more than two million visitors paid tribute to the relics. From there, those were brought to *Dharmarajika Vihar* in Calcutta and kept for two weeks. People of all religions came to pay homage. Prime Minister Nehru handed

Syama Prasad holding Buddhist relics with Dr. S. Radhakrishnan

them over to Dr. Mookerjee on 14 January, 1940 in Calcutta amidst the sound of sacred music and Buddhist sutras.

Dr. Mookerjee wanted the strengthening of religious, cultural ties with another world of India. He wanted to see India as a robust allied nation internationally. Dr. Mookerjee visited Buddhist countries with the holy relics and souvenirs of the disciples of Lord Buddha, where he established sound bridges of ideas and culture. At the request of countries like Burma, Vietnam, Sri Lanka, Myanmar, Cambodia, Tibet, etc., Dr. Mookerjee travelled to those countries with sacred ashes before re-establishing the souvenirs in Sanchi. The people there saw the saint in Dr. Mookerjee, who had come to awaken their faith and belief. During his visit, Dr. Mookerjee also visited the famous Buddhist temple of Angkor Wat.

In Burma too, there was a rush of people from Mandalay to Rangoon carrying the holy ashes. The recitation of divine Buddhist sutras continued all the way. In Cambodia, with unprecedented enthusiasm, more than 1 million Buddhist monks and common men were present on the way from Phnom Penh Airport to the Silver Pagoda, an important religious site. Burma and Sri Lanka requested that they should also be given one part of the sacred ashes as a permanent loan. Dr. Mookerjee wrote a letter to Prime Minister Nehru about this, Nehru agreed for Burma, but he objected for Sri Lanka.

Dr. Mookerjee believed that doing so would create excellent and sound relations with neighbouring countries, however, respecting the sentiments of the followers of Buddhism there, Pt. Nehru would not mind giving 1-1 part of the holy relics as a permanent loan. Eventually, Pandit Nehru accepted. Dr. Mookerjee's request for both Burma and Sri Lanka. The relics were established in Burma's World Peace Pagoda known as Kaaba-i-Jada and in the Mahabodhi Society, Colombo, Sri Lanka.

On 30 November 1952, the sacred relics and souvenirs were installed in Sanchi at the new *Chettiyagiri Vihar* (before this they were kept in Sarnath). The ceremony was presided over by the then Vice President of India, Dr. Sarvepalli Radhakrishnan. Thakin Nu, the Premier of Burma, attended the ceremony and told Dr. Mookerjee, "You do not know what a great service you have rendered to my country. Your visit with the relics brought about a wonderful change in my people. They have found their souls."

On 23 February 1953, the Buddhist Association, Vietnam also appreciated Dr. Mookerjee's work and wrote a letter of thanks to him.[12]

Syama Prasad as President, Mahabodhi Society of India, handing over the relics of Lord Buddha to Thakin Nu, Prime Minister of Mayamar at the Society premises at Calcutta

Interestingly, Nicholas G. Thatcher, an American Vice Counsel who attended the meeting of the Mahabodhi Society in September 1950, was so impressed with Dr. Mookerjee that he brought a reference letter from Thomas W. Siemens, an American friend of Dr. Mookerjee, so that he would get some time from Dr. Mookerjee to discuss the philosophical ideas.

Syama Prasad with Pandit Jawahar Lal Nehru and Thakin Nu, the Burmese Prime Minister

Syama Prasad addressing a meeting in Cambodia – 1951

Syama Prasad in Cambodia – 1949

King Narodam Sinhahoke, Cambodia—1951
(When Syama Prasad handed over Buddhist relics)

Indian Institute of Science, Banglore

Dr. Mookerjee had distinguished contribution to the administration of the Indian Institute of Science, Bangalore. In the year 1935, he played the role of a member of the Court and Council. Court and Council were critical units of administration. While holding the post of Vice Chancellor of Calcutta University; he used to spare time for the Indian Institute of Science in his busy life. He used to attend meetings or send his valuable suggestions through letters. He was also a member of the Finance Committee of the Institute. Whether to buy high-quality new equipment or recruit new staff for the organisation, he took full interest in them. In those days, the Institute's Director was Sir C.V. Raman. He was the first Indian Director there. Probably this thing offended some Britishers. In particular, an English scholar working in the same institution, Mr. Watson, felt very bad as he had thought that he would be made Director after Sir Martin Foster. This time was a bit difficult for Sir Raman. Many people of the Institute were not supporting him. In 1937, Sir Raman resolved to devote himself to full-time research in Physics and resigned as Director.

The application of Dr. J.C. Ghosh of Dhaka University for the post of Director was received. Vice Chancellor of Dhaka University said that Dr. Ghosh has the qualities of a good administrator. He became the Chairman of the chemistry department at the age of only 28. The Vice Chancellor of Dhaka University told Dr. Mookerjee that Dr. Ghosh had set up Agricultural Chemical Science and Soil Science Department. Dr. Ghosh had introduced new schemes one after the other and was instrumental in establishing the Faculty of Agriculture and Faculty of Pharmacology. Dr. Mookerjee wanted that one such Indian Director should be chosen for the Indian Institute of Science, who could actively implement new schemes and take the Institute to the pinnacle of success with his innovative ideas. So, Dr. Mookerjee immediately wrote a letter to another member of the Council, Professor V.N. Chandrawarkar, and told him that this opportunity to provide a stable foundation to the Institute should not be missed and should send an appointment letter to Dr. Ghosh after talking to the Tata representative.

It is known that the Institute was also facing financial problems at that time. Paying according to the ability of the new Director was also a problem. Ultimately, on the request of the Council, Dr. Mookerjee spoke to Dr. Ghosh and convinced him for less salary. However, Dr. Mookerjee accepted his other conditions—free housing, an appointment for ten years, personal lab staff and financial support for research work. It was Dr. Mookerjee's experience that took the Indian Institute of Science to new heights.

After the appointment of the new Director, Sir Raman's working did not get affected. Dr. Mookerjee along with Sir Vishveshwaraiah, assured Sir Raman that the facilities provided to him earlier (when he was Director) would not be withdrawn on assuming the post of Head of the Department of Physics, although the salary of the new Director was lower than Sir Raman. Dr. Mookerjee accepted that our nation had very few scientists like Sir Raman and that we should give them the best facilities. Sir Raman also ensured that he would carry out his duty with full devotion. This event happened in 1938. Sir Raman took over the Physics Department, and the Council approved his terms (proper place for Physics Lab, permission to stay in his bungalow).

On 12 June, various issues were discussed, and a total of 21 resolutions were passed in the council meeting of the Institute. An important issue was raised in the Council. The Senate was violating its jurisdiction. A committee was constituted under the chairmanship of Dr. Mookerjee to evaluate the resolutions and decisions of the Senate. There was a Senate member who used to leak the matters to the press without taking consent from the Council. Dr. Mookerjee informed the press that only the authorised releases should be published in the newspaper. Dr. Mookerjee made it clear that after every meeting of the Council, an authorised press release should be sent through the Director. The problem of indiscipline of students was also discussed. Dr. Mookerjee's views on discipline were apparent; he found people without discipline obnoxious. He made it clear to the leader of the student union through the Committee that indiscipline would not be tolerated. Apart from Dr. Mookerjee, the Committee also included N.S. Subbarao, Prof. S.S. Bhatnagar, J.S. Bhatt, and V.N. Chandravarkar.

Dr. Mookerjee kept bringing excellent academicians to whatever educational institution he was associated with. Dr. Mookerjee agreed with the appointment of Prof. H.S. Sen, Director of the Indian Natural Resin and Gum Institute, Ranchi, as Professor in the Department of Chemistry of the Indian Institute of Science. With his consent, Dr. Armstrong was also appointed as a visiting professor in the Chemistry department.

Vishwa Bharati, Shanti Niketan

Dr. Mookerjee was a member of various committees of Vishwa Bharati, Shanti Niketan like Executive Committee, Assembly, Granth Vibhag Committee, Music Committee, etc. He was also regular in touch with Rathindranath Tagore, executive secretary of Vishwa Bharati through correspondence and personal visits. He used to take part in the meetings of Vishwa Bharati, Shanti Niketan. He also presided over its Annual committee in December 1950.

Addressing the Annual Convocation of Vishwa Bharati over which he presided as its Vice President Dr. Mookerjee referred to the far-sighted wisdom, vision and patriotism of Poet Tagore in finding for the first time in modern India a seat of learning that could be genuinely called international. Education must be a matter of joy and not a burden. It could only prosper in the right atmosphere, which Tagore helped in creating. He firmly believed in combining the best Indian traditions with the wholesome gifts of the West. He emphasised the use of one's mother-tongue at every stage. The students, after taking comprehensive education in subjects, like arts and letters, science and agriculture, etc., bore upon them the impression of Tagore's idealism and practical realism. Art, architecture, philosophy, languages, literature, religion—all could be and should be studied from a comparative standpoint to discover that great unity in diversity which must ultimately form the basis of a lasting international understanding, at once peaceful and harmonious. Dr. Mookerjee was committed to spreading Tagore's above thoughts on the actual grounds.

It is but natural that if a university in India has to keep so high a purpose in view in the sphere of international relations, it must be able to lay a firm foundation in respect of studies connected with Indian culture and civilisation. Dr. Mookerjee observed, "until and unless Vishwa Bharati is in a position to represent the highest traditions of Indian scholarship in all their varied aspects and maintain teachers and scholars, museums and libraries worthy of the cause, it cannot possibly attract workers from countries outside India."[13] He further said that Tagore was a born revolutionary and he naturally claimed for himself the right to do experiments in all spheres with which he was connected. He considered freedom as the life-breath of education. The rigid rules and regulations make the working of an educational institute, wooden and artificial. Tagore was at first unwilling to have any connection with any statutory Indian university or with the government of the day. However, at a later stage, Tagore and Vishwa Bharati came into closer contact with Calcutta University,[14] whereby his freedom of action remained undisturbed, and at the same time, Vishwa Bharati became entitled to specific academic and administrative advantages.

Annual Convocation at Vishwa Bharati on 24-12-1950, Syama Prasad delivered the Convocation address

Syama Prasad giving awards to the students of Vishwa Bharati in the Convocation in 1950

Syama Prasad delivering Convocation address at Vishwa Bharati in 1950

Syama Prasad delivering a speech at a meeting held at Vishwa Bharati

Dr. Mookerjee said that Vishwa Bharati represented a type of its own which was different from any other Indian University. Further, he said that there was no reason why India should not maintain a different type of universities located in various sites, each fulfilling its purpose and serving the cause of progress. There should be no attempt to mould all on a similar pattern. He announced that the Radhakrishnan Commission had supported the proposal of the statutory recognition of Vishwa Bharati and soon it would be recognised by the Indian Parliament. He said that the Vishwa Bharati had zealously to guard against the possibility of it turning into a mere machine or a lifeless administrative body overloaded with laws and bye-laws. He asked them not to make the university a golden cage.

Dr. Mookerjee said that the wisely planned and rightly executed education would be the principal factor on which the future peace, progress and paradise of Indian people would rest. Primary, secondary and higher education—all stages demand equal attention from the state and the public. Expansion and not curtailment must be the motto. Preservation of equality must be the constant aim. Education is one sphere of activity on which the state can never be accused of overspending. If the planning is sound and administration correct, the larger we spend, the more robust will be the result leading to national prosperity and solidarity, said Dr. Mookerjee. The state government and the private benefactors should come forward to give money for developing the Indian universities so that the task of rediscovering the Indian mind, fully conversant with the rich heritage and adequately equipped with science and technology be undertaken by the universities in a spirit of courage and devotion. Dr. Mookerjee wished that the Vishwa Bharati might fulfil the enormous task of the reawakening of the soul of India and thereby fulfil the dream of its illustrious founder, Rabindranath Tagore.

Dr. Mookerjee concluded his speech by quoting the words of Tagore, "...this institution may be a perpetual creation by the cooperative enthusiasm of teachers and students, growing with the growth of their soul; a world in itself, self-sustaining, independent, rich with ever-sustaining life, radiating life across space and time, attracting and maintaining round it a planetary system of dependent bodies. Its aim should lie in imparting life-breath to the complete man who is intellectual as well as economic, bound by social bonds, but aspiring towards spiritual freedom and final perfection."[15]

University College of Science, Calcutta

Dr. Mookerjee has made an unprecedented contribution to the development of University College of Science, Calcutta. The foundation of the college was laid on 14 April 1914 by Sir Asutosh Mookerjee. Dr. Syama Prasad Mookerjee formed a committee to celebrate the college's silver jubilee. Sharing his dream with all the members of the college, he said that this college should prepare such professionals who can meet the needs of industries, make such teachers, who can fulfil the needs of schools and colleges and create such professors and researchers who bring glory for India. His dream was to expand the industry department of the college. He wanted that the functioning of the college should be restructured. His dream has come true in the form of the 'Industry Institute Partnership Program' being run at University College of Science.

Dr. Mookerjee wanted to establish a science museum in this college. His idea was that the Science Museum would popularise science and technology, which would make the road to India's development easier. His dream could not be fulfilled during his lifetime. The first science museum was opened in BITS Pilani. The National Science Museum Council (HQ in Kolkata) was established in April 1978. University Science College has many departments, Dr. Mookerjee wanted to build a common library for all departments. A working committee was formed under the chairmanship of Dr. Mookerjee, whose aim was to collect funds to fulfil all these objectives.

He had set another goal through University College. He wanted to construct a building like Burlington House, London which would have several auditoriums and sections, where the entire scientific society of India could join together.

Where all India scientific committees like National Institute of Science, Indian Chemical, Physical and other Scientific Society could gather.

Saha Institute of Nuclear Physics, Calcutta

Dr. Mookerjee was doing everything possible for the development of India. Bringing a high-quality scientist like Dr. Meghnad Saha to Calcutta University and paving the way for his research was one such endeavour. Dr. Saha took charge of Physics Palit Chair. Dr. Meghnad Saha expressed his gratitude to Dr. Mookerjee, saying that he provided him facilities to travel to different countries and facilitated his path to the work of atomic energy. It is known that Dr. Saha used to share the impediments coming in the way of his organisation with Dr. Mookerjee. He knew that Dr. Mookerjee is such a nationalist leader who wants to see the multifaceted development of his nation. Dr. Mookerjee used to get his problems resolved. A new wing of Nuclear Physics was to be established in the University College of Science, but there was a shortage of space. The teaching of Nuclear Physics was also to be started in the University College of Science, which required space. The air training corps had taken some part of that building, but that part was not being used. With his proficient speech skills, Dr. Mookerjee got that part vacated by them.

Dr. Saha wanted to pursue research in atomic energy. Dr. Saha, while expressing his gratitude towards Dr. Mookerjee, said, "I am able to complete this research work in Palit Physics Laboratory (1940-48) through Dr. Mookerjee's efforts."[16] Dr. Saha wanted to get his report on Atomic Energy recommended by Dr. Mookerjee. Therefore, he sent this report to Dr. Mookerjee through his colleague Sir J.C. Ghosh for evaluation.

Dr. Saha wrote a letter to Dr. Mookerjee on 10 April 1948, to draw his attention to the fact that in the House, Pt. Nehru had introduced a provision in the Atomic Energy Bill which would prove to be negative. Pt. Nehru wanted all research to be more or less concentrated. Dr. Saha asked him to have a talk with Pt. Nehru and get this clause deleted. Dr. Mookerjee's viewpoint was that research should not be concentrated if the country wants any progress at all. In the USA and UK, there was no provision that research would be focused in one place or one man. The research centres were distributed all over the country. Dr. Mookerjee was in favour of linking research centres with educational institutions. Pandit Nehru agreed with him and removed this provision. When Dr. Mookerjee laid the foundation of the Institute of Technology on 21 April 1948, Dr. Saha expressed gratitude towards Dr. Mookerjee and told everyone that Dr. Mookerjee had laid the foundation of the Institute 7 years ago when he persuaded the Senate of Calcutta University to be prepared to receive financial support from Tata Charity to install Cyclotron in Physics Laboratory, however, the representatives of the state government were entirely against this aid because they thought that financial assistance (₹60,000/-) was low. He believed that once the *Yajna Kund* is established, the people who offer sacrifices in the *havan* would come by their own. Prof. Pramathanath Banerjee (Vice Chancellor, Calcutta University) presented a brief introduction to the new project at the time of the foundation of the Institute. In his lecture, Dr. Mookerjee referred to the utility of atomic energy and the various experiments that can be done in its future. He said that the world had become conscious of atomic energy since the atomic bomb fell on Hiroshima and Nagasaki. That sad event had blanketed the positive uses of atomic energy. He said that atomic energy could prove to be a blessing of God in peaceful times. He further said:

- This energy is a source of unlimited energy accessible in every region of the world.
- It is a new weapon for the study, control and treatment of diseases. Radioactive will prove to be very useful in this field.
- By this, we will be able to know how plants and animals grow.
- It will prove very useful in the field of best food products and nutrition.

The thinking of Dr. Mookerjee about Nuclear Physics was quite clear. Institute of Nuclear Physics, Calcutta started wo i.

in 1950. At the Institute's inaugural ceremony on 11 January 1950 in addition to the world-renowned scientist Marie Curie (Madame Irene Juliet), other intellectuals were also present. Prof. Madame Curie inaugurated the Institute. Scientists like Dr. Bhabha, Dr. S.S. Bhatnagar etc. appreciated this work of Dr. Saha. Dr. Mookerjee laid the foundation of the Institute. He also contributed as a member of the executive body of the Institute. The Institute of Nuclear Physics was dedicated to Nuclear Chemistry, Bio-Physics and Atomic Energy research. Dr. Saha said that this Institute would serve as a nursery school for future scientists. After the death of Dr. Saha in the year 1956, this Institute was renamed as 'Saha Institute of Nuclear Physics'.

Diverse Schemes

Dr. Mookerjee remained sensitive to the needs of the education sector until his last breath. He believed in Sanskrit saying:

हर्तृ र्न गोचरं याति दत्ता भवति विस्तृता।
कल्पान्तेऽपि न या नश्येत् किमन्यद्विद्यया विना॥

Education is a gem which no one can ever steal from us. Education is the invaluable gift of God to man, a wealth that increases when it is distributed. The solution to every problem is hidden in education. During the famine, Chandpur faced much suffering. Chandpur was one of the backward areas where there was no high school. Chandpur was getting help from good people in financial terms, but the permanent relief to sufferers was education. In the year 1944, Dr. Mookerjee proposed to open an H.E. school in Chandpur to eradicate its anguish. He asked Ashwini Kumar Dev to devise a scheme that would prove beneficial in opening a training centre for agriculture, industry and science where students could get free training.

In 1945, the All India Soap Makers' Association offered a scheme to start a diploma in the art of soap-making under Calcutta university. The diploma was introduced for the B.Sc. students, having Honours in chemistry. Factory training was also arranged. All such schemes got positive support from Dr. Mookerjee. He also urged the Ramakrishna Mission to support him in fulfilling his dream of improving the level of education in India and present a better plan format for providing adequate education to the youth. As desired by Dr. Mookerjee, Promode Kumar Bhattacharya, Principal, Nadia college prepared a scheme for opening a training centre. It was an experimental scheme of training pupils for re-establishing the solidarity of Indian society. He desired that Institutes for Research and Graduate Training should be established to take cognisance of all phases of human activity. The aim of such institutes should be to sketch out principles, policies and plans after drawing upon all relevant material and experience available in the world outside; to sift this material in the atmosphere of detached scientific approach proper to a university, and when necessary to initiate new research. In the year 1945, a scheme was presented to Dr. Mookerjee for preparing a postgraduate course of study and research in Agricultural Chemistry and Soil Science at the University of Calcutta. He was ready for immediate implementation of the scheme.

Secondary Board of School Education, West Bengal

He was the one who first suggested the formation of a Board of Secondary Education. Dr. Mookerjee envisaged primary education, secondary education and university education to be the backbone of our nationalistic education. He showed the path of progress and democratic control in the sphere of education. He attempted meticulous curricular revision and renewal of primary and secondary education.

The academic preparation should be appropriate at every stage so that they can confidently frame the emerging challenges of the next stage. This is a permanent academic challenge, and Dr. Mookerjee was one of the first Indians to realise this.

On 3 May 1951, the Governor of Bengal, Dr. K.N. Katju, inaugurated the Board of Secondary Education, West Bengal. The Chairman of the Board was Mr. Apoorva Kumar Chadda. Dr. Syama Prasad Mookerjee, as a member of the Executive Council Board of Secondary Education, gave invaluable guidelines based on the experience gained in the education sector in his past years. The first meeting was held on 12 June 1951 in the Cabinet Room of the West Bengal Secretariat. Subsequently, these meetings were held on 14 June, 5 July 10 July, 17 July 24 July, 28 August, 4 September, 20 September and 25 September 1951. All these meetings became evidence of Dr. Mookerjee's presence. The purpose of these meetings was to develop the secondary education of the state and formulate policies for that. The following main points were decided in the meetings:

- That the Middle Scholarship Examination, 1951 would be conducted by the Board and that the Examination Committee was asked to take necessary steps. The Director of Public Instruction would assist the Board in every possible way.
- That the School Final examination to replace the Matriculation Examination conducted by the Board in 1952. Calcutta University would help in conducting the School Final Exams.
- That the grant to Anglo Indian Schools recognised by the Board should be distributed by the Board and that Government should be requested to allocate a proportionate amount for giving grants to recognised Anglo-Indian Schools.
- For recruitment of the Staff, the committee under the leadership of Dr. Mookerjee formed to consider the applicants. Other members of the committee were Dr. T. Sen, Dr. N. Sanyal, and Shri J.K. Sengupta.
- The resolution was taken on the important issues of Recognition and Grants committee. Dr. Mookerjee suggested such guidelines that only the schools which meet the eligibility criteria would be able to fall in the recognised category.
- A manual was prepared for the Board.
- Students who were studying under Dacca programme were allowed to appear in the examination according to their syllabus. It was also decided that the Board will not charge any migration fee from the refugee students.

- Executive Council welcomed the idea of holding a well-organised 'Education week'.
- Dearness allowance should be given to teachers of non-government secondary schools at the same rate as dearness allowance being given to government teachers.
- In the case of non-admission in any school, private examination facility was provided to the students. The Board would not demand fees from them. The goal was that the students should not have any discomfort, and they could complete their studies.
- A course committee was formed.
- Dr. Mookerjee was deeply interested in the development of the personality of the students. This goal was hidden behind conducting an oral examination along with a written examination. They wanted the students to present their ideas with confidence. All students can get this opportunity by conducting an oral examination. He also insisted on conducting an oral examination/Viva-voce at Calcutta University with a written examination. The same rule was implemented in the Board.
- Subjects were fixed for the school final examination. There was a particular emphasis on languages, such as Bengali, Hindi, Urdu, Nepali, English. Students were free to opt any one language for which two papers of 200 marks were fixed.
- Must pass General Bengali or General English examination.
- Options were also given from ancient languages, such as Sanskrit, Pali, Arabic, Persian, Latin or Greek.
- Options were placed as foreign languages—English, French, German and Spanish literature.
- General Hindi or any other Hindustani language will also have to pass.
- Apart from subjects like Mathematics, Science, General Science, Social Knowledge, Geography, History, Administration, some of the essential and optional

subject were Engineering, Drawing, Elements of Engineering, Workshops, Shorthand and Typing, which were enough to provide skills to the students and enable them to pursue higher education. Dr. Mookerjee's experience helped the Board greatly, and by adopting his suggestions, the Board was able to conduct tests successfully. Post-partition educated refugees were also given jobs in the secondary Board.

Central Advisory Board of Education

The first meeting of the Central Advisory Board of Education was held in New Delhi in December 1935. Apart from Dr. Mookerjee, its leading members were Shri B.G. Kher, Education Minister, Bombay; Dr. Syed Mohammed, Minister of Education, Bihar; Pt. R.S. Shukla, Minister of Education, Central States and Berar; Sir Girija Shankar Bajpai, Rajkumari Amrit Kaur, Sir Ziauddin Ahmed, Kunwar Sir Jagdish Prasad, Shri V.N. Chandavarkar etc.

The Central Advisory Board constituted a committee to consider the Wardha Education Scheme. The committee met in Shimla on 28-30 June 1938. In addition to Dr. Mookerjee, Rajkumari Amrit Kaur, Shri B.G. Kher, Dr. Zakir Hussain attended the meeting.

The problems of the then academic world were discussed in the meeting. Criticism of the erstwhile education system was with the issue that it was not matching with the change of time and even did not match any positive ideals. In 1937, Gandhiji introduced a new system, whose main principles were:

Elementary education should be tied up in a seven-year curriculum, and general knowledge should be taught till the tenth standard. Students should also be given vocational education, and the use of English should be reduced. It is known that considering the restructuring of the matric syllabus in the 1920s, Dr. Mookerjee had emphasised the use of mother-tongue. Also, a fundamental change in school education was discussed. Dr. Mookerjee wanted that the Tenth class certificate should be given only when the students could produce a certificate of merit in any one of the vocational subjects.

This thinking of Dr. Mookerjee is reflected in Mahatma Gandhi's Wardha Scheme. The Central Advisory Board of Education also acknowledged the same point, but India's youth continued to bear the brunt of unemployment for many years after independence. What could be the purpose of these patriots behind making the students skilful in vocational education or any craft? When every youth is skilled in some vocation, he can lead a life of conviction.

The foundation of Gandhiji's Wardha Scheme rested on the mantra of *'Sarvadharma Sambhav'*. The Wardha scheme was mainly designed, keeping in mind the rural areas. The Central Advisory Committee was of the view that after implementing the scheme in villages, it should be implemented in cities also with some changes in it. In Wardha Scheme, the minimum age of students was kept seven years. Dr. Mookerjee and other members of the committee agreed to a minimum age of five to six years. They were also agreed on the idea that state governments should start nurseries and playschools to prepare children for formal education and their all-round development. The committee accepted that education should be made compulsory for children between the ages of six to 14 years. All were unanimous on the idea that the medium of instruction should be the mother-tongue.

The training of teachers should be reorganised. It should be remembered that ever since Dr. Mookerjee entered the field of education (from the 1920s), he started stressing the importance of teacher training programs. He believed that if the teacher is trained, he will be able to transfer knowledge in the students smoothly.

The second annual meeting of the Central Advisory Board of Education was held in Delhi in December 1936. Kunwar Sir Jagdish Prasad presided over the meeting. Besides Dr. Mookerjee, Dr. Tejbahadur Sapru, Lala Shriram, V.N. Chandravarkar, Bengal Education Minister Khan Bahadur M. Aziul Haq, etc. also participated in the meeting. The Board decided that a National Commission on Intellectual Cooperation should be established and the Board itself would function as the National Centre of Education Information. It is known that the above things were also decided in the February 1936 meeting of Inter-University Board. Dr. Mookerjee was a member of that Board also.

The meeting emphasised scientific and professional education. Discussions were also made on sending students abroad for the best education. The unique thing is that all these advancements can be seen in Dr. Mookerjee's academic speeches.

In India, it was decided to consult the Inter-University Board for the uniformity and standardisation of university degrees. The discussion was held on focussing the education of specially-abled children.

Its four standing committees were formed:

1. Women's Education Committee.
2. Secondary Education Committee.
3. Regional Language (Vernacular) Committee.
4. Committee on Vocational and Professional Education.

Dr. Mookerjee was included in the Second and Fourth Committee for imparting his important views and guidelines. Dr. Mookerjee has talked about the classical restructuring in periodical speeches, discussion sessions, convocation ceremonies, etc., at the same time. He believed that a change in the basic structure of education is necessary, as India is facing unemployment.

Most of the members of the Inter-University Board and the Central Advisory Board wanted to proceed with this view. The Board was unanimous in making education essential for all up to the primary level so that the country becomes literate. At the lower secondary level, general knowledge of education and practical reasoning ability should be developed among students, however, the emphasis was laid on the establishment of various vocational training centres at the higher intermediate level. Dr. Mookerjee's voice was vocal in the Education Council of Bengal. He set up separate vocational training centres after school, and that is we can see it as an ITI today.

Dr. Mookerjee laid particular emphasis on the establishment of polytechnic institutions to fight unemployment. Necessary changes were made in the curriculum of secondary schools in Bengal. Simultaneously, training was also started in Agriculture and Horticulture, Carpentry and ironsmith etc. Dr. Mookerjee used to think ahead of time. This was the exceptional quality that he used to foresee the problem and used to get rid of it. Dr. Mookerjee believed that to make the society literate and to instil education interest in the students; the teachers must be trained and satisfied. They should experience pleasure in their business i.e. teaching; however, the public should also be made aware of the importance of education. He has made unique contributions in board meetings by sharing his views.

In 1937, the Inter-University Board and the Central Advisory Council decided that the council would also serve as the Intellectual Cooperation Committee.

In the year 1938, Dr. Mookerjee was nominated as the representative of India in the Committee of Intellectual Cooperation of the League of Nations. Dr. Mookerjee placed India's attitude towards education before the whole world. The foreign government realised that they would never be able to use education to fulfil their repugnant motive in India, as there were education leaders like Dr. Mookerjee, whose confidence was unwavering. Dr. Mookerjee became the voice of Indian education and teachers.

Inter-University Board of India

In 1934, Dr. Mookerjee became a member of the Inter-University Board of India;[17] later he held the post of Chairman. Dr. Mookerjee made his full contribution in fulfilling the Board's objective.

On behalf of the Board, Dr. Mookerjee also took over the membership of All India Council of Technical Education in 1946. Dr. Mookerjee made a significant contribution to the conference organised by the Board from 1 to 3 March 1939. The conference was attended by scholars including Azizul Haque, Vice Chancellor, Calcutta University, Dr. Saha, V.N. Chandavarkar (Bombay University), Dr. K.L. Mudgil (Travancore University) etc. The important issues that Dr. Mookerjee presented in the conference were:

In all universities, the regional languages should be included in the syllabus.

- Diploma course in public administration should be included.
- Dr. Mookerjee emphasised the utility of military training and pushed the Military Bill forward. Military science should be kept as an optional subject in the degree course. The services of Military officers should be availed to provide military training facilities to schools. All colleges and universities should be given military training facilities.
- Dr. Mookerjee wanted students to be disciplined. The problem of discipline among students was also discussed at the conference. These ideas culminated in the form of NCC[18] in 1948. Dr. Mookerjee supported the following points in the conference:
    1. Industry and commerce should be linked to the university curriculum.
    2. The university should prepare students for the promotion of general and health education in rural areas.

Academic institutions can fill qualities of social service in students. At present, we can see NSS[19] as a representation of these thoughts.

The literature world of India was also discussed in the conference. Dr. Mookerjee supported the preparation of the catalogue of entire literature available in India. Dr. Meghnad Saha insisted on providing scholarships to the researchers, and everyone agreed.

The subject of 'Sanitary Engineering' (already taught at Calcutta University) was decided to be taught in all universities. Dr. Mookerjee himself paid much attention to cleanliness. He believed that every human being must keep the environment around him clean. Men like Dr. Mookerjee and Gandhi dreamt of Clean India. To fulfil the same, our current Prime Minister Shri Narendra Modi launched the *Swachh Bharat Abhiyan* on 2 October 2014.

It was decided in the conference that modern Indian languages and ancient eastern languages will be recognised and will be added as a subject. It was also decided to include particular subjects like home-science, etc., in the syllabus for women. It was agreed to implement air training courses and entomology courses for students. Dr. Mookerjee emphasised to promote Indian literature and languages; he said that mother-tongue should be made the medium of studies till graduation. It was his devotion towards the nation, which compelled him to save the existence of Indian languages. He knew that on the basis of the Indian languages, we would be able to bind India into the thread of unity, and it was essential for us to be free from the British rule.

Overall, this conference proved to be very useful, where scholars have come together to promote research in science, while scholars emerged to protect literature, art and culture. The result of this conference was the establishment of the Council of Scientific and Industrial Research. After the independence of India, Dr. Mookerjee became the first Vice- President of the Council. He served CSIR from 1947 to 1950.

In addition to this conference, as a member of the Inter-University Board, Dr. Mookerjee kept guiding the Board from time to time with his developing ideas. Dr. Mookerjee was also a member of the 'Teaching Sub Committee'. Dr. Mookerjee attended the Board meeting held in Colombo in December 1945 and mesmerised everyone with his speech at the Colombo Town Hall. During the same visit, Dr. Mookerjee accepted the invitation of Ramakrishna Mission and Vivekananda Society, Colombo to be a speaker in the events organised by them.

The Quinquennial Conference of India Universities, Bombay, March 1939

International University Centre, Pondicherry (Now Known as Shri Aurobindo International Education Centre)

Dr. Mookerjee had a great reverence and honour for Shri Aurobindo and 'Mother'. The impression of Shri Aurobindo's thoughts and ideas can be easily seen in the personality of Dr. Mookerjee. As per 'Mother', Dr. Mookerjee was a master of a strong character and could have contributed significantly to fulfil the dream of Shri Aurobindo.

Remember that Aurobindo had great affection and reverence for France after India. His dream was to make an International University to be utilised as the venue of the permanent meeting of India and France, which would be located in Pondicherry. In this context, the discussion started in May 1947, but Nehru was initially hesitant to establish any such university. Many ministers iike K.M. Munshi, Pt. G.B. Pant, M.K. Vellodi, etc., tried to move this discussion forward. In the end, a conference was held under the direction of Dr. Mookerjee. This conference was held in Pondicherry on 24-25 April 1951. Dr. Mookerjee had already begun preparations for the success of the conference. He started sending letters of invitation to assemble distinctive influential people of the society in the conference. He wrote in the message that it was necessary to analyse the ideals of Shri Aurobindo in order to influence the progress of human civilisation properly. He further wrote in the letter that people should come to the 'Aurobindo Ashram' to see how it has developed into a living centre. He said that the objective of this conference was to establish an international university whose aim is to assist in the development of the intellectual, emotional, moral, spiritual level of the student and his entire personality.

Syama Prasad unveiling the plaque at Alipore Central Jail in the cell where Rishi Aurobindo was imprisoned – 17 August 1950

Syama Prasad unveiling the statue of Rishi Aurobindo at Aurobindo Bhavan Calcutta on – 17 August 1950

Dr. Mookerjee thought that this University should be unique just like Shantiniketan; there should be variation in the way of education.

While giving the presidential address on 24 April 1951, Dr. Mookerjee said that the coordinated system of ideas that emerged from the best efforts of human beings is contained in the philosophy of Shri Aurobindo. He said that we had lost our way of culture. Shri Aurobindo used to talk about the tripartite culture. The first aspect is thoughts, ideas, ambitions and spiritual desires; the other side is creative self-expression and appreciative aestheticism, intellectualism and imagination; the third aspect is functionality and external order.

Dr. Mookerjee said that philosophy and religion belong to the first aspect; Art, poetry, and literature are related to the second aspect; and society and politics are related to the third aspect. He said that because we have deviated from these sacred thoughts, it is the need of the hour to teach the eternal values of life in the university.

The Upanishads present coordination in 3 words—*'Shantam, Shubham, Advaitam'*. Shri Aurobindo has also explained this doctrine. Dr. Mookerjee said that the purpose of this conference is to start the era of the cultural renaissance of India and the world. Only internal freedom can establish a proper human order. This university will reincarnate new theosophy and will help us get out of the conflicts of malice and doubts.

At the concluding ceremony of the conference on 25 April Dr. Mookerjee said that the policy of the government should be to encourage such experiments. He said that this university would be presenting cultural coordination. With the efforts of Dr. Mookerjee and others, the bill to establish the university was passed.

A radio talk was presented by Dr. Mookerjee on 15 August 1950 in which he paid his tribute to Shri Aurobindo. He said that the spiritual light of Shri Aurobindo is of permanent importance not only in strengthening our culture but also for our character and actions. Dr. Mookerjee said, "It is clear that the song 'Vande Mataram' exercised a profound influence on his mind and gave his patriotism a transcendental spiritual character which transformed the valiant fighter for freedom into a recluse, then a yogi, a seer and a prophet."

Throughout the long period of our national suffering, We tried to understand the real meaning of our life. What is real life, ultimate reality, and how to attain divine perfection? Shri Aurobindo is the pillar and the prophet of patriotism, but not of narrow parochial type. He has taught us that patriotism is only a Milestone on the road to the Life divine. Shri Aurobindo is the philosopher-king who has given a new orientation to our culture and has made it clear that the answer to all the questions lies in the Indian culture.

Delhi School of Economics

Syama Prasad Mookerjee was one of the founding members of the Delhi School of Economics. All the founding members also donated 43,000 rupees donations to the Delhi School of Economics. Other main members were—Pandit Jawaharlal Nehru, Shri Krishnamchari etc. The first meeting of the founding members was held on 15 October 1952, when its director was Professor VKRV Rao. Professor Rao spoke to Dr. Mookerjee about the future of the institute. He told Dr. Mookerjee that the school would be working at the All India level, and he had no doubt that the association of Dr. Mookerjee with the school in the capacity of a founding member would give it a high strength and enable it to develop and expand its activities in the field of advanced economics studies and objective research in economic problems. After some time, Professor Rao became the Minister of Education of India. Delhi School of Economics is one of the country's specialised educational institutions. Amartya Sen has been a student of this renowned institution. The institutions thrive in association with generous mind scholars. Such an association gives a strong base to the organisations.

Asutosh College, Calcutta

(South Suburban College established by Sir Asutosh in the year 1916 was named Asutosh College after his death.)

Dr. Syama Prasad Mookerjee also took a keen interest in the work of Asutosh Mahavidyalaya. In the year 1934, he was made the President of the 'Governing Body' of the college. He remained in this post till his last time. In the year 1935, he got the new college building constructed. Dr. Mookerjee continued to pave the way for the students and teachers of the college while holding the post of President of the executive body of the college.

He was always ready to solve all kinds of problems for teachers. Despite being in Delhi, Dr. Mookerjee remained connected with Khagendra Nath Sen, Principal, Asutosh College, Jatin Mohan Majumdar, etc. through correspondence. In a letter on 13 June 1949, Dr. Mookerjee told Jatin Mohan Majumdar that he would reach Calcutta on the morning of 26 June. He requested him to call an executive meeting on 26 June and asked him to send a note regarding the financial position of the college. He also asked for the representations given by teachers.

The teacher association of Asutosh College showed their gratitude towards Dr. Mookerjee in words, "...we are proud of your association with the college which we have the privilege to serve and we hope you will inspire us to greater vigour by your active encouragement and display of sympathy."

In the year 1932, Dr. Mookerjee established a separate section for women at Asutosh College and named it 'Jogmaya Devi College'. In the year 1957, a different college was formed, which was called 'Asutosh College for Women', but after the demise of Lady Jogmaya, it was renamed Jogmaya Devi College.

Dr. Mookerjee wanted to provide various employment opportunities for the students that students should also study subjects like Commerce and trade. Syama Prasad College, founded by Dr. Syama Prasad Mookerjee, was established immediately after the end of World War II in 1945 at Kolkata. It was then named as Asutosh College of Commerce (evening section). This college has its genesis in Asutosh College and has primarily been designed to meet the growing demand for higher education in Commerce. This Evening Section was delinked from Asutosh College and acquired the status of a full-fledged independent college in 1958 with a separate Principal and separate management (i.e. Governing Body) under instruction from University Grants Commission and with the approval and affiliation of University of Calcutta. After the immature demise of Dr. Mookerjee, Calcutta University resolved to perpetuate the memory of Dr. Mookerjee by renaming the college founded by him as Syama Prasad College in 1962. The college is situated at 92, Syama Prasad Road, Kolkata.

Asutosh Mookerjee Memorial Institute, Bhawanipore

77, Asutosh Mookerjee Road, Bhawanipur, which witnessed the development of personalities like Sir Asutosh Mookerjee and Dr. Syama Prasad Mookerjee, gradually converted into an educational and research institution unannounced. The residence of eminent Vice Chancellors of Calcutta University has now been converted into a duly research institution. Many students come to this temple of knowledge with the desire to make their future golden. Dr. Reena Bhaduri, the granddaughter of Sir Asutosh Mookerjee, retired professor, Calcutta University, and Justice Chittosh Mukherjee take charge of this institute. On the second and third floor of this building, Asutosh College of Communication and Management of Bharatiya Vidya Bhavan had been established. Due to fund shortages now, this college has been shifted to some other building. It seems that the government of Bengal didn't pay attention to this great institution in the past years.

The institution was conceived at a commemorative meeting held on 25 May 1935 at Harish Park, Bhawanipur (on the occasion of Sir Asutosh's first death anniversary). Deshbandhu Chittaranjan Das, the then Mayor of Calcutta, chaired the meeting. Mahatma Gandhi also participated in this meeting, along with many dignitaries. Mahatma Gandhi had said in the memory of Sir Asutosh, 'I never got the privilege of meeting him, but while living in far-off South Africa, information about his great works kept getting received. I had heard with great joy and pride the account of his quarrel with the Viceroy (Lord Curzon), I feel very proud to remember how he had boldly favoured the interests of education in this country."

In this meeting, it was decided to build a hall and library in memory of Sir Asutosh. In 1927, the Asutosh Mookerjee Memorial Committee was established. For many years, the activities of this institute were conducted from the building of Asutosh College. In the year 1960, this institute was shifted to his ancestral residence, 77, Asutosh Mookerjee Road.

Asutosh Memorial Library was established in 1927 as a public library. Dr. Syama Prasad Mookerjee shifted the library on 1 September 1935 from 38-A Rusa Road (Presently Asutosh Mookerjee Road) to 92, Rusa Road (Presently Syama Prasad Mookerjee Road). The Cottage Library and Bhawanipur Institute were also added to this library in 1935. Presently, there are more than 10,000 books in this library. There is a vast reading room in the library.

Asutosh Memorial Hall (estd. in 1935), Syama Prasad Foundation (estd. In 1953), Rama Prasad Children Library (est. In 1984), and Shivatosh Mukherjee Science Centre (estd. in 1994) established under Asutosh Mookerjee Memorial Committee at the residence of Dr. Mookerjee. A research, writing and publishing unit has also been found here. This unit supports Asutosh Mukhopadhyay Museum, National Library, Asiatic Society, Kolkata and Nehru Memorial Museum and Library, New Delhi, as well as other institutions like Calcutta University, and Asutosh College.

The institute has also established an exhibition of paintings related to the life of Sir Asutosh and Dr. Syama Prasad Mookerjee for the general public at the ancestral residence of Dr. Mookerjee. More than 100 pictures taken by Uma Prasad Mookerjee on the Himalayas are also displayed here. In short, there is a lot of valuable information related to research and other educational and cultural purposes in Asutosh Mookerjee Memorial Institute.

Sir Asutosh College, Jadavpur, 1950

After partition, the education and culture of the refugees

who came from East Bengal were in deep crisis. 40 lakh Hindu refugees came from East Bengal to the land of West Bengal while sidestepping communal forces. Most people reached Calcutta because it was the focal point of education. The schools and colleges were full. The refugees established the National Welfare Association to rehabilitate themselves and their education. It aimed at protecting the educational and cultural rights of the people. Shri Gangadas Pal, a generous nobleman of the locality, donated his land to open the College in Jadavpur. Sir Asutosh College was established in Jadavpur. Dr. Syama Prasad Mookerjee was made the President of the executive body of Sir Asutosh College and other pre-existing educational institutions (Jadavpur Technical College, Indian Science Association, various high schools).

All India Lighthouse for the Blind

Dr. Mookerjee was the Vice President of the All India Lighthouse for the Blind. The Lighthouse was established in 1940-41. Currently, this institution also trains needy youth in education, vocational education, music, craftsmanship, etc.

Through the correspondence of Dr. Mookerjee, we came to know that at that time it was the only institution of its kind. This institution was used to spend on education and living of needy youth. To meet the expenses, the organisation had to resort to donations. Dr. Mookerjee used to talk to the eminent people of the society for this.

Dr. Mookerjee used to say that our future generations will never forgive us if we deprive even the needy of the light of education. Dr. Mookerjee wrote letters to Shri S.C. Roy (Aryasthan Insurance Company Limited), Surya Bose (Dhakeshwari Cotton Mills Limited), Chhoturam Harilal Ram Limited and Bahadur Kamaksha Narayan Singh, Maharaja of Hazaribagh regarding this.

Relation with Other Institutions

Dr. Mookerjee executed the responsibilities of the Institute as a member of the Executive Council of the Indian Association for the Cultivation of Science[20] (1948-53). In that period, Dr.

Saha was in the role of chairman of the council. Dr. Mookerjee was also a member of the Executive Council Committee of the following institutions: National Council of Education, Bengal; Vice President of CSIR; Banaras Hindu University;[21] Indian Statistical Institute Research Society, Jaipur; Trustee of All India Military, Arial, Naval Preparatory School and College Society; Member of All India Save the Children's Committee; and Bengal Religious Education Society. Dr. Mookerjee was also the chairman of the Swami Sachchidanand Smriti Samiti. Swami Sachchidananda[22] was a dedicated personage for society. After his death in 1944, Dr. Mookerjee pledged to fulfil his dream (establishing a Hospital for Sannyasis). He also supported the 'United Nations Committee on Teachers and Students'. Dr. Mookerjee appealed to the country to bring 'new changes' in the education sector from various educational and cultural forums.[23] He believed that a new education policy for youth and children should provide excellent service in the creation of a united India. He boosted the morale of the youth in his every speech given at the educational institutions. His addresses are the heritage of the country.

Apart from the scholars of Political Science, and Social Science, the scholars of Literature should also come forward to take up research on the speeches given by Dr. Mookerjee. The literary value of his lectures is profound. His language is powerful, and the impressions of English, Bengali, Sanskrit, and Hindi literature are visible in it.

Lok Sabha M.P., Prakash Veer Shastri wrote in one of his memoirs that when he invited him to Gurukul University to give a convocation speech, Dr. Mookerjee laughed saying, "Hey brother, the most beautiful and important convocation speech that the sages of Upanishads have given—*'Satyam vada; dharmam chara; svãdhyãyãn mã pramadaha'*—'Speak the truth. Abide by your dharma. Never be idle in your studies'. It is said there itself. What more can I say than this?" Seeing his exclusive allegiance to this ancient culture, Prakash Veer Shastri was surprised.[24] On 9 March 1947, Shankaracharya of Dwarka Peetha while blessing Dr. Mookerjee through a letter said that 'you are doing a great job of coordinating ancient Indian culture and modern education and knowledge'[25].

Dr. Mookerjee had given earnest thought towards life-long education, the interests of teachers and learners. He bestowed the sole wisdom of life to the future responsible citizens of the country. He proved to be a genuinely excellent academician. Dr. Mookerjee told the youth, "...success can never be achieved by any 'short-cut' process. You have to toil and work hard during this formative period of your career, and you will find that it will turn into a profitable investment. Whatever work you undertake, do it seriously, thoroughly and well, never leave it half-done or undone, never feel satisfied unless and until you have given it your very best. Cultivate the habits of discipline and toleration. Surrender not the points of view of your opponents. Remember that respect for and obedience to your superiors constitutes no sign of weakness in human character. Abandon everything false, sham and hypocritical. Forget not that labour and social service form the two fundamental principles of life in society. Contempt for labour and indulgence in luxury make a person a parasite and perpetuate national subjugation. Use all in your power to assist others by doing at least one good deed everyday, thus paving the way for the more important work of national reconstruction. Remember that the blessed work of helping the world forward does not wait to be done perfect men and you are fully equipped for this task. Form the spirit of love and charitable sympathy for your friends, neighbours and different communities, endeavouring to work together in righteousness and to co-operate to the best of your ability.

Pray, do not misunderstand me while I am speaking to you in this strain. I am addressing you as the future masters of your country's destiny, and it is the duty of each one of you to understand the position clearly and thoroughly. If you shoulder this responsibility in all earnestness and strive hard to restore our beloved country to its position of honour and freedom, the era of humiliation and hardship will cease, the glory of our race will be enhanced, and this glory will be yours. Let me hope and pray that under the fostering care of your college and university, under the influence of your home, you will train yourselves physically and morally, widen your intellectual activities and capacities, develop the spirit of bravery and perseverance, inculcate noble ideals and patriotism;—in short, mould yourselves into good citizens of a united and regenerated India."

Endnotes

1. Gurukul Convocation, 25 April 1943.
2. Ibid.
3. V-VII instalment; sr.no. 11 (Speeches by Dr. Mookerjee)
4. V-VII instalment; sr.no. 4 (Speeches by Dr. Mookerjee)
5. M.K. Gasndhi Papers(Pyarelal Collection) Subject file 27, 30, NMML
6. Educational Speeches, Calcutta University, convocation address, 1935, p. 13
7. Nagpur University Convocation, 5 December 1936
8. Under the leadership of Shri Narendra Modi, the present Prime Minister of India, Government of India established the *National War Memorial* on 25 February 2019 near India Gate, New Delhi, to honour the Indian Armed Forces. The memorial is spread over 40 acres of land..
9. The Asiatic Society was founded by civil servant Sir William Jones on 15 January 1784 in a meeting presided over by Sir William Jones, Justice of the Supreme Court of Judicature at Fort William at the Fort William in Calcutta, then capital of the British Raj, to enhance and further the cause of Oriental research. At the time of its foundation, this Society was named as 'Asiatick Society'. In 1825, the society dropped the antique *k* without any formal resolution and the Society was renamed as 'The Asiatic Society'. In 1832 the name was changed to 'The Asiatic Society of Bengal' and again in 1936 it was renamed as 'The Royal Asiatic Society of Bengal'. Finally, on 1 July 1951, the name of the society was changed to its present one. The Society is housed in a building at Park Street in Kolkata (Calcutta). The Society moved into this building during 1808. In 1823, the Medical and Physical Society of Calcutta was formed and all the meetings of this society were held in the Asiatic Society. (One

of the main activities of the Asiatic Society was to collect the old manuscripts of India. There was an enormous collection of Sanskrit manuscripts with the society. At present, the library of the Asiatic Society has a collection of about 117,000 books and 79,000 journals printed in almost all the major languages of the world. It has also a collection of 293 maps, microfiche of 48,000 works, microfilm of 3,87,003 pages, 182 paintings, 2,500 pamphlets and 2,150 photographs. The earliest printed book preserved in this library is Juli Firmici's *Astronomicorum Libri* published in 1499.[1] It has in its possession a large number of books printed in India in the late 18th and early 19th centuries. The library also possesses many rare and scarcely available books. The library has a rich collection of about 47,000 manuscripts in 26 scripts. The most notable amongst them are an illustrated manuscript of the *Qur'an*, a manuscript of the *Gulistan* text, and a manuscript of *Pa shah Nama* bearing the signature of Emperor Shahjahan. The number of journals in the possession of the library is about 80,000 at present.

10. Under the leadership of Sir Asutosh, the society was registered in 1915.
11. In 1851, the British archaeologist Sir Alexander Cunningham was excavating at the Ashokan Buddhist complex in Sanchi, near Bhopal, M.P., which dated to the 3rd century BCE. In the famous Third Stupa, he uncovered the bodily relics of Sariputra and Mahammoggallana. At approximately the same time, more relics of the two arahants were found in a stupa at Satadhara, about ten kilometers from Sanchi. The relics from both locations were taken to England and placed in the Victoria and Albert Museum,
12. II-IV instalment, Private Papers of Dr. Mookerjee Correspondence Nay Kinh Hoi, CHU-HOI PGVN.
13. Speeches by him, s.n.15, p.4
14. It was at the request of Dr. Mookerjee that Tagore established a relationship with the Calcutta University.
15. Speeches by him, p.7
16. Dr. Meghnad Saha Private Papers, I instalment (letter dated 11 December, 1947) NMML.
17. The Inter-University Board (later known as the Association of

Indian Universities) was established in 1925 to promote university activities, by sharing information and cooperation in the field of education, culture, sports and allied areas. The first attempt to formulate a national system of education in India came in 1944, with the Report of the Central Advisory Board of Education on Post War Educational Development in India, also known as the Sargeant Report. It recommended the formation of a University Grants Committee, which was formed in 1945 to oversee the work of the three Central Universities of Aligarh, Banaras and Delhi. In 1947, the Committee was entrusted with the responsibility of dealing with all the then existing Universities.

18. National Cadet Corps (special contribution of Pt. H N Kunjru, Col. G.G. Bevur, Pt. Nehru)
19. National Service Scheme (The contribution of Dr. Radhakrishnan, Pt. Nehru, C.D. Deshmukh, Khwaja Gulam Saiyyadan), established in 1969.
20. The oldest research institute of India, Sir C.V. Raman did his famous research 'Raman effect' in this institute..
21. I instalment, subject file 13.
22. Before sanyas, Dr. Devendranath Mukherji, Professor, Pharma Science, Cuttuck.
23. II-IV instalment, speeches, sr no. 20.
24. Prakashvir Shastri; *Kasmir ki Vedi Par*, p. 20.
25. Correspondence, Dr. Mookerjee, NMML, New Delhi.

□

8

The Relevance of Dr. Syama Prasad Mookerjee's Ideas on Education in the Contemporary World

"Through education, more than through anything else, we can attain these our cherished hopes and aspirations, and let us stand united to serve its sacred cause. I hope and pray that in the years to come, it may be given to us all in whose hands rest responsible powers, to leave aside disputes and differences, to put our shoulder to the wheel of progress and to help in inaugurating an era of constructive work."

—Dr. Syama Prasad Mookerjee

(Excerpt from the Calcutta University Convocation address on 5 March 1938)

"Education must spread and penetrate the poorest among us."

—Dr. Syama Prasad Mookerjee

(Excerpt from the Leaves of My Diary)

To ascertain the greatness of a leader perhaps, one of the best indicators can be the impact of his deeds beyond the geography he was born in. Another indicator can be the timelessness of his ideas that coax the world to work for a better future.

Blessed with the art of simple and immensely meaningful communication, Dr. Syama Prasad Mookerjee as we have already discussed was an academician par excellence who delineated the blueprint of the Indian education system and advocated his thoughts on education vociferously. Efforts were made to recast and give a fillip to the education system by the regime which assumed office after independence, ironically, with some deviations from what Dr. Mookerjee had envisaged. He thoroughly understood and discussed the problems plaguing the Indian education system under British rule. His stint as the Vice Chancellor of the Calcutta University equipped him with first-hand knowledge of all the dimensions of the Indian education system, including its challenges and above all its importance in the process of nation-building. In fact, he was one of the visionaries who could foresee what kind of education the country would require in times to come. He, therefore, not only ideated but also delineated an outline for an education system which was futuristic in approach and pragmatic still for the time he was to shape as an educationist.

Dr. Mookerjee relentlessly engaged himself in the dissemination of his ideas on the Indian education system. He utilised every given opportunity, both personal as well as professional, to propagate how education could be made a potent instrument to strike the much-needed changes in the Indian society. As Vice Chancellor of the very prestigious Calcutta University, Dr. Mookerjee was often invited to deliver convocation lectures and national and international seminars on education. In fact, his lectures on such academic occasions form the bulk of his ideas on education system. Apart from academic gatherings Dr. Mookerjee also used political platforms to promulgate his thoughts on what was required to address the challenges in education to turn it into a fertile soil for all-round development of the county which took much pride in its scholarly achievements of the past. It is interesting to note that even his personal diary marked a large number of entries on his thoughts on education. In fact, as Vice Chancellor, he was able not only to comprehend the limitations of contemporary education, but he also got the opportunity to place his reforming ideas on the anvil. And by doing this, he was simultaneously waging a battle against present lacunae and propounding an outline for the future of Indian education.

If we analyse his work as the Vice Chancellor of the Calcutta University and his writings and lectures we can easily understand a simple fact that his ideas on the development of Indian education were carrying the seeds for future. Even after more than three-quarters of a century his thoughts and works seem pioneering and relevant for the policy-makers of our times. His ideas can act as a guiding force for shaping the Indian education in the 21st century to make it an all-encompassing and enriching learning experience for the students and scholars. Perhaps this foresight and its resultant relevance in our times are the hallmarks of Dr. Syama Prasad Mookerjee's greatness not only as a political leader but also as an academician who provided seeds of his thoughts for the future of Indian education.

As we have already discussed in earlier chapters, the education in India under the colonial rule was intended to serve the British interests rather than aimed at the amelioration of the Indian people. Dr. Syama Prasad Mookerjee was well aware of this servile nature of education propagated by the British to create brown replicas of the white sahibs. Moreover, Dr. Mookerjee also understood the fact that a multifaceted transition in education was working silently. This was something which, if overlooked or not understood in its entirety, would lead to unprecedented backwardness of the education. This was bound to have an impact on the economic well being of the people who were already witnessing oppression and starvation at the hands of their colonial masters.

The transition which was affecting Indian education the most was the drive to bring the education under the nationalist banner as the freedom fighters rightly believed that the British had been tempering it for their own benefits. Noticeably, Syama Prasad Mookerjee during his formative years saw many institutions being founded by the nationalist leaders. Then there was an immense change in the education at the world level post-Industrial Revolution. The revolution changed the requirements of society on a large scale. The machines powered by steam and electricity needed new skill sets. This new milieu relegated the traditional subjects to a great extent while science and technology, and subjects which could prepare human resource in confirmation with the machines and tools of the rapidly growing industries grew by leaps and bounds. The machines needed a skilled workforce to handle them and maximise production. The shift in focus for all the countries was a must so as to keep pace with the new changes which became synonymous to economic growth in an ever-increasing competitive world. Unfortunately, India was in no position to assert her rightful needs as the imperialist policy-makers never intended to see India grow on its own as it would have had an adverse impact on their primary goal of amassing wealth avariciously even at the bare minimum cost of human welfare. Dr. Mookerjee's understanding of this multilayered transition led him to take a few steps, as the Vice Chancellor of Calcutta University, which were destined to prove pioneering and significant even after three-quarters of a century. He was a resolute administrator who could translate his ideas into actions.

Dr. Mookerjee was in favour of balancing the binaries of ancient and modern so far as education was concerned. He had an unwavering faith in India's time tested practices in education which continued across millennia. However, he was also in favour of bringing the changes to make education pertinent to the future of the country as he felt that without bringing required changes, education would become like stagnant water. Thus, for him, judicious assimilation of the past and the present practises was the solution through which the wisdom acquired through the toils of the times of yore could be preserved without compromising the benefits of new trends in education. Perhaps, this was the reason why he staunchly advocated that education should consist of the subjects dealing not only with literature, history, philosophy, etc. but also with subjects which could cater to the other fundamental requirements concerning the material well being of the countrymen.

Dr. Mookerjee's ideas of connecting Indian education with the employability has not only become the most sought after policy plank of almost all the recently formed Indian governments but also a major initiative to use the huge untapped human resource. He urged the University that "an employment bureau should be established not as a pure university body but also consisting of a representative of Government and of various commercial and industrial interests".[1]

A robust initiative in that direction has been taken up under the scheme known as the Skill India programme. What is being tried out now can be traced back to an outstanding initiative taken by Dr. Syama Prasad Mookerjee in the 30s of the last century. Under the guidance of Dr. Mookerjee, the Employment Bureau was founded in the Calcutta University with an objective to link education with employment. This pioneering step taken long ago was unprecedented and would have reaped far-reaching results in making education employment centric had there been a well-formulated policy in place. Sadly enough, the gulf between the two could not be bridged even after almost 8 decades when Dr. Mookerjee experimented with the very idea with considerable success. Whatever ground the policy-makers have covered so far can at best be termed as little with a lot more still to cover. This is true with the private institutions too barring a few as they struggle when it comes to the employability of their students. The education system has not yet been able to provide a proper structure for employment-related information, interview preparation for the students and a proper connection to the potential employers. As a result, the human resource loses a potential symbiotic relationship with employers even before it is formed. By establishing the Employment Bureau, Dr. Mookerjee was trying to emphasise the need to connect educational institutions with the industries so that both the stakeholders remain on the same page about their requirements from each other. To further understand this aspect by taking an empirical view around us today. Almost every major industrial and trade and commerce association like Federation of Indian Chambers of Commerce and Industry (FICCI) and the Confederation of Indian Industry (CII) has opined on the yawning gap between the education and adequate preparedness of the students for a job. Very recently, N.R. Narayan Murthy, the founder of the world's leading software company Infosys, has vociferously said that more than 70 per cent Indian graduates are unemployable for their human resource-related needs of various industries have changed and the existing curriculum is obsolete. And as we have said, the efforts of Dr. Mookerjee were aimed to address the same challenges in the 1930s. He was insisting on a long-lasting relationship between the academic institutions and the industries. Unfortunately, the policy-makers in the post-colonial era had neglected this facet of education for about half-a-century.

There was another twist in the tale of the colonial education system which attracted Dr. Syama Prasad Mookerjee's attention. This was the growing rate of unemployment in colonial India which was crumbling financially and otherwise under the snowballing defence expenditure. Although the number of newly founded educational institutions was not at all high that a limited number of pass outs from these colleges and universities were not getting employment. Dr. Mookerjee, realising his responsibility as an educationist, resorted to a novel initiative when he took up the mantle as the Vice Chancellor of the University. His initiative bore fruit in the form of Information and Employment Board that helped the students stay abreast with the employment opportunities and guide them to bag the jobs. This board was also conceived as a platform for the students and the potential employers from the world of trade, commerce and industries. This platform also became a stage for ideating the issue of creation of more employment opportunities for the unemployed youth. In other words, this was one of his outstanding initiatives aimed at bridging the gap between education and the industrial requirements of the country. The immediate and indicative result of this experiment of founding the Information and Employment Board was that in the very first year of its foundation, forty enrolled students were successful in getting employment.

However, a little progress could be made in this direction in post-Independence India save the last couple of decades, when the country has seen some conscious efforts on the part of the policy-makers to introduce changes in the education system. In fact, the leaders of the Indian industries have been voicing their concerns since long to update the pedagogy and curriculum so that the students are equipped with the right skill sets.

Dr. Mookerjee also believed that by setting up departments of new disciplines in new institutions and universities and imparting students the necessary training for employment, students could be polished efficiently in various tasks. He said that the capacity of students should be increased by giving training in technical and economic fields. According to him, this is the path through which youth can participate in the upliftment of the nation. Today, when India's population has crossed 1 billion, creating new employment opportunities and educating and training large people are enormous challenges. The establishment of new educational institutions cannot be found a solution to the problem just by opening new departments in the already run university, Dr. Mookerjee had foreseen the possibility of such dire circumstances appearing in the future.

According to Dr. Mookerjee, this problem cannot be successfully dealt with only through the youth trained by the new institutes and departments, for this, the Government and other official departments will have to keep constant efforts and change their policies from time to time.

Another crucial thing which we find very relevant is the Student Exchange Programme. Dr. Mookerjee made arrangements for students and teachers to go to foreign seats of learning in various countries in Europe, USA, South America and the Far East. These scholars were advised to take up subjects relating to technical and industrial training as well. Besides these distinguished scholars of the university were duly invited to deliver specialised courses. This very process is widely practised by the universities today, without which knowledge dissemination is impossible. Regarding the field of Medicine and Engineering, Dr. Mookerjee took the task of revising the entire syllabus and raise its standard and extend its scope and utility.

Dr. Mookerjee was undoubtedly an outstanding figure in the emergence of a national system of education in India. He can be acclaimed as one of those leaders who triggered the reorientation of a colonial system to a nationalistic system of education. He brought about several fundamental changes for which we stand on a firm footing today. First of all, Syama Prasad very rightfully felt the need for scientific and technological study and its bonding with the industrial sector of the country. He went on to inaugurate quite a few scientific-educational organisations, which have these influence felt, still today. One of the most significant steps he took was the introduction of the mother-tongue as a language in the core education system, without which mass education would not have been possible.

Apart from the ideas related to vocational and technical education, analysis of Dr. Mookerjee's views related to the promotion and dissemination of knowledge is also necessary here.

From 1 April 2010, the 'Right to Education' was added to our list of Fundamental Rights through the Parliamentary Act, but the story of the inclusion of fundamental components like education into the Fundamental Rights legally is a series of conflicts and ups and downs.

At the time of implementation of the Indian Constitution, the subject of fundamental importance like Education was not kept in the fundamental rights by the framers of the Constitution and placed it among the Directive Principles of State Policy. This situation was better than the education policy directed by the British in colonised India, but the time was not going to prove favourable in the coming years. With the increasing population and the lack of necessary economic support, the gap between education and the general population increased gradually due to policy oddities. The rate of admission in schools was worrisome; after admission, the dropout rate of the school started to become even more frightening. In the ever-increasing population of the country and changing economic environment, education should be expanded appropriately in every part of the nation. It is a well-known fact that the human resources of the country are essential in the primary tasks of the progress of a nation. Dr. Syama Prasad Mookerjee understood this very well. He kept insisting on the universal availability of education. He believed that education should be easily accessible to every citizen of the nation. He was also aware that it would be difficult for people to bear the expense of education. Hence, Dr. Mookerjee used to insist on providing education for free or at a low cost.

As a result of the continuous economic degradation of India in the form of a subjugated country, a large part of the country's population was struggling for the availability of food. In such a situation, education or any other subject could easily be placed in the category of luxury. The ideas related to simplifying the general public's access to education in these difficult circumstances demonstrate Dr. Mookerjee's strong will to promote Education. Not only this, his views confirm to be relevant in today's time. The strong foundation of decisions by the last few governments such as the *'Sarva Shiksha Abhiyan'*, the National Secondary education Campaign and the Primary Education in the list of Fundamental Rights of the Constitution are visible in the education-related suggestions of Dr. Syama Prasad Mookerjee.

Dr. Mookerjee believed that with more significant publicity of education, people get opportunities to increase their abilities qualitatively. Quality education is the most accurate response to all social, religious and regional disparities.

The discussion of Dr. Syama Prasad Mookerjee's educational ideas being relevant at present is incomplete without the *'Sarva Shiksha Abhiyan'* approved by the Atal Bihari Vajpayee government and the National Curriculum Framework 2005 consequently. *'Sarva Shiksha Abhiyan'* has emerged in front of us as a vital and ambitious program given India's simple level of literacy. It is to be noted here that the then Prime Minister Shri Atal Bihari Vajpayee, the founder of *'Sarva Shiksha Abhiyan'*, run by the Government of India in 2000-2001, was one of the closest persons as his partner in the last years of the life of Dr. Syama Prasad Mookerjee. The resemblance between Dr. Mookerjee and Atal Bihari Vajpayee can be seen in the *'Sarva Shiksha Abhiyan'* at the level of educational ideas. The main objective of *'Sarva Shiksha Abhiyan'* gives a clear glimpse of the views expressed by Dr. Syama Prasad Mookerjee on the reform of education.

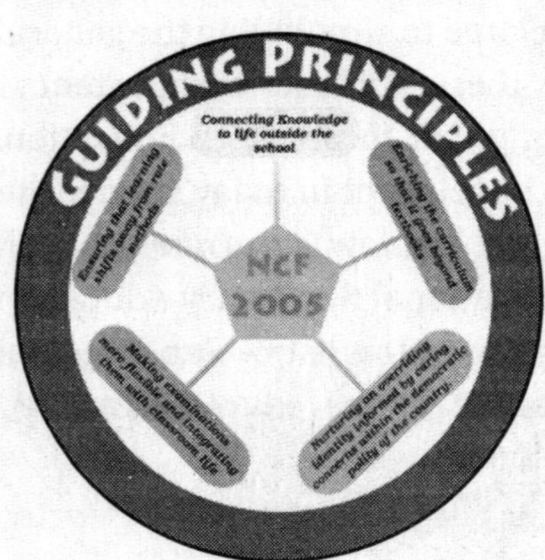

Dr. Syama Prasad Mookerjee as Vice Chancellor of Calcutta University called for the restructuring of school education. The apparent reason behind doing this was that the University could not produce good results on a weak foundation of primary and secondary education.

As a result, Dr. Mookerjee was emphasising on the spread of quality accessible education at all sections of society at least cost. Precisely this objective is the focal point of *'Sarva Shiksha Abhiyan'*. The *'Sarva Shiksha Abhiyan'* also presents a framework for the implementation of the dissemination of quality education with a specific time frame for universal elementary education. Another important objective of *'Sarva Shiksha Abhiyan'* is to promote the spirit of social harmony through education, and Dr. Syama Prasad Mookerjee presented this idea in his statement. According to him, education is a temple that provides equal opportunity for students of all religions, classes, *varnas* to study and grow in life.

He condemned the propagators who attacked the roots of the ideal of 'service and equality' and recommended to provide Education for all to form a society on the idea of equality.

Dr. Syama Prasad Mookerjee, a strong advocate of all-round reform in education, believed that India's education system should develop on the principle of uniformity.

One of the main difficulties in the way of spreading educational programmes in today's India is the acute shortage of trained teachers, which has resulted in the dreaded situation of compromising the quality of education. In the last few years, it has been the effort of the Government of India to accept this challenge and make efforts to deal with it. Dr. Syama Prasad Mookerjee was speaking very loudly in the 1930s on this burning problem of 21st-century education. Dr. Mookerjee was not only talking about the educational quality training of teachers, but was also clearly expressing his views that an ideal teacher should be compassionate towards the student and understand all their problems. Moreover, if our education system can encourage such teachers, then the education institute will be able to bring forth such students who will be skilled and bring out the talent inside them ultimately. Only such students will become capable and responsible citizens of the country.

We can see the views of Dr. Mookerjee, as mentioned earlier in the education schemes currently being formulated. In 2005, in the

National Curriculum Framework, the student's mental strength, as well as physical strength, had been discussed. Dr. Mookerjee in his address at the convocation ceremony of the University of Calcutta on 2 March 1935 (which was Dr. Mookerjee's first occasion to address any convocation), "What is Education worth if our youth, in general, are physically weak or unfit, unable to stand the stress and strain of modern life? What is Education worth if we cannot turn them into men physically strong and well-equipped as they should be intellectually sane and robust?"

To achieve this objective, Dr. Mookerjee was providing medical facilities to the students as well as arranging physical education for them based on sports and the new scientific method, so that the disease of disability could be eradicated.

After the end of the British rule in 1947, the leading leaders and political thinkers of Indian independence paved the way for democracy for independent India. It is worth noting here that at that time all major democratic nations of the world were governed by this governing system through large groups of literate citizens. Unlike these nations, Indian democracy was the story of a long struggle of slavery. Among the many challenges before the new nation, a large percentage of citizens was not literate. How they would be able to understand the meaning of democratic system properly and how they would use this system suitably for their interests? The apprehensions surrounded almost all scholars. In fact, it was for this reason that one of the points of the First Five-Year Plan (started in 1951) by the Government of India was to make literate even those citizens who for some reason were left out of the purview of school and higher education and by the beginning of the 21st century important and ambitious schemes like 'Adult Education Campaign' and *'Saakshar Bharat'* were also done to make a large percentage of Indian people literate.

Dr. Syama Prasad Mookerjee was quite vocal on the matter of opening the doors of education even for the adult citizens in the subjugated India; while the British Government was hell-bent on narrowing the spectrum of education by reducing the number of educational insitituions. The British Government was not giving education in India to benefit Indian citizens, but it was trying to build an army of obedient employees for their Government. In such a situation, the idea of educating adult illiterates by Dr. Mookerjee was ahead of his time. According to Dr. Mookerjee, "We strongly feel that the door of the University should be thrown open wider still so that it might elevate the nation and rouse the self-respect of the people of this land. The influence of the University in this democratic age cannot safely be limited to the period of youth but must include systematic and organised effort for the education of adults."[2]

These views of Dr. Mookerjee seem even more contemporary in today's perspective. According to Dr. Mookerjee, along with the spread of general education, expansion in adult education would be seen as to literate the ideological power of common people.

In the recent years, a great scheme implemented by the Central Board of Secondary Education with a sense of proper development of students at the centre is Continuous and Comprehensive Education (CCE). One of the essential reasons for implementing this system is to motivate students to understand the syllabus rather than rote learning.

Dr. Mookerjee did not find it appropriate to memorise the subject matter repeatedly or in other words, to make the student a '*rattu tota*', and that is why he continued to discuss the practicality of the course. According to Dr. Mookerjee, the 'Cram book spirit' impedes the overall development of the students' intellect. Pressing the burden of books on the student cannot be called development. What is the purpose of such knowledge of books which is not practical? The ability of thinking should be developed in the students.

Dr. Mookerjee was in favour of the all-round development of

the student. For students, sports, cultural activities, crafts, etc. are equally important subjects as academics. Albert Einstein's says, "Education is not about learning facts but thinking about ideas." People like Dr. Mookerjee and Einstein always believed in learning beyond facts and concentrate more on ideas.

Along with the appropriate significant changes in the policies of education, what Dr. Mookerjee wanted to emphasise was the revival of Indian culture and civilisation through the Sanskrit language. The time has come when his thoughts should be given importance. Many such gems are hidden in the womb of Sanskrit, which has the potential to lead India to the pinnacle of success. In his diary, he had revealed that he is more concerned not for politics but education policy:

"I have not been able to decide on any future course of action. I do not want to get involved in political factionalism. It can serve no purpose. I am sick and tired of all the disputes and quarrels. I will try to do something that will give me peace. I do not aspire for glory anymore, but I have the desire to do something constructive. I do not have the resources to enable me to do my duty to my family and still have enough left to give my dreams a concrete shape. I wish I could build an organisation which would train at least twenty-five people every year, who could pledge their lives for the service of society. Where are the noble workers who could bravely take on the challenge of nation-building? The country cannot be redeemed by political wranglings. My organisation would be a centre for the study of Sanskrit; not merely to learn the language, but to explore the vast resource of knowledge enshrined in it and spread it to the people and the world at large. Whatever is of abiding value in our culture is preserved in Sanskrit—which is still inaccessible to the people. The erudite English and German scholars tried to kindle this lamp of wisdom for us, but we, in our eagerness to imbibe Western education, shied away from appreciating our own culture. What a shame! This nation can never come into its own if its search from identity is not founded on its own culture."[3]

In the education policy that is being prepared at present,

if any co-ordination of Science and Sanskrit syllabus is brought forth, then it seems to us that it will help in accelerating the development journey of India. It seems inevitable to study the vast scientific literature available in Sanskrit. By doing this, India's education strategist will fulfil the dream of Dr. Mookerjee and proffer a priceless gift to India. Education Policy should be such that in which education should be made available to the most disadvantaged person; the light of education should reach every corner of India. If the flag of the higher education hoisted on the sound foundation of primary and secondary education, it would spread the message in the whole world that India was the *Vishwa Guru* and will remain the *Vishwa Guru*.

Endnotes

1. V-VII Instalment, Speeches by him, S. No. 6, p.4
2. Dr. Sarvepalli Radhakrishnan, ed., Educational Speeches of Dr. Syama Prasad Mookerjee, p.15
3. Dr. Syama Prasad Mookerjee: 27 January, 1946; Leaves from a Diary; P.165

□

9
Epilogue

After the arrival of the British in India, the traditional Indian education system was facing a multi-faceted transition.The English colony had deep roots in India in the nineteenth century, politically and economically. Now there was an attempt to confine the settlement with the robust chains, that is, mental hegemony. Declaring Indian *sanskaras* and education as second-class and making black-skinned British with the promotion of English education and ensuring long suzerainty over the colony was the implication of the new education policy. In such a situation, a group of scholars like Dr. Syama Prasad Mookerjee were able to understand the intent of the education policy of the British properly and were using their arguments against it. For this, it was necessary to understand the characteristics and shortcomings of both the Indian education system and the English education. Dr. Mookerjee's understanding of it was terrific. He was able to understand the limitations and potential of ancient educational traditions of India and the latest requirements of education in their entirety. The blueprint that he had prepared for the future of Indian education should be apparent and precise according to the needs of the time. Giving clear evidence of being an ideal thinker, Dr. Mookerjee was not only discussing and analysing problems prevailing in education, but was also making efforts in that direction along with presenting suggestions to solve problems.

While addressing Nagpur University, Dr. Mookerjee said that education is not static. It must always be closely related to the life of the people. Otherwise, it becomes stagnant and soulless, and instead of uplifting society tends to retard progress. The modern Indian scholar must have the training and the vision to connect our ancient history and civilisation with our present needs and condition and to suggest rules of conduct and formulate the outlook on life which the Indian society of today can worthily accept. He believed that ideas suited to the traditions of a country should enrich the education of that country. Dr. Mookerjee was continuously in favour of incorporating the high ideals of Indian culture and reasonable knowledge of the West in Indian education policy. Coordination of the best ideas of Indian culture, tradition, heritage, and western knowledge is significant in an educated youth.

Dr. Mookerjee's insistence on making the mother-tongue a medium of instruction ensured that he was well aware of the sufferings of the subject admissibility of students. At that point, educated Indians were only 10%, broadly because a foreign language was the medium of education. Due to the Swadeshi movement at the beginning of the twentieth century, the people started denouncing the westernisation of education. A lot of English schools were established by the late 19th and early 20th centuries. The gap between the educated English community and the general public was increasing. The average students used to pass the examination by rote learning. The understanding of subjects was not developing in the students. The attempt to teach through mother-tongue was made in 1840 in the Tatvabodhini Pathshala, established by Devendranath Thakur. Bankim Chandra was also expressing his concerns about the language through his literature. Rabindranath Thakur led the supporters of the mother-tongue. Mohandas Karamchand Gandhi was also discussing the importance of mother-tongue in imparting education.

The National Education Movement of the Swadeshi era of Bengal accepted the need for making Bengali a medium of education. However, the journey to implement this was yet to be itinerated. With the efforts of Sir Asutosh Mookerjee, Bengali got a place as a subject in the university curriculum. His talented son, who won a gold medal in B.A. English (Hons.), immediately decided that he would do M.A. in Bengali language. Syama Prasad, who was growing up during the Swadeshi movement, was witnessing the ill-treatment of the Britishers towards Indian languages. He observed other severe challenges in the field of education. As the custodian of Indian culture and civilisation, Dr. Mookerjee restored the pride of the regional languages of India. He made the mother-tongue the medium of teaching and examination so that more and more Indians might take education. His residence was a concourse of Indian and Western education system. Various streams of academic thoughts used to gather there. Syama Prasad's life was progressively strengthening as he was witnessing the exchange of ideas of education sector veterans at his residence 77, Rusa Marg. When he was a teenager, he took the role of assistant of his great educationist father. The father's last sermon for his son was that he should be ready to bring revolutionary changes in the education sector because the land of India was in great need of his services.

Dr. Mookerjee linked education to India's independence, integrity, improvement and necessities. According to Sir Asutosh, the last war of independence of India was to be influenced by Indian education. Dr. Mookerjee introduced new practises in the field of education. One type of education was not suitable for all people. He reiterated the need for reconstitution of the former education system on three things—adequate funding, expansion of education, and full autonomy for educational institutions.

If it is said that receiving an education at that time was like a luxury, then there would be no exaggeration, because the British government did not grant sufficient financial aid for education. Though the government used to spend money on English schools so that Macaulay's followers could be born there and they get clerks for their work. The government wanted to limit the expansion of education for obvious reasons so that farmers could learn nothing more than becoming a good farmer. The government felt that university education is the main reason for unemployment. So, the British Government wanted to keep it repressed. Curriculum subjects were also limited, and education was not accessible to the general public. Not everyone was able to read in English medium schools. The government wanted to increase check over education. Efforts were being made to destroy the autonomy of the education sector completely.

Just at the age of 23, Dr. Mookerjee started discussing all these essential points in the Senate and Syndicate of Calcutta University. There was a confluence of high intellectualism with youthful energy. At the same time, he started raising issues like recognising the mother-tongue and incorporating army training into the curriculum for the youth. Soon after becoming the Vice Chancellor, he made the mother-tongue the medium of education and training. The mother-tongue helped in spreading education. Now it was set to reach the masses. Dr. Mookerjee gave rapid pace to the works like preparing textbooks and vocabulary in the mother-tongue. He believed that all students should have practical knowledge of Hindi and English along with the knowledge of their native language. Sanskrit should not be neglected. It is not only the source of Indian languages but also of our cultural heritage. Dr. Mookerjee took the responsibility of preserving Sanskrit, Pali, Prakrit, Persian languages along with the development of indigenous languages. At that time, there was a section of people who wanted to adopt the western education system.

On the other hand, some people were in favour of complete denial of the Occidental system. They wanted the old school system of 'Tolls' and 'Maktab'. However, even the orthodox people generally understood the importance of vocational education and began to accept that industrial training should be given in a modern way.

Dr. Mookerjee combined the focal points of Indian culture and civilisation with the most suitable aspects of western education in the reconstruction of education. While on the one hand, it gave impetus to the development of languages; on the other hand, English and other foreign languages were also encouraged. The chief aim was that students should get proper knowledge of the whole world. He made arrangements to send students abroad to study the subjects which were not available in Indian Universities.

The departments of Sanskrit, Pali, and Prakrit languages were given importance, while on the other hand, modern subjects like Radio, Commerce, Management, Soil Science, Agricultural Science, Geography, History, etc., were added to the university curriculum. The mother-tongue was made the medium of study not only at the primary and secondary level but also at a higher level. Mother-tongue was recommended as a medium of education for other Indian universities as well at the conference of the Inter-University Board. He eliminated the maximum age limit for entrance to the university courses intending to educate more and more people.

The communal policy of 'divide and rule' adopted by the British rulers after the great uprising of 1857 was also taking hold of educational institutions. Dr. Mookerjee was firmly against the communalism in education. He said that the temple of education is open to students of all religions, classes, colour and sects. Any religion or creed should not influence the character of education. Gandhiji recommended this form of education in the Wardha Scheme. Gandhiji was of the view that the educational institutions should keep religious education outside, but they can teach the highest and best ideas of all religions to the students. Dr. Mookerjee said pointedly in the assembly that "I will never allow communalisation of education". He wanted to make educational institutions the establishment of free and progressive ideas, where people of all religions, sects, colour and classes are duty-bound to develop education in an atmosphere of cooperation and goodwill. He strongly opposed the 'Secondary Education Bill', which was communal in nature and introduced in the Bengal Legislative Assembly. He prevented it from becoming law. Due to this bill, he had entered politics wholly by giving his 'scholastic solitude'. Mahatma Gandhi welcomed his entry into politics. In the eyes of Gandhiji, Dr. Mookerjee was a priceless asset of India, who had the power to speak on communal issues. He believed in social harmony but was not a conservative. Dr. Sarvepalli Radhakrishnan described his spiritual vision as liberal and broad-minded.

According to Dr. Mookerjee, a promoter of Indian values, '*aham*' is the root cause of sorrows. He always sought happiness in 'service', not in materiality. His goal was clear from his student life—'to serve'. He believed that we should have full dedication towards God, only then a man will get inner strength, and he will be able to take proper measures to achieve 'happiness and peace'. Dr. Mookerjee's life philosophy was coordinative, taking everyone along. He embodied the sense of 'service' of each community in his 'philosophy'. Rabindranath Tagore said the same—"I slept and dreamt that life was a joy. I awoke and saw that life was service. I acted and behold; service was a joy."

This is the philosophy of Vedanta, mutual relation of 'service and bliss'. Bliss is God Himself and to achieve Him; service is the standard belief. Stalwarts like Shri Aurobindo, Acharya Vinoba Bhave, Swami Ramakrishna Paramahamsa, Swami Vivekananda, Mahatma Gandhi revived these Indian ideals. Dr. Mookerjee's religious service was magnificent. He taught "सेवा अस्माकं धर्मः" (Service is my creed) to the future masters of India by presenting the ideal of his own life. He was giving an excellent example of service to the nation through the promotion of education.

Dr. Mookerjee was a staunch opponent of making educational institutions a political arena. He believed that the student can be influenced by any opinion and can also have an independent ideology, but as long as he is getting education, he should focus his attention on education with concentration, so as to enter political life in future, he could gain the ability to present his ideas in a more robust way. At present, his views seem relevant when we can see the efforts made to make educational institutions the platform of politics. It is worth mentioning that how prudent Dr. Mookerjee's thinking was. His predictions seem to be very accurate.

While revealing his education philosophy, Dr. Mookerjee also had an in-depth discussion on the relationship between teacher and learner. He believed that the teacher and students' relationship should be like father and son. Rabindranath's opinion used to say the same. The close personal relationship of *Guru-Shishya* was an ideal thing in his eyes. Dr. Mookerjee believed that the teacher should also play the role of a counsellor for the student. A teacher should discuss the problems of the political and social life of the country along with the syllabus in the classroom. The teacher must show the right path to the student. He urged that the ratio of students to teachers should be reduced. If there are abundant students stuck in the lectures, the teacher will not be able to give them his best. He, therefore, favoured a fair percentage of the availability of teachers over students and also promoted a 'tutorial system' to solve this problem. At present, almost all universities have adopted this system. Dr. Mookerjee wanted that if a student had a personal problem, then he could also put it in front of his teacher so that the student would not suffer from any frustration and could also solve the problem and avoid taking any antisocial steps. He used to keep a close watch on meeting the smallest requirements of the students.

For this reason, subjects which seemed secondary to others also attracted him. He opined that a Central Bureau should be set up for the benefit of the students, which would focus on the health and character development of the students. He favoured creating common rooms and unions for the students. His idea was that students should be allowed to exchange their ideology with one another freely.

Dr. Mookerjee considered 'healthy and active' students important for independent India. He started 'military training' in colleges and universities and established 'physical education' as a compulsory subject in schools. They wanted military training to be attached to the curriculum as an essential subject in all colleges. He also urged that the students must compulsorily do social work for some time before attaining graduation. The National Service Scheme is a by-product of his ideas, which many enlightened people understood and embodied his thinking.

While Dr. Mookerjee was sensitive to the needs of students, the problems of the 'teacher community' were also not unknown to him. They knew that the teacher is the pivot of the 'educational process'. Therefore, the administration must provide him with a strong foundation. He started 'teacher training courses'. With the advent of various new subjects in the syllabus, teachers also required 'refresher courses'. He also stressed the 'exchange programme of university and college teachers' so that it could benefit the students at postgraduate level. He also favoured conducting various seminars, workshops for teachers. He believed that from time to time, university teachers should keep lecturing on their field of interest. Teachers have to become lecturers of Indian heritage by becoming rich in learning and character. He said that the teachers should be trained and reliable because they have to be the creator of true, brave, honest and patriotic, leader and worker, man and woman. He raised the issue of giving proper pay scale, facilities and freedom to teachers in the Bengal Legislative Assembly. He was in favour of giving due respect to teachers.

In all teacher organisations, he gave his views on autonomous and independent education. He believed that the three levels of education—elementary, secondary and higher education—should be developed independently. It should be clear that the three should not violate each other's interests. Education should be cheap and accessible to the common man; it is a basic need, not a luxury. He considered the means spent on learning to be spent on nation-building. He urged the government to provide monetary funds more generously for education.

Dr. Mookerjee viewed the reconstruction of education in the context of nation-building. He made it clear that the problem of education cannot be solved until it is completely freed from foreign influence and handed over to the government of a nation. Without proper education, we cannot achieve freedom, and without freedom, we cannot rebuild our education system according to the needs of the country. Addressing the universities, he said that they should build such youth who are capable of meeting the challenges of creating a new India. While presenting his model of education, he said, "Our ideal is to make the widest provision for a sound liberal education, and vocational and technical training, always remembering that no nation can achieve greatness by turning its youth into a mere machine-made product, with nothing but a material end in view."

Consigned to flame at Shahnagar Burning Ghat (Kewrahtala) on 24 June 1953

Dr. Mookerjee was an outstanding and exceptional educationist. His thinking was far-reaching and, at present, the relevance of his ideas puts him in the category of immortal figures. Just at the age of 52, on 23 June 1953, while fighting for India's integrity and uprightness, his death in Srinagar under unfortunate and mysterious circumstances was an irreparable loss to India.[1] The unprecedented inspiration that Dr. Syama Prasad Mookerjee has provided to teachers and learners through his life and teachings is our legacy, which cherishes topical values in itself, which every country needs.

Syama Prasad with mother Lady Jagmaya Debi, 1947

I am not dead
I have just slept in mother's lap
I will wake up like the sun in the east
Just recognise me
Those who live only for themselves
Die
We descend like avatars
Behold, I fly in the clouds
Just recognise me
I am not gone

I am in people's mind
From Himalaya to the Indian Ocean
In the dreams of the people
In the bottom of the soul
Just recognise me
I am not wiped out
I laugh in flowers and buds
I am running like a gleam
In the streets of the starry race
I have become a wind
In the jungle of the valley
Just recognise me
I am not extinguished
I burn in the youth
I blow the bugle
In the Army's hustle[2]

Endnotes

1. Lady Jogmaya kept requesting Pandit Nehru to set up an inquiry commission to find out the cause of her son's death, but even after her appeal and request, no steps were taken by the then Government of India to investigate his death.
2. Translation of Bharat Bhushan's poem (done by authors) from *'Mere Chuninda Geet'* (Amarsatya Prakashan; 2009, p.238).

□

Appendix-I

Correspondence with Netaji Subhash Chandra Bose

To
Syama Prasad Mookerjee, Esqr., M.A.,
Charlemont, Darjeeling.

Dear Sir,

With reference to your telephone message informing the proposed date and hour of an interview with Mr. Subhash Chandra Bose for an hour as permitted by the Government, I write to inform you that the Officer-in-Charge, Kurseong P.S. will remain present at Kurseong Railway station on 11.6.36 at 3.30 P.M. to accompany you up to Giddhapahar.

The interview should take place in the presence of the Office-in-Charge, Kurseong P.S. for one hour only on 11.6.36 at 4 P.M. as fixed by you.

Yours faithfully,
(Sd.) Superintendent of Police,
Darjeeling.

c/o The Superintendent of Police
Darjeeling.

17.7.36

My dear Syama Prasad Babu,

I was very glad to receive your letter of 27th June, together with a list of the University Publications. I am enclosing herewith a list of the books I would like to have.

Dr. Dinesh Sen's *'Brihat Banga'* arrived here the other day. Many thanks.

I am keeping the typed list of the University publications with me for the present, for future use.

I hope you are now back from Banglore and all of you are doing well.

It is rotten weather here.

Encls.:

A list of university publications.

Yours affectionately,

(Sd.) Subhash C. Bose

Syama Prasad Mookerjee, Esq.

Calcutta.

Correspondence with Rabindranath Tagore

Senate House
Calcutta.
16th January, 1936

Dear Dr. Tagore

It has been proposed that the University should invite some eminent persons to deliver a short address at the ensuing Convocation which will be held on 22 February 1936. It is the unanimous wish of the members of the Syndicate and also of His Excellency the Chancellor that you should be invited to deliver this address. I shall only add that if you will kindly agree to do so, it will not only give the University a sense of satisfaction and honour but will also be greatly appreciated by the entire student community of Bengal.

I know the present state of your health is anything but satisfactory. But the address need not be a long one. You need not speak for more than 20 minutes. It will be an address mainly to students of the University who will feel inspired by your presence at this important annual function of the University.

I shall be obliged if you will kindly let me have an early reply signifying your acceptance of the proposal.

Yours sincerely
Sd.
Syama Prasad Mookerjee

17 January, 1936

Ref. D.O. No. 450

My dear Syama Prasad,

I feel grateful for the honour you have done me by asking me to deliver the Convocation address this year, but unfortunately, I shall not be in Calcutta then. As I am leaving on the 9th February for a long tour in Delhi and the north. In the circumstances I have to deny myself the pleasure of accepting the invitation, you have so very kindly accorded to me on behalf of the university.

Yours sincerely,
(Sd.) Rabindranath Tagore

14 November 1936

Ref. D.O. No. 707 of 11th November

My Dear Syama Prasad,

I appreciate very much your kindness in thinking of me again in connection with Convocation address at the university and I feel I cannot deny you this time. But, I would accept the honour only on a special condition.

You know of my life's great desire of seeing our language firmly and finally established as the medium of instruction in the University. Your great father started the movement, and perhaps it will be given to you to complete his noble task. If you are going to break a tradition by asking me, an outsider, to address the convocation, you will have to break yet another convention and permit to address in Bengali. If the University would accede to this, I shall gladly take the responsibility, even though the engagement will mean a great physical strain.

As regards the University marching song, I shall like to discuss the matter with you when I meet you next. In the meantime, I shall try to do something for you in the latter.

Yours affectionately,

(Sd.) Rabindranath Tagore

Sj. Syama Prasad Mookerjee.

Senate House
Calcutta.

17 December, 1936
D.O. No. 730
Dear Dr. Tagore

I am sorry for the delay in replying to your very kind letter, agreeing to deliver the next Convocation Address I was absent from Calcutta on several occasions during the last few weeks.

The University can certainly have no objection to your delivering the address in Bengali. There is however one difficulty which you will no doubt consider. We shall have among the members of the audience many who do not know Bengali. There will be such people among members of the Senate, including His Excellency, Principals of colleges, guests and also students. If you finally decide to deliver your address in Bengali and we shall abide by the noise which you may make, it will be desirable to have the English rendering of the address beforehand so that it may be printed and placed in the hands of those who do not know Bengali. Kindly consider this matter and let me know how you finally decide. We shall be glad to print the address in the University press according to your directions. The Convocation will be held on 13th February and I shall be grateful if a copy of the address including the English translation, if you speak in Bengali, is sent to me confidentially about three weeks before that date.

I wonder if any progress has been made with regard to the composition of the marching song. When will you be coming to Calcutta next time?

Yours sincerely
(Sd.) Syama Prasad Mookerjee

Correspondence with Dr. Meghnad Saha

Madhupur
28.10.1936

My dear Dr. Saha,

Welcome book home! I any received your letter from the Steamer and also the one from Allahabad. I hope you had a fully successful four.

I shall return to Calcutta after 8 or 10 days. I am leaving this place tomorrow and shall stay a few days at Banaras and Hazaribagh, I shall have to leave for Banglore on 13th Nov, at the latest.

There have been great developments at Banglore, and I do not know what the govt. of India intends to do. We shall discuss these trips when we meet. Pl. let me know at my Calcutta address when you propose to visit Calcutta.

It will be a great pity science and culture has to be discontinued for want of funds and Bengali enterprise. We must devise a way out of this possibility.

I hope you are keeping fit.

Yours sincerely
(Sd.) Syama Prasad Mookerjee

11 December, 1947

My dear Dr. Mookerjee,

I am preparing my report on Atomic Energy. I shall send a copy to you.

Many thanks for having kindly arranged my passage for return and having given me facilities to visit different countries.

You are probably aware of how cramped we are in University College of Science for space.

Kindly contact on a higher level and get the release-order (of building which was Sci. College building, Air training corps put up the building under lock and key) issued.

Yours Sincerely

(Sd.) M.N. Saha

Translation of a letter written in Bengali by poet Kazi Nazrul Islam to Dr. Syama Prasad Mookerjee, which speaks for the great respect the famous poet had for Dr. Mookerjee as a true nationalist and the country's foremost leader.

Madhupur
17.7.42

Most Respected Sir,

Please accept my most respectful salutations. After coming to Madhupur, I am feeling considerable relief and relaxation. My headache has considerably lessened. Numbness of my tongue has also slightly abated. Had you not so promptly arranged this change for me, I would have perhaps died prematurely, like poet Madhusudan, in a hospital. My wife is stricken with paralysis and is completely bedridden for nearly five years. I have brought her here with great difficulty. I had to incur a debt of about seven thousand rupees to meet her medical expenses which still remains outstanding. I had to borrow the money mainly from Marwaris and Kabuliwalas. When Haq Saheb came to me and lamented that "Mussalman youths are preventing me from coming out of my house" and pleaded, "please save me", I then pacified the leaders of the students and youths belonging to Muslim League. Thereafter, I appealed to all the Muslim members of the legislative assembly. Seventy-four members agreed to extend support to Haq Saheb.

Shortly before I accepted the editorship of 'Nava Yug' I was offered Music Directorship in a film and I had asked for seven thousand rupees contract. I was then assured by Haq Saheb and many of his Hindu and Muslim supporters that they would repay my debts. Relying upon this assurance I then cancelled the contract as the music director in the film. Later on, when even after two/ three months, I did not receive the promised sum, I entreated Haq Saheb, "Please arrange a loan for me from a bank on low interest and deduct half of my salary every month till the loan is repaid." Haq Saheb was pleased and said, "everything will be arranged within fifteen days." Thereafter, further seven months passed dilly-dallying. His supporters also remained indifferent. Even after one lakh rupees were sanctioned for augmenting Hindu-Muslim Unity and Haq Saheb received this amount, even he did nothing to help me. You are aware, what Haq Saheb stated in the secretariat in your presence, 'Kazi's' debt has to be repaid." You also assured me saying, "this will be done." I replied that I would now be able to work with peace of mind. You are aware that through my numerous poems, songs and other literary compositions, I have appealed to my countrymen for Hindu-Muslim Unity. My songs are widely sung in various villages, towns, cities and countryside in Bengal. I have tried to keep together the students and young men of Bengal, belonging to both Hindu and Muslim communities. If the Haq Ministry falls, this will be because of the Coalition Ministry. The other day Haq Saheb asked me you are mentioning about which sum of money?" I became silent and left his place. After this incident, I have not paid any more visit to him.

Since you said me at the Secretariat "This will be arranged", I have been under the firm belief that I was certain to receive the money. I have whole-hearted respect only for you and I also have a sincere affection for you—I have no respect for others. I believe that one day we shall make India fully independent. On that glorious day, Bengalis will remember foremost you and Subhash Bosh—you will be the Country's true Leaders.

Please accept my whole-hearted gratitude and regards. I trust that I shall receive the necessary sum from Hindu—Muslim Unity Fund to enable me to repay my debts. Your words of honour can never fail. I have received five hundred rupees. Kindly send me further five hundred rupees as early as possible, or bring with you if you happen to come to Madhupur. This amount is for satisfying the decree passed by the Court of Law and which I was not able to pay during the last three/four months. Perhaps, the Court may issue a warrant against me.

Your magnanimity, generosity, genuine affection for me, your courage, uprightness, and bravery are all intermingled with every particle of my body and spirit.

Kindly accept my affectionate regard and salutations to your lotus feet.

Yours most respectfully,
Kazi Nazrul Islam

Note made by Dr. Syama Prasad—'Spoken to Zulfikar Hyder about arrangements. He returned fully cured.'

Appendix-II

Delhi University Convocation Address (13 December 1952)

—Dr. Syama Prasad Mookerjee

The University of Delhi, though of a comparatively recent origin, has certain unique features of its own which strengthen its possibility of development and service to the nation. Situated in the capital city of our country, it naturally receives special attention at the hands of the central government and no less a person than the President of our Republic is its Visitor. One can venture to express the hope that this association may lead to generous state-aid to enable the University to carry on its plans for progressive expansion. The proximity of a university to the seat of the central government is sometimes fraught with the danger of unnecessary and irritating state interference which, it is to be earnestly hoped, will be avoided. Delhi attracts people from all parts of India, and this University, therefore, can well develop into a seat of learning which will seek to harmonise diverse elements of the inhabitants of this great land, whose sons and daughters may assemble to receive their training in different branches of knowledge. Further, a number of all-India institutions have sprung up in and near Delhi which is fast becoming the centre of useful studies and research in the domains of Arts, Science, Technology, Medicine and Agriculture. These may well afford to the teachers and advanced students of the University opportunities for collaboration which will be of lasting benefit to all. Momentous problems arising out of government's policies in respect of administration and the passing of laws are constantly coming up, affecting the welfare of the entire nation. Sometimes they may even have international significance as well. Teachers and advanced students of the University and its colleges in Delhi have, thus, a great opportunity to study these problems at close quarters in a spirit of critical analysis and non-partisanship. Delhi is also often the centre of all-India and even of international activities in such fields as sports, athletics and drama and, thus, hold out before its alumni various models of superior performance which are bound to act as healthy and powerful incentives to them. If full advantage is to be taken of all such varied opportunities for self-development and national service, the University and its colleges, their staff and students must receive generous aid from the state and the public. With the limited opportunities available today, the University has succeeded in making its mark in such departments of study as Economics and Science, thanks to the zeal and devotion of the distinguished staff associated with them.

Since the attainment of independence, the role that the universities in India are destined to play has been emphasised by both official and non-official spokesmen. The Radhakrishnan Commission has submitted a valuable report dwelling on the need for a planned and thorough re-orientation of university administration and teaching. Unfortunately, like other distinguished Commissions that had previously reported on Indian universities, this report also is in danger of being pigeon-holed on account of want of financial resources. It is not through changes only in the external pattern of the administrative machinery of universities that we can expect to see the ushering in the new era of reform and expansion. Their vital needs relate to improved methods of teaching and research and abundant facilities, both academic and extra-academic, to the staff and the students for performing their essential duties. This can hardly be fulfilled without adequate state aid. A university that has to depend for its existence principally on its fee income can never meet its obligations, however much it may compromise with sound academic principles for artificially raising such income.

A Universities Grants Committee appointed by the central government serving not only the central, but also the state universities is a most urgent necessity. The committee should be so composed as to command the confidence of the universities as well as the public. It must have at its disposal adequate funds for distribution amongst the universities in accordance with a planned and systematic development on a national basis. There is a general tendency to believe that grants and control necessarily go together. The need for maintaining the autonomy of the universities and not making them subservient to the state on the plea that they receive state grants must be emphasised by all well-wishers of the country. We can generally accept the standard adopted by the Universities Grants Committee in Grant Britain which has evolved a sound and efficient system of work, earning the praise of enlightened public opinion not only in Great Britain but in other advanced countries as well.

No external authority set up by the government can ever hope to secure co-ordination of work or enforce a common standard among all universities in India. It will thus become a super-university by itself, developing extremely complex machinery, deadening the soul of all universities in India and making them rigid and stagnant. If such an authority is to enjoy executive powers, it will lead to the regimentation of university education which even totalitarian countries or autocratic regimes dared not experiment in. I don't ignore the need for co-ordination. I do not minimise the importance of maintaining adequate standards of university instruction and examinations. I appreciate the urgency of avoiding wastage and unnecessary duplication. All these necessary reforms have to be undertaken, first by each university acting in a rational manner, balancing regional requirements with national progress; secondly, by the Inter-University Board which, though having advisory powers, must be helped to develop healthy conventions and whose well-considered recommendations cannot be easily flouted by any university; thirdly, by well-informed deliberations in state legislatures and Parliament at the time of voting of demands on grants and lastly, by the Universities Grants Committee, which, functioning on the model of the British Grants Committee, can always exercise a healthy and decisive influence on both the administrative and the teaching activities of the universities concerned.

The universities of modern India have very little in common with ancient or mediaeval centres of learning. It is well known how the British authorities planned the establishment of universities in India about one hundred years ago mainly for their own administrative purposes. Western education itself was then visualised as the only passport to service and the learned professions, and also the means through which enlightened knowledge could elevate the people belonging to what was said to be a rusty and backward civilisation. The very system of education which was deemed essential for forging bonds of unbroken alliance with the British power succeeded in unleashing revolutionary ideas and thoughts which, ultimately helped to throw off the yoke of alien rule in India. If we take a dispassionate view of what happened during the last century, we must acknowledge that this has been an era in which good has been mixed with evil. The contact between the Indian mind and western thought and civilisation did not enslave the soul of India. In every domain of thought, in arts and architecture, in science, in history, philosophy and letters, in social services and religious thought, great Indians gave their best, maintaining their stamp of originality as well as imbibing and assimilating fruits of western skill and knowledge. Though the number of Indians affected by such spread of knowledge was comparatively small, many of them assumed a much-needed political leadership and became the instruments of agitation and mass movements, leading ultimately to the political liberation of their country. The cultural Renaissance preceded and created the silent political Revolution. We must not, however, overlook the debit side as well. The masses were neglected. Villages were stagnant. Poverty reigned supreme. Elementary education remained in the background. Our languages were under-nourished; especially neglected was that great store-house of Indian knowledge and wisdom, the mother of most of our languages, Sanskrit. The aims and purposes of education were inconsistent with national aspirations. Respect for the noblest features of our great culture and civilisation dwindled away due to ignorance and disbelief. The pattern of society based on equality and justice, on contentment, and self-sufficiency, that true education must foster and strengthen, hardly took shape. Can we honestly maintain that after freedom, have we been able to uproot these and other salient defects in our educational system?

Education must be examined from an organic standpoint. Free India must be able to cater to the needs of all stages of education as parts of one comprehensive national system. There need not be any conflict amongst primary, secondary and university stages, nor amongst literary, scientific, technical, vocational and agricultural courses of study. A national system of education must conceive of a balanced structure where the due and proper emphasis will be laid on every section so as to maintain its harmony, its strength and solidarity. Today, after freedom, the universities must be conscious of a much wider conception of their duties and responsibilities than before. There is an urgent need for adequate leadership in the professions, in commerce and industry, in politics and administration. Millions of teachers and workers are needed for institutions of various types. There awaits the solution of the problem of freeing the masses from want, disease and ignorance. There still remain untapped and hidden the vast natural resources and raw materials of India and it will be for the universities to create knowledge and to train minds which could bring together material resources and human energies which lie latent today. I lay great stress on the need for developing the research activities for our universities. No doubt the importance of scientific study and research in the modern age must not be overlooked. It may not be possible for every university to specialise in every department of science; indeed want of resources and man-power will debar this.

Yet the basic science must be a common factor and specialisation may be shared region-wise. Every university should offer facilities for study and residence to deserving students coming from the other regions where smilier facilities may not be available. There is a great need for encouraging research on subjects which have a special relation to the Indian problems of today or to the basic conception of Indian culture and civilisation. Indian History, Indian Thought and Philosophy, Indian Art, Architecture and Music, and Indian Sociology afford fields for laborious work by hundreds of scholars. The fruits of their study and investigation are bound to produce new light which will help us in remodelling the structure of our society and the pattern of our lives in a worthy manner. Information on these subjects is widely sought for today by people coming from distant lands and we fail to give them a correct and co-ordinated answer regarding many problems affecting our civilisation. To unearth the hidden wisdom of our country is not to seek benefit for ourselves alone, enabling us to appreciate our heritage, but also to share it with the rest of the world. Similarly, the gigantic problems relating to our social and economic reconstruction based on a comparative study of what exists here and the successful experiments made elsewhere have yet to be tackled. Political freedom, if not followed by social and economic emancipation, will be utterly meaningless and the guidance for this purpose must emanate in an appropriate measure from our teachers and advanced students, untrammelled by any dogma as such. It has been truly said that the main motif in India's history is her unity amidst diversity. What serious study, I ask, has been made of the urges, habits, outlook and mode of life of millions of men and women, of diverse castes and tribes, living under varied conditions, in plains and hills, in towns and villages, speaking a multitude of languages, but all cheerfully owning themselves as the sons and daughters of mother India, and swayed by common spiritual impulses? Some British administrators and experts and later on some renowned Indian scholars have, no doubt, dealt with some aspects of Indian Sociology and Anthropology, but much yet remains to be done before we can formulate a sound and progressive basis of true national consolidation. No country has ever spent too much on research either in the domain of Arts or Science. It matters little if we do not get a quick return, for we can never render a commercial account of research and investigation. Let our universities provide for basic training according to approved standards and maintain fellowships and scholarships on a well-planned basis. Let research for truth and knowledge be carried on in a spirit of harmony and co-operation, under the guidance of enlightened Indian teachers selected for their merit and efficiency.

A controversy faces us in respect of languages. While Indian languages must be fostered and developed in the widest possible manner, we need not and we must not take a hostile attitude towards English. Up to the second stage, the medium of instruction should be the mother-tongue of the students or where it is not feasible, due to the paucity of numbers, the regional language should be the medium, with full facilities given to them to study their mother-tongue. In many states, the regional languages will be rich enough to be the medium of instruction at collegiate and university stages also. By such encouragement of the Indian languages will they be endowed with creative force and be able to compete with each other, and enrich the heritage of Indian literature. Hindi which has been accepted as the official language of India should be learnt by all without any hesitation. It will act as a powerful unifying force. The teaching of English should be revised so that less emphasis may be given on the compulsory study of English literature and more on current and spoken English, using it as a vehicle for general study and expression of views. We should have no prejudice against the English language as such. It no longer represents the language of our rulers. It is one of the greatest languages of the world through which we can make ourselves familiar with essential knowledge and information, to exclude which would render our education imperfect. Without lowering our sense of patriotism in any way we can well utilise our two centuries' old acquaintance with the English language to our best national advantage, increasing our capacity to compete with the rest of the world in spheres of higher education and international contacts. I similarly urge the systematic study of some at least of the important Indian languages at each university centre. A comparative study of Indian languages will be greatly facilitated, if under state patronage a scheme is formulated for bringing out a well-known publication from different Indian languages in their original texts but printed in Devanagri script. I would urge also the revival of the study of Sanskrit and grant of special facilities for this purpose. I am not suggesting for a movement that these linguistic studies should be made compulsory, but the existence of such facilities is bound to attract the intelligent curiosity of a large number of our students and also to create a healthy foundation for proper appreciation of our cultural unity and heritage.

I would plead for exchange of university teachers on a planned basis along with programmes for visits of teams of university students from one centre to another. While our universities must be so equipped and administered as to make it unnecessary for Indian students to go abroad for studying ordinary subjects, our scheme for foreign scholarships and fellowships should be more liberal than at present. Care must be taken to ensure that we send abroad only those advanced students for whom facilities for specialised training do not exist in India. Such a rationalised scheme will save wastage of time and money. The system of examinations now in vogue also needs thorough revision. The increasing percentage of failures in the examinations of many universities is a matter of deep public concern. I do not wish to enter into controversy and discuss how far it is due to the faults of students and how far to the prevailing system of study and examination. In any case, we are accepting as inevitable the colossal wastage of human efforts and energy followed by deep frustration and sullen discontent amongst a large section of our youth. The rigidity of our university examinations can be removed only if we can provide for a more extensive tutorial system and make the final results dependent not on one examination, but the performance of students during the entire session. This matter has been examined in details by many foreign countries and no final and satisfactory solution has been found, although changes of various kinds have been periodically made. This has also to be examined in relation to our courses of study, our syllabus and methods of teaching. I do not ignore that any large-scale provision for tutorial work involves increased staff and hence additional expenditure which the educational authorities cannot by themselves meet without extra state-aid.

No university can exist unless it can evoke a spirit of affection and loyalty in the minds of students. Such an atmosphere of good-will and cordiality cannot come into existence merely by means of extraneous rules and regulations of discipline. Our country was rightly proud of the traditional relationship of deep understanding between the teachers and the taught in days gone by. The present system of education and modern conditions of living are not always helpful for the maintenance of this relationship. The training that we give to our youth must be purposeful. If our goal is liberty and democracy, then we must undertake the responsibility for teaching them the arts of being free and of governing themselves. If we teach them instead, the arts of bullying and passive obedience, we will not achieve liberty and democracy at which we are aiming. Today the economic sufferings of the majority of our people are reflected in the attitude and outlook of our students. Grants of scholarships must be more liberal for the backward sections of our people and we must ensure that poverty does not stand in the way of any deserving youth from receiving the highest education. Many of our educational institutions are so large-sized that it is impossible to look after individual needs. Want of books and of guidance and half-hearted participation in sports and physical activities, want of food and nourishment depress the minds of the students. Want of aim and purpose in pursuing a particular type of education darkens their future. They also cannot but often share the sense of general frustration that dominates peoples' outlook today. Over and above these considerations, sometimes a wave of agitation, perhaps born out of a minor event, sweeps them away and they may lose valuable weeks or months. The contents of our education have yet to be remodelled so as to give them sufficient impulse for facing the perils of life with greater courage and success. The steadily increasing number of women students in our colleges and universities is bringing to the forefront the special claims of women's education and the role they may play in the service of the people. It is a supreme task for university administrators and teachers today to read into the minds of the youth of re-awakened India and to place before them not only well-regulated courses of studies and well-thought-out programmes for extracurricular activities, but also rousing in them a true scientific spirit and a deep impulse for devoted service to the cause of national well-being. A compulsory provision for three months of intensive social work for at least every intending graduate may narrow the gulf that divides the so-called educated class from the illiterate masses.

The great task of reconstruction is in front of us. The army of selfless and patriotic youths that must take up this challenge is also standing by. The only task is to link the two together, by giving the youth the training that they and the country deserve and to canalise and enthuse their selfless efforts in this noble task. Today unemployment has become one of the curses of Free India. Apart from millions of our countrymen who continue to remain in the dark abyss of ignorance, disease, poverty and superstition, we have thousands of educated youths who have passed out of colleges and universities and even received much-coveted degrees and diplomas in science, engineering and medicine or have been otherwise qualified, who for want of work and opportunity are slowly withering away. They feel neglected, sullen and frustrated. No university can solve the problem of unemployment. Its main task is to impart a system of education that will not produce a race of unemployable. I admit even in this respect much yet remains to be done by our universities. But the main task is for the state to see that they may be absorbed in employment and occupations made available to every son and daughter of India according to his or her ability. Economic depression chills the soul of man. What contribution can our educated youth make to serve society or to revive the glorious aspects of our culture and civilisation in accordance with the needs of the modern age, if we cannot provide for them a decent standard of living?

Let the universities be the mouthpieces of the liberty of thought and expression which a true democracy must uphold. Let our students sweep away the cobwebs of mistrust and of the miasma of hatred from the minds of the people. An eagle alone can train an eaglet. If teachers themselves are partisans and swayed by dogma how can youth be expected to uphold free thought or righteous conduct? Let us declare that to us justice and liberty are meaningless if they do not include other men and other nations. It is not so much what our students learn, not so much what they know, as what they are which should concern us. Do we love liberty, love it so much that we will fight for it, die for it and will accord it to others as well as claim it for ourselves? Nations live or die according to the character of the people. Wealth, arms, munitions, disciplined armies and navies and air forces are of splendid service but the character of the people, the character into which the youth is growing, determines the life or death of the nation. "Liberty," says Manu, the great law-giver or our race, "is happiness and dependence is misery." With our ancient heritage, with the spirit of India still ennobling the mind of man, with our vast resources of man-power and buried wealth, with our undoubted capacity for assimilation of new ideas, let us, irrespective of all differences, make a supreme co-operative effort to raise our motherland to a high and a nobler life of existence, bringing joy and contentment to all and making her a mighty instrument for the maintenance of world peace and freedom.

□

Educational Re-Construction

—Dr. Syama Prasad Mookerjee

(Presidential Address at the eleventh session of the India Educational Conference, Nagpur—27 December 1935)

I must at the outset express to you my deep thanks for the honour which you have done me by asking me to preside over the 11th session of your conference. Last year I was unexpectedly prevented from fulfilling a similar obligation at Delhi. I feel grateful to you for continued confidence which you have reposed in me.

The All-India Federation of Educational Associations under whose auspices this conference meets enjoys a representative character. Its objects include the investigation of educational problems affecting our future welfare from the lowest to the highest stages. The Federation cannot, however, remain satisfied with its present status. I would urge the extension of its sphere of influence, especially by the establishment of active provincial centres in all parts of India, which would examine important local needs and problems and pursue a progressive policy in the light of general principles enunciated by the parent body. The Federation is capable of turning itself into a most powerful and beneficent organisation, which may legitimately demand to be heard on all appropriate occasions. It must in its turn continue to be body fully alive to the varying needs of the provinces which it claims to serve; it must call forth the services of men representing different academic interests, irrespective of class, creed or political dogma, and be inspired with the sole desire of advancing the cause of educational expansion.

In India, education has recently been receiving close attention at the hands of people belonging to diverse schools of thought, and we have confronted today with a long catalogue of criticism, suggestions for reform and reconstruction, almost bewildering in character. This situation is capable of logical explanation. Valuable as education is at all times in the history of every civilised nation, to us, Indians, it is of paramount importance at the present juncture. Differences there exist as to the means which should be adopted fot the realisation of India's political rights, but there is complete unanimity of opinion that no real and permanent advancement is possible unless education of the right type spreads far and wide till it saturates the teeming millions of this vast sub-continent. I believe it is this aspect of our future national growth that has inspired many, though not all, of the recent reports and utterances on education.

One of the criticisms with which we have grown familiar is that education in India has been a complete failure. I have no desire to underestimate the evils inherent in the present system, but I believe there has sometimes been a definite tendency to overstate the case. It would be idle for us to ignore the fact that, but for the education which we and our forefathers have received, we could not have made the progress achieved by us in different fields of thought and activity. There can be no question that Western education has brought us into closer contact with the culture and civilisation of progressive countries other than ours. There can be no question that it has laid the foundations of Indian nationhood; it has helped to awaken our national consciousness, to broaden our intellectual horizon and to kindle in our dreams of a better and a mightier India which we all long to see realised. It has taught us self-respect and has inspired us with a sense of equality and fearlessness prompting us to stand up as men, demanding justice and fair play. We need not feel unduly nervous if it has helped to disturb the placed contentment of our people or if it has shaken accepted beliefs and dogmas, for it is only through such unsettlement that the right path of future reconstruction can be discovered.

I am not a suggestion for a moment that everything that our educational system has to offer is good, or that all products of western education are animated by the spirit of service, culture and patriotism. The system has undoubtedly its weak points and a change in its outlook and objective is imperative. But let us not minimise, much less forget, the great contribution it has made.

One of its gravest defects is to be traced to historical reasons. The growth of Universities in India marked a definite stage in the progress of Indian education was introduced primarily for the supply of the agency for running the administration of a bureaucratic government stood in need of central organisations which could test the capacity of the students, educated in schools and colleges, on the basis of public examinations and the Universities were brought into existence. They were not meant at the first stage to be seats of culture and learning, nor were they intended to foster higher teaching and research or to train leaders of a democratic community. More than seventy-five years have come and gone; Universities have undergone vital changes and not to-day exist only for conducting examinations. They have adopted other ideas more appropriate to their true functions and are trying to discharges their obligation with varying degrees of success and efficiency. But, a machine-like spirit still persists and continues to deprive these institutions of their full share of life, faith and vigour without which they cannot contribute to national wealth and welfare.

English was deliberately chosen as the medium of instruction and examination to the deplorable neglect of the vernacular languages. Indigenous institutions suffered decay and existed merely as shadows of a bygone past. It was apparently thought that a new race of Indians would gradually grow up who would become influenced by the culture and civilisation of their rulers and out of feelings of loyalty and gratitude would be the strongest champions of British interests in India. I need not enter into the details of this aspect of the history of Indian education. That our vernaculars should be developed and given their rightful place in any scheme of national education is now widely recognised. We cannot at the same time forget that our economic and political progress and cultural advance are closely bound up with western science and literature through the medium of Western languages, especially English. Reconciliation between these two points of view is possible and must be found for the sake of our future national growth.

There is another matter which deserves notice. Primary education was neglected until recently and that in a manner which gave rise to widespread resentment. It was thought at one stage that higher education, if extensively given, would itself become an instrumend for the spread of primary education among the masses. This hope has not materialised to any satisfactory extent. It is now recognised that the spread of free and compulsory elementary education is one of the pressing needs of the day and, in many provinces, ways and means are being discussed for giving effect to this idea. Lack of funds is usually advanced as the reason for the delay in fulfilling this sacred obligation which rests on Government. But, we refuse to believe that money cannot be found if there is a will to find it. I voice your united demand when I say that there should be no further delay on the part of Government to remove this stigma which has attached itself to its administration, namely, that after more than 150 years of British rule in India only about 9 per cent of her people enjoy the benefits of literacy.

I would here refer to one line of criticism which is often adopted in certain quarters. It is said that we should spend more on primary education by depriving other branches of education of the financial assistance derived from the state. The question is whether we are spending such colossal sums on secondary and higher education that they will without loss of efficiency permit of reduction. The answer here is definitely in the negative state-help for education in India is meagre compared with that in other progressive countries. It is also out of proportion to the contributions made by private non-official agencies in India. We should deprecate any attempt to create a division among the different branches of education. If we are to advance as a nation, we must meet the legitimate demands of all stages, for it is only thus that we may hope to build a complete edifice, a temple of learning with a foundation deep-rooted, a base broad and strong, and a crown of glory reflecting India's highest culture and civilisation.

Another defect which has received its due share of criticism in recent times is the disproportionate attention paid to literary education. It is now recognised that our students must be given ample opportunities for following varied lines of study, theoretical and practical, devised in accordance with our needs and resources. One of the problems now engaging the attention of educational authorities, official and non-official, is the establishment of institutions which may provide for training in diverse branches of practical skill and knowledge. This reform is urgently called for in order to meet the question of middle-class unemployment. It will, however, be a mistake to take an exclusive view of vocational or technical education. We must devise means of shaping our policy in such a way as not to neglect the supreme value of a sound liberal education. There must also be ample provision for scientific education and for the spread of technical knowledge. While the emphasis may be laid on one or the other, in accordance with the aptitudes and requirements of different classes of students, we must not encourage one aspect to the detriment of any other.

It is important for us to bear in mind that a mere supply of trained youths, qualified in various scientific or technical pursuits, will not solve the question of unemployment. Opportunities must be created for absorbing the services of such young men, who must also be encouraged to take to trade, commerce and industry. There must be a closer association between the state and the educational authorities on the one hand, and representatives of capitalist, of trade, industry and commerce on the other. The state must also pursue a policy of a fairer and more equitable economic distribution and strive for the utilisation of India's vast natural resources in the interests of the people of this land. Neither can our aspirations be ever satisfied unless we succeed in breaking through the barriers which at present restrict our entrance to certain careers, such as the army and the navy, which absorb not a small percentage of youths of other civilised countries.

Suggestions are now and again put forth to limit admissions to universities, either directly or indirectly, mainly with a view to alleviating the increasingly distressful problem of unemployment. While, as I have said, it is the duty of the state and the people to explore new avenues which could absorb our trained young men, I must affirm that it is a retrograde measure to seek to solve the problem by reducing the number of educated men. We must not forget that the percentage of university-trained men in our country in relation to our population is deplorably lower than in other civilised lands, and any attempt to reduce still further even this small number will bring about national deterioration. Crude and mediaeval standards of life yet prevail in most villages and in many towns and call for immediate redress at the hands of trained and skilled workers. With the development of electric power, broadcasting, cinema, to mention only a few, scientifically trained men can, with the help of the state, making them eminently useful to society. Cultural and political awakening due to the influence of Universities still calls for their services. Educational institutions must not regard themselves as factories for the production of clerks and subordinate officers but they have also to supply the country with the leadership and skill in different branches of activity—economic, commercial and industrial; municipal, provincial and national. India stands in urgent need of university men, animated with the ideals of service, imagination, courage, the catholicity of outlook and resilience of nature.

There can be no question of reducing the existing educational facilities on the plea that re-orientation of education is vitally necessary. We do not believe that the present number of schools and colleges is too large for the requirements of the country. Those who urge their reduction on the ground that the education imparted by them is defective, must, in the first instance, secure the foundation of a sufficient number of institutions where the right type of training will be provided for the children of the soil. The schools and colleges of to-day may be enabled to adapt themselves gradually to the altered demands of the educational reformers. The situation becomes extremely dangerous when a reduction in their number is advocated on the plea of educational reform. Let us not follow the path of destruction so easy of access until the materials for reconstruction and expansion are generously made available to us.

No far-reaching reforms, aimed at increased facilities for education, which will be varied in character, will ever be accomplished without larger financial assistance from the state. The central Government recently distributed to the provinces a crore of rupees for rural reconstruction. For this, it has earned the gratitude of the people of India. The same Government has just inaugurated a Central Advisory Board of Education for India; it rightly regards education not merely as a provincial concern but also as a national problem of supreme importance. Let us put forward a united demand that Government should set apart at least a crore of rupees annually for several years in succession for distribution among the provinces, in proportion to what they themselves may raise, to be spent for the improvement of primary and secondary education, principally the latter in relation to the problem of unemployment. This expenditure will be productive of national efficiency and will yield results far more valuable than what some other departments of the state, which absorb not one but several crores of rupees from the public exchequer, can ever hope to achieve. This is the only practical way in which Government can realise the object it claims to have in view, namely a wide expansion of sound education; and it can do it far more speedily and effectively than by the periodical publication of reports, resolutions and schemes, however exhaustive, elaborate and learned as they may be. Let me turn for a moment to the intricate problem of education of girls. One of the noteworthy features in recent times has been the rapid growth of female education. Our responsibility in this sphere becomes all the greater because it is left mostly to us, men, to discover the best methods for educating the future mothers of our race. We must not perpetuate the blunder of training them under the same system as governs the education of our boys. In these days of female emancipation, I do not urge that women should not be treated with equality, but it must be recognised that however insistent their demand for equal treatment may be, there are certain differences which cannot with any effort be obliterated. Our ideals should be, generally speaking, to give our women an education which will make them the main-spring of spiritual force in our society. They must be rendered fully qualified for discharging those sacred obligations which constitute the heritage of Indian womanhood. From them will radiate the great virtues of strength, of purity and devotion, of truth, joy and beauty, of patience under suffering, reminiscent of the glorious past of India, which will constitute irresistible forces in the future development of our mind and character. From this, it does not follow that we should discourage women who may enjoy special aptitudes from following particular branches of knowledge or professions, now mostly the prerogative of men. It is, however, essential for us to remember that if our society is to be held together and not be broken to pieces, Indian women must be so educated as to enable them to take their rightful place in family and social life, peculiar to the traditions of this country, which with suitable improvements must in their fundamental features be worthy maintained in future.

Before I close, permit me to emphasise that true education consists more in the spirit it conveys then in the instruction it imparts. The question is whether we have been able to strengthen those invisible bonds of understanding which unite man to man, irrespective of caste, creed and community, or whether we have betrayed this ideal and imposed artificial restrictions on natural sympathies and brotherhood. Judged by this test, I am sorry to have to say that many of our educated men are today often the victims of narrow provincial and communal feelings. Pray, do not think for a moment that I am casting a reflection on any province or community in particular. I must make every teacher pause and think when he finds that uneducated men are often free from these trammels and we, who claim to be educated, are trying to inoculate them with this severe poison. So long as the present environment of distrust and suspicion continues, we can never hope to attain our cherished goal of a united and regenerated India. It makes us sometimes despair of our future when we realise how our education often fails to check the growth of better communal feuds and increasing inter-provincial ill-feeling. I do not ignore that the present economic and political condition of the country is also responsible for this state of affairs. While the teachers have little to do with these aspects of the matter, I would implore them, with all the emphasis at my command, to ask themselves every day whether the influence they transmit and the atmosphere they create are likely to strengthen the separatist tendencies or to break them down. The success of their teaching will be judged not by the result of examinations or the careers which their students may obtain, but by the qualities of patriotism, self-sacrifices courage, and freedom from communalism and from sectarian instincts which they develop. If the members of this association, and through the teachers in general, interpret their functions in this more catholic and spiritual way and inculcate upon our youths, the masters of our future destiny, the right relation between their provinces and community on the one hand and their heirs of the great teachers of this ancient hand to whom we almost all that we know and live by.

Let us all be true to our salt, and let us so strive and so act in the sight of all men that if we fall, future generations might at all events love us and bless us as brave loyal souls that fought for the right. If we believe what culture is the essence of the best that man, toiling through the ages like 'an infant crying in the night, like an infant crying for the light with no language but a cry' has felt and said and done; if we believe that culture is the summation and harmony of things as they should be; that it is the divinely appointed principle of Evolution forever dynamic, growing from more; that it ministers, unites, elevates and saves—if thus strong and radiant be our faith, it is still possible that we shall be able to get the better of communalism. And we shall do so if sternly we resolve to honour men according to their quality and character, regardless of the sect or camp they come from, and to stamp our mint-mark on great thoughts and deeds as such, uninfluenced by the colour and creed of the thinker and doer. Communalism, cliquisim, cabalism are but cultural nullities—from them come only freaking growths and perverted performances. May we be endowed with strength and courage to regard ourselves, however humble and unworthy, as soldiers in the war of liberation of humanity, marching proudly for the promised land of the swaraj of the Intellect, the mental emancipation of man!

□

Convocation Address

—Dr. Syama Prasad Mookerjee

Delivered at Gurukul Viswavidyalaya
(25 April 1943)

I am deeply grateful to you for the honour you have done to me in asking me to address your Annual Convocation. This is my first visit to this great seat of learning which we feel proud to regard as a national asset. Let me pay my tribute of respect to the memory of your illustrious founder and his renowned successor, who had not only the courage and vision to propound new educational ideals but also the capacity and determination to translate them into practise by the establishment and development of institutions dedicated to the cause they held so dear and sacred. Today, we stand at the crossroads of history. Our beloved motherland, rich with an ancient heritage, struggles for the attainment of that free status which is her birthright. It is through education that the ultimate battle of Indian freedom will be won. The gigantic task of reconstruction, culture, social, economic and political can be rendered possible through the coordinated efforts of bands of trained and disciplined Indians. Armed with the knowledge of India's past glory and greatness, her strength and weakness, it is they who can place before their country a programme of work, which while loyal to the fundamental traditions of Indian civilisation will be adapted to the changing conditions of the modern world.

If the history of education in British India is traced by an impartial historian, the record will be hardly creditable to our ruling class. We have suffered not for want of zeal and devotion for the cause of education on the part of children of the soil, but on account of the colossal blunder made by our rulers while formulating their educational policy a little over a century ago. That policy, determined in the days of Bentinck and Macaulay, was influenced not by considerations of the welfare of the Indian people but of the advancement of the interests of the ruling class. In no country has education properly developed unless it has drawn its inspiration from the foundation of its own national life. Education with its roots cut off and superimposed by the edicts of an alien power is doomed to ultimate failure. Applied to a subject-race which has not entirely lost its intellectual curiosity and virility, such a system may for some generations foster an artificial growth; it may even produce a race of able imitators but it can never inspire or elevate the people as a whole, far less advance their permanent welfare.

When Bentinck decide to concentrate State aid and support on European education alone, he started an era of cultural conquest of the Indian people. Afraid of the possible dangerous results of the spread of knowledge among the masses of the people, Macaulay and his co-workers chose to favour a select class of Indians and train them on Western ideas, not with a view to help them develop into self-reliant and patriotic Indians, but as Macaulay himself said, to form a class of persons, Indian in blood and colour but English in taste, in opinions, in morals and in intellect. Contemporaneous records of those days disclose a lamentable lack of knowledge of our masters of the greatness of India's past civilisation. They indeed portray a remarkable over emphasis on the so-called virtues of Western culture and unconcealed contempt for everything Indian. What we deplore is not that the gate of western knowledge was thrown open to Indians, but that such knowledge was imported to India at the sacrifice of our own cultural heritage. What was needed was a proper synthesis between the two systems and not neglect, far less destruction of the Indian base India's chequered history amply demonstrates that during a period when many of the European countries remained steeped in ignorance and barbarity, our great seers, savants and sages, backed by royal support, had attained an intellectual eminence which might well be the envy of any highly civilised nation. In this country was developed a state of society which encouraged not merely scholastic learning, philosophy and religion, but also art, architecture, medicine, science, astronomy and engineering. Education must be nourished by ideas and thoughts consistent with the tradition of the country which it claims to serve. The sustaining force of Western education in India was chiefly the glamour of State service. Education was encouraged not for its own sake but for the opening avenues of employment essential for the successful functioning of bureaucratic machinery.

I have no desire to trace here the growth of the educational system in India in detail. Macaulay's prophecy was partially falsified by the results that followed its adoption. The national consciousness of educated Indians could not be suppressed and far from being blind supporters of an alien rule, they themselves became the torch-bearers of revolt. The education of the masses was neglected in a manner unprecedented in the history of any civilised administration. The educational system failed to serve the real needs of India and its defects were soon manifest to patriotic Indians. Attempts have no doubt been made from time to time to introduce far-reaching changes into the educational system in accordance with the needs and aspirations of the people. In the field of higher teaching and research, in arts and science, it has been demonstrated that the power of original thinking of Indian scholars has not been demonstrated not been extinguished and they are capable of holding their own against any foreigner. Partial success has been achieved in some spheres of thought and activity but a general dissatisfaction is an evidence suggesting a thorough overhauling of the entire system.

The problem of education can never be fully solved in a manner acceptable to self-respecting Indians until and unless it is left in the hands of a government representing the national will and freed from foreign domination. We move indeed in a vicious circle. Without education properly outlined and directed, we cannot easily attain our freedom. Without freedom and full control over our own destinies, we cannot re-shape our educational policy entirely according to our will and requirements. So long as the present situation continues, however, it is obvious we have to make the best use of the existing machinery and by constant efforts and agitation secure changes and improvements which will bring us as near our goal as possible. Acceptance of our national languages as the media of instruction and examination up to the highest standard is a fundamental condition which has yet to be fulfilled. You have rightly adopted this course in developing your activities. Each province has its own major language and this should be accepted in its own educational sphere. If there is another language which has a substantial number of adherents, this may also receive recognition under suitable conditions, although the multiplicity of languages within the same provincial zone may lead to obvious complications. A bureau should be set up in each province under the supervision of well-trained scholars and working in close co-operation with government and universities, it should undertake the preparation of books in all subjects of study in the provincial language. A working knowledge of English at the post-elementary stage is sufficient for our ordinary purposes, except in the case of that limited number of scholars who may choose to study the English language and literature as part of their academic training. Similarly, a working knowledge of Hindi is essential so that direct contact among peoples of different provinces may be maintained. The study of different subjects has to be re-organised in a manner suited to the conditions of our country. Subjects like History,

Economics and Social Science have to be dealt with in relation to Indian environments. With regard to science which knows no geographical boundaries, the nomenclature should not be divorced from what is in use in other parts of the world, for only thus can we keep ourselves in touch with world-progress, and retain contact with co-workers outside our own sphere of activity.

While we cannot but emphasise the need for well-equipped libraries and laboratories, seminars and museum in any system of national education, we have to keep down unnecessary expenditure on buildings and hostels. In a poor country such as ours, we should aim at minimising expenditure in every possible manner so that money thus released may be utilised for the progressive expansion of education. The conditions of living and training of our alumni should be such as to render it possible for them on the termination of their studies to identify themselves without any pang with the environments amidst which they had been previously accustomed to living. Nothing is more ruinous to the cause of our country's progress than to create a separate class of so-called educated Indians, entirely out of touch in outlook and mode of living with the vast millions of their less fortunate fellow-countrymen to whose service they must dedicate their lives.

Education can hardly be separated from the social and economic surroundings of the people. While those responsible for imparting education cannot guarantee employment to all students, the system should be so regulated that the training given is a help and not a hindrance to them in their struggle for existence. For this reason, education must be many-sided and institutions of various types must grow up so as to train people in manifold directions suited to the economic and industrial progress of the country. It is in this sphere that a National Government will deem it a supreme duty to co-ordinate effectively the activities of academic institutions with trade, commerce, agriculture and industry. There can be no clash of interests among these agencies only if all strive to achieve one ultimate end—the service of the nation as a whole.

The relation between teacher and student must be such as between father and son. It is only by the fulfilment of this condition that a correct standard of education can be maintained and its objects properly fulfilled. Obedience that grows out of spontaneous loyalty and affection is permanent; enforced discipline born of the fear of rules or rods fails to mould the character of the students. Your basic concept of Gurukula—the home of the teacher—is a gift of the ancient Indian mind and has seldom penetrated into the artificial atmosphere of residential schools, copied from the Western pattern in many parts of India. An Indian Gurukula cannot separate education from the mainsprings of Indian Dharma, interpreted in its broadest sense. The heritage that belongs to an Indian youth must be clearly and boldly held before his mind's eye. The eternal value of the teachings of the ancient seers must be explained to him—not for lowering his vision or choking his spirit of inquisitiveness, but for making him judge for himself their fundamental values. Civilisation in our society meant progressive socialisation of our lives by developing all the finer feelings which helped us to realise our own selves in others and others in our own selves. This is why, our social life had been dominated more by moral conscious rather than political. If today we suffer from divisions and disruptions, the fault lies with those interpreters who for historical reasons clung to forms and practises and narrowed the base of the original structure of our society striking at the root of service and equality, so manifest in the teachings of our ancient seers. Pride in one's national heritage such as ours which transcends all barriers of race and creed must be implanted in the heart of our youth, for by this alone will he shake off an inferiority complex and lack of self-confidence, fatal to the cause of our progress. We claim that instead of turning westwards we can rebuild our society fundamentally on our own model. In a country such as ours with people following different religions and faiths, we must so adjust our movements as to permit full scope for intellectual and cultural development to all essential units, each remaining loyal to its creed, helpful to and trustful of each other, and all owing allegiance to the imperishable spirit of Indian unity.

Today, the world is faced with a crisis unknown in the history of human civilisation. Western civilisation has failed to give the world peace and freedom. In spite of material advancement and scientific and industrial progress, the ruling classes in Europe were dominated by the triple forces of power, prestige and possession. The future happiness of the world will depend on the outlook of the men who control the destinies of the stronger and more powerful nations. Whatever lip-sympathy they may pay to the doctrine of equality, democracy and freedom, if in their actions they allow themselves to be dominated by a policy of aggression and exploitation of weaker or less fortunate countries, they can never hope for the inauguration of a better world-order. The future of the world lies in a federation of free countries where each will have the scope of developing its national life in accordance with its best ideals and traditions. If this goal is acceptable to all, the educational system in all parts of the world must be so moulded as to encourage the growth of correct international behaviour and understanding. Among the fundamental moral qualities, man must have a deep concern for the good life of his fellows. Every person should be given a fair chance of growing up sound in mind and body and making the best of his natural faculties. He must have a sense of social responsibility and the will to sink his personal interest and that of his class in the common good. He must be a man of independent judgement, respect the individuality of others and be tolerant to opinions in conflict with his own. He should realise that he has a responsibility not only as a citizen of his own country, but also as a citizen of the world, that there must be equal justice for all, that Government should be based on general good-will and support rather than on brute force.

One of the urgent problems confronting us is preplanning of a system of national education suited to our needs and aspirations. We do not yet know when political conditions will permit us to give effect to such a reformed scheme. But this must form a major part of the post-war reconstruction. We should lose no time in setting up competent machinery, fully representative of all interest, which should explore the lines of our future educational program. The matter will not be an easy one. Problems relating to languages, traditions, needs of different communities, and employment will require the closest examination. The aim of education has to be defined with clearness and precision. Briefly put, our object should be to develop every Indian child as completely as possible so that he may feel himself consciously at one with his community, share in its traditions of past, its life and action in the present and its aspirations and responsibility for the future. A vast country like India will present problems peculiar to particular provinces. Our aim should be to inculcate in the mind of every child a passionate loyalty to the spirit of Indian unity and so to regulate the daily work that he may become aware that what he is doing is for the advancement of his nation and through his nation of humanity at large.

Your great institution will contribute in no small degree to the solution of the Indian education problem. Regimentation of rules and adoption of a rigid pattern in the sphere of education virtually give it a death blow. They strike at the root of its life and lead to deadly stagnation. You have demonstrated that education in this country can be organised by a correct synthesis between the fundamental aspects of Indian civilisation and the true requirements of a scientific age. The influences for the good which alone can save human civilisation from the destructive forces of arrogant and selfish materialism have been steadily nurtured by you in spite of grave obstacles. In the task of reconstruction of Indian society, you are bound to play a dominant part and your experiences will influence in no small measure the future course of educational policy and administration in this country. India amidst all her diversities presents a unity of thought and action which is indeed remarkable. In spite of political bondage, we have been able to keep our heads erect because of the inherent power of assimilation that the Indian mind has shown itself capable of. The aim of our culture has been the complete realisation of life. Nature, man and God make for life entire knowledge; and service and love are the materials which go to the making of man complete. In the firm belief that the cause of Indian advancement is just and righteous, and standing at the foot of the Himalayas and near the Holy River that have from time immemorial witnessed the mighty career of Indian civilisation, which no alien Power can crush, let us draw inspiration from the Glorious Past, sustain fortitude and strength to face the trials and tribulations of the present and fearlessly contribute our humble share in the re-building of a free and united India of the Future. Let us gather in our own the voices of India's oppressed millions and proclaim in the words of our beloved poet our determination to march along the path of truth and justice and to consider no sacrifice, no preparation too great for the emancipation of our Motherland:

Where the mind is without fear and the head is held high
Where knowledge is free
Where the world has not been broken up into fragments
By narrow domestic walls
Where words come out from the depth of truth
Where tireless striving stretches its arms towards perfection
Where the clear stream of reason has not lost its way
Into the dreary desert sand of dead habit
Where the mind is led forward by thee
Into ever-widening thought and action
Into that heaven of freedom, my Father, let my country awake

Excerpted from: V. Bhatia (ed.) 1994. Rabindranath Tagore: Pioneer in Education. New Delhi: Sahitya Chayan.

□

Appendix-III

'The Parrot's Tale'

—Rabindranath Tagore

Once upon a time, there was a bird It was ignorant. It sang all right, but never recited scriptures. It hopped pretty frequently but lacked manners. Said the Raja to himself: 'Ignorance is costly in the long run. For fools consume as much food as their betters, and yet give nothing in return.' He called his nephews to his presence and told them that the bird must have sound schooling. The pundits were summoned, and at once went to the root of the matter. They decided that the ignorance of birds was due to their natural habit of living in poor nests. Therefore, according to the pundits, the first thing necessary for this bird's education was a suitable cage. The pundits had their rewards and went home happy. A golden cage was built with gorgeous decorations. Crowds came to see it from all parts of the world. "Culture, captured and caged!" exclaimed some, in a rapture of ecstasy, and burst into tears. Others remarked: "Even if culture be missed, the cage will remain, to the end, a substantial fact. How fortunate for the bird!" The goldsmith filled his bag with money and lost no tune in sailing homewards.

The pundit sat down to educate the bird. With proper deliberation, he took his pinch of snuf, as he said: "Textbooks can never be too many for our purpose!" The nephews brought together an enormous crowd of scribes. They copied from books, and copied from copies, till the manuscripts were piled up to an unreachable height. Men murmured in amazement. "Oh, the tower of culture, egregiously high! The end of it lost in the clouds!" The scribes, with light hearts, hurried home, their pockets heavily laden. The nephews were furiously busy keeping the cage in proper trim. As their constant scrubbing and polishing went on, the people said with satisfaction: "This is progress indeed!" Men were employed in large numbers and supervisors were still more numerous. These, with their cousins of all different degrees of distance, built a palace for themselves and lived there happily ever after.

Whatever may be its other deficiencies, the world is never in want of fault-finders; and they went about saying that every creature remotely connected with the cage flourished beyond words, except only the bird. When this remark reached the Raja's ears, he summoned his nephews before him and said: 'My dear nephews, what is this that we hear?' The nephews said in answer: "Sire, let the testimony of the goldsmiths and the pundits, the scribes and the supervisors be taken if the truth is to be known Food is scarce with the faultfinders, and that is why their tongues have gained in sharpness."

The explanation was so luminously satisfactory that the Raja decorated each one of his nephews with his own rare jewels. The Raja at length, being desirous of seeing with his own eyes how his Education Department busied itself with the little bird, made his appearance one day at the Great Hall of Learning. From the gate rose the sounds of conch-shells and gongs, horns, bugles and trumpets, cymbals, drums and kettledrums, tomtoms, tambourines, flutes, fifes, barrel-organs and bagpipes. The pundits began chanting mantras with their topmost voices, while the goldsmiths, scribes, supervisors, and their numberless cousins of all different degrees of distance, loudly raised a round of cheers.

The nephews smiled and said: "Sire, what do you think of it all?" The Raja said: "It does seem so fearful like astound principle of Education!" Mightily pleased, the Raja was about to remount his elephant, when the fault-finder, from behind some bush, cried out: "Maharaja, have you seen the bird?" Indeed, I have not! exclaimed the Raja. I completely forgot about the bird.

Turning back, he asked the pundits about the method they followed in instructing the bird. It was shown to him. He was immensely impressed. The method was so stupendous that the bird looked ridiculously unimportant in comparison. The Raja was satisfied that there was no flaw in the arrangements. As for any complaint from the bird itself, that simply could not be expected. Its throat was so completely choked with the leaves from the books that it could neither whistle nor whisper. It sent a thrill through one's body to watch the process. This time, while remounting his elephant, the Raja ordered his State ear-puller to give a thorough good pull at both the ears of the faultfinder. The bird thus crawled on, duly and properly, to the safest verge of insanity. In fact, its progress was satisfactory in the extreme. Nevertheless, nature occasionally triumphed overtraining, and when the morning light peeped into the bird's cage, it sometimes fluttered its wings in a reprehensible manner. And, though it is hard to believe, it pitifully pecked at its bars with its feeble beak. "What impertinence!" growled the kotwal. The blacksmith, with his forge and hammer, took his place in the Raja's Department of Education. Oh, what resounding blows! The iron chain was soon completed, and the bird's wings were clipped. The Raja's brothers-in-law looked black, and shook their heads, saying: "These birds not only lack good sense, but also gratitude!" With textbook in one hand and baton in the other, the pundits gave the poor bird what may fitly be called lessons! The kotwal was honoured with a title for his watchfulness, and the blacksmith for his skill in forging chains. The bird died. Nobody had the least notion how long ago this had happened. The fault-finder was the first man to spread the rumour. The Raja called his nephews and asked them, "My dear nephews, what is this that we hear?" The nephews said: "Sir, the bird's education has been completed." "Does it hop?" the Raja enquired. "Never!" said the nephews. "Does it fly?"

"No." "Bring me the bird", said the Raja. The bird was brought to him, guarded by the kotwal and the sepoys and the sowars. The Raja poked its body with his finger. Only its inner stuffing of book-leaves rustled. Outside the window, the murmur of the spring breeze amongst the newly budded Asoka leaves made the April morning wistful.

□

Bibliography

Primary Source:

1. Private Papers of Dr. Syama Prasad Mookerjee (Nehru Memorial Museum and Library, New Delhi).
2. Mookerjee, Syama Prasad, *Leaves from a Diary*. Calcutta: Oxford UP, 1993.
3. A Diary of Sir Asutosh Mookerjee, Calcutta : Asutosh Mookerjee Memorial Institute, 1998.
4. Mookerjee, Syama Prasad, (ed. Dr. Reena Bhaduri). Selected speeches in Bengal Legislative Assembly 1937—1947. Calcutta: Asutosh Mookerjee Memorial Institute, 2002.
5. Roy, Tathagat. *The Life and Times of Dr. Syama Prasad Mookerjee*. New Delhi: Prabhat Publication, 2012.

Secondary Source:

1. Banerjee, Anil Chandra. *A Phase in the life of Dr. Syama Prasad Mookerjee* 1937-46. Calcutta : AMMI, 2000. Print.
2. Banerjee, Purnendu Kumar. *Sir Asuthosh: Our Grandfather*. Bombay: Bharatiya Vidya Bhavan, 1992. Print.
3. Gupta, S.P. Das. *Asutosh Mookerjee*: 1st ed. India: National Book Trust, 1986. Print.
4. Pal, Bipin Chandra. *Sir Asutosh Mookerjee: A Character Study*. Calcutta: Kuntaline Press, 1922. Print.
5. Sarkar, Sumit. *Aadhunik Bharat*. Delhi: Rajkamal Prakashan, 1992. Print.

6. Upadhyay, Vishvamitra. *Bharatiya Krantikari Aandolan Aur Hindi Sahitya*. Delhi: Pragatisheel Janprakashan, 1989. Print.
7. Singh, Ayodhya. *Bharat Ka Mukti Sangram*. 3rd ed. New Delhi: Granth Shilpi, 2012. Print.
8. Sinha, Shashdhar. *Asutosh Mookerjee*. New Delhi: Prakashan Vibhag, Ministry of Information and Broadcasting, Govt. of India, 1973. Print.
9. Kohli, Ritu. *Dr. Syama Prasad Mookerjee Aur Kashmir Samasya*. Delhi: Prabhat Prakashan, 2016. Print.
10. Verma, Mohan. *Dr. Syama Prasad Mookerjee: The Great Hindu Nationalist*. New Delhi : Lucky International, 2015. Print.
11. Arya, Anita. *The Lion of Parliament: Dr. Syama Prasad Mookerjee, 1901-53*. New Delhi: Gyan Publishing House, 2001. Print.
12. Chatterjee, Prashanto Kumar. *Syama Prasad Mookerjee and Indian Politics*. Rev. ed. New Delhi: Foundation Books—Cambridge UP India, 2015. Print.
13. Gajrani, Shiv and S. Ram, eds. *Dr. Syama Prasad Mookerjee*. New Delhi: Commonwealth, 2009. Print.
14. Palit, Chittabrata, and Kabita Ray, eds. *Bengal Miscellany* Vol. 3 Delhi: B.R. Publishing Corporation, 2011.
15. Bhattacharya, Sabyasachi. *The Defining Moments in Bengal, 1920-1947*. New Delhi: Oxford UP, 2014.
16. Sarkar, Sushobhan. *Bengal Navjagran*. Trans. S.N. Kanoongo. New Delhi: Granth Shilp. 1997. Print.
17. Sarkar, Sumit. *Bengal Mein Swadeshi Aandolan*. Trans. Aaditya Narayan Singh. New Delhi: Granth Shilpi, 1997. Print.
18. Vijay Tarun, ed. *Thus Spoke Syama Prasad : Selected Quotes from the writing and speeches of Dr. Syama Prasad Mookerjee*. New Delhi: Dr. Syama Prasad Mookerjee Reasearch Foundation (SPMRF), 2009. Print.

□□□